D1234117

DISCARD

INTERNATIONAL POLITICAL ECONOMY SERIES

General Editor: Timothy M. Shaw, Professor of Political Science and International Development Studies, and Director of the Centre for Foreign Policy Studies, Dalhousie University, Halifax, Nova Scotia

Recent titles include:

Seamus Cleary
THE ROLE OF NGOs UNDER AUTHORITARIAN POLITICAL SYSTEMS

Robert W. Cox (*editor*)
THE NEW REALISM: Perspectives on Multilateralism and World Order

Stephen Gill (*editor*)
GLOBALIZATION, DEMOCRATIZATION AND MULTILATERALISM

Jacques Hersh and Johannes Dragsbaek Schmidt (*editors*)
THE AFTERMATH OF 'REAL EXISTING SOCIALISM' IN EASTERN EUROPE, Volume 1: Between Western Europe and East Asia

Staffan Lindberg and Árni Sverrisson (*editors*)
SOCIAL MOVEMENTS IN DEVELOPMENT: The Challenge of Globalization and Democratization

Anne Lorentzen and Marianne Rostgaard (*editors*)
THE AFTERMATH OF 'REAL EXISTING SOCIALISM' IN EASTERN EUROPE, Volume 2: People and Technology in the Process of Transition

Stephen D. McDowell
GLOBALIZATION, LIBERALIZATION AND POLICY CHANGE: A Political Economy of India's Communications Sector

Ann Seidman, Robert B. Seidman and Janice Payne (*editors*)
LEGISLATIVE DRAFTING FOR MARKET REFORM: Some Lessons from China

Geoffrey R. D. Underhill (*editor*)
THE NEW WORLD ORDER IN INTERNATIONAL FINANCE

International Political Economy Series
Series Standing Order ISBN 0–333–71110–6
(*outside North America only*)

You can receive future titles in this series as they are published by placing a standing order. Please contact your bookseller or, in case of difficulty, write to us at the address below with your name and address, the title of the series and the ISBN quoted above.

Customer Services Department, Macmillan Distribution Ltd
Houndmills, Basingstoke, Hampshire RG21 6XS, England

The European Science Foundation is an association of its 56 member research councils, academies and institutions devoted to basic scientific research in 20 countries. The ESF assists its Member Organizations in two main ways: by bringing scientists together in its Scientific Programmes, Networks and European Research Conferences, to work on topics of common concern; and through the joint study of issues of strategic importance in European science policy.

The scientific work sponsored by ESF includes basic research in the natural and technical sciences, the medical and biosciences, the humanities and social sciences.

The ESF maintains close relations with other scientific institutions within and outside Europe. By its activities, ESF adds value by cooperation and coordination across national frontiers and endeavours, offers expert scientific advice on strategic issues, and provides the European forum for fundamental science.

This volume arises from the work of the ESF Scientific Programme on European Management and Organizations in Transition (EMOT).

Further information on ESF activities can be obtained from:

European Science Foundation
quai Lezay-Marnésia
F-67080 Strasbourg Cedex
France
Tel. (+33) 88 76 71 00
Fax (+33) 88 37 05 32

Industrial Transformation in Eastern Europe in the Light of the East Asian Experience

Edited by

Jeffrey Henderson
Manchester Business School
England

Assisted by

Karoly Balaton

and

Gyorgy Lengyel

First published in Great Britain 1998 by
MACMILLAN PRESS LTD
Houndmills, Basingstoke, Hampshire RG21 6XS and London
Companies and representatives throughout the world

A catalogue record for this book is available from the British Library.

ISBN 0–333–68208–4

First published in the United States of America 1998 by
ST. MARTIN'S PRESS, INC.,
Scholarly and Reference Division,
175 Fifth Avenue, New York, N.Y. 10010

ISBN 0–312–21190–2

Library of Congress Cataloging-in-Publication Data
Industrial transformation in Eastern Europe in the light of the East
Asian experience / edited by Jeffrey Henderson, Károly Balaton, and
György Lengyel.
p. cm. — (International political economy series)
Includes bibliographical references and index.
ISBN 0–312–21190–2 (cloth)
1. Europe, Eastern—Economic policy—1989– 2. Europe, Eastern–
–Economic conditions—1989– 3. China—Economic policy—1976–
4. China—Economic conditions—1976– 5. East Asia—Economic policy.
6. East Asia—Economic conditions. I. Henderson, J. W. (Jeffrey
William), 1947– . II. Balaton, Károly. III. Lengyel, György.
IV. Series.
HC244.I495 1997
330.947086—dc21   97–38221
                                                    CIP

This book is printed on paper suitable for recycling and made from fully managed and
sustained forest sources.

10   9   8   7   6   5   4   3   2   1
07   06   05   04   03   02   01   00   99   98

Printed and bound in Great Britain by Antony Rowe Ltd, Chippenham, Wiltshire

Contents

List of Tables

Preface

The intellectual project, of which this book is a major product, developed from a concern about the social consequences of the course of economic transformation on which the state-socialist societies of Europe had embarked since their decisive turn to capitalism in 1989–91. I, like others, became convinced that the dramatic downturn in the economic fortunes of the various societies of Eastern Europe and its consequences for living standards, was partly a product of the inappropriate models of industrial capitalism – legitimated by orthodox economic theory – that had been allowed to inform the transformation process there. Prior to my engagement with Eastern European development I had spent many years studying East Asian experiences of industrialization and as a result I was conscious of the fact that there were other ways of constructing dynamic industrial capitalist societies than those enshrined in orthodox economic theory and communicated worldwide by the IMF, World Bank and other international agencies. Indeed I became persuaded that aspects of the East Asian experience were potentially highly relevant as guides to the construction of successful industrial capitalism and generalized prosperity in Eastern Europe.

My involvement with the European Science Foundation's 'European Management and Organizations in Transition' (EMOT) Programme provided me with the opportunity to bring together a number of scholars from Europe, Asia and the United States to debate the extent to which East Asian experiences might be relevant to Eastern European realities. Facilitated by the good offices of the Budapest University of Economic Sciences our meeting took place in May 1995. Earlier versions of the essays collected in this volume were among those presented at that meeting. Since then, and in preparation for publication, they have undergone extensive revision.

In preparing this volume I am especially grateful to my collaborators, Karoly Balaton and Gyorgy Lengyel. They were largely responsible for organizing the meeting in Budapest, and subsequently provided important editorial assistance as the book began to take shape. Furthermore, I wish to thank them and our other joint coordinator of EMOT's 'industrial transformation' stream, Gert Schmidt, for supporting my idea that a workshop exploring East European – East Asian comparisons would be valuable, and the Directors of the EMOT Programme, Anna Grandori and Richard Whitley, and their colleagues on the Programme's Board, for approving financial support.

In addition to these colleagues and organizations I am grateful to Ivan Szelenyi. It was he who first stimulated my interest in a serious scholarly engagement with problems of Eastern European development during my first visit to Hungary – at his invitation – in 1988. Since 1993 my intellectual involvement in Eastern Europe has been deepened and enriched by a number of colleagues and friends. These include Jolanta Kulpinska (who sponsored my first visit to Eastern Europe in 1980) and Witold Morawski (Poland), Milan Matejka (Czech Republic), Zdravko Milnar and Drago Kos (Slovenia) and Csaba Mako (Hungary). Research collaboration with Laszlo Czaban, Richard Whitley, Gyorgy Lengyel and more recently Marko Jaklic, has been especially important to this intellectual journey. I am most grateful to them all for helping me to understand this most fascinating of regions.

My final word of thanks goes to Suet Ying Ho and our son, Alexander Boman Henderson. They suffered with good grace my frustrations as an editor and my despair with collapsing computer software.

JEFFREY HENDERSON
Manchester and Leeds

Notes on the Editors and Contributors

Wladimir Andreff: Professor of Economics and Director of the Research Programme on Reforming and Opening Post-Socialist Economic Systems (ROSES), University of Paris I, Pantheon-Sorbonne, France.

Karoly Balaton: Professor of Management Studies, Budapest University of Economic Sciences, Hungary.

Laszlo Czaban: Lecturer in International Business, University of Leeds, England.

Nigel Harris: Professor of Development Planning, University College, University of London, England.

Jeffrey Henderson: Professor of International Economic Sociology, Manchester Business School, University of Manchester, England.

Eun Mee Kim: Associate Professor of Sociology, University of Southern California, USA.

Gyorgy Lengyel: Head of the Department of Sociology, Budapest University of Economic Sciences, Hungary.

Dic Lo: Lecturer in Economics, School of Oriental and African Studies, University of London, England.

David Lockwood: Lecturer in Russian and Soviet History, University of Melbourne, Australia.

Victor Nee: Goldwin Smith Professor of Sociology, Cornell University and Fellow of the Center for Advanced Study in the Behavioral Sciences, Stanford, California, USA.

Peter Nolan: Siny Professor of Chinese Management and Fellow of Jesus College, University of Cambridge, England.

Hugo Radice: Lecturer in Economics, University of Leeds, England.

Richard Scase: Professor of Sociology and Organizational Behaviour, University of Kent at Canterbury, England.

Sijin Su: Researcher and Consultant on Chinese Business, Berkeley, California, USA.

John Thirkell: Senior Lecturer in Industrial Relations, University of Kent at Canterbury, England.

Sarah Vickerstaff: Senior Lecturer in Social and Public Policy, University of Kent at Canterbury, England.

Richard Whitley: Professor of Organizational Sociology, Manchester Business School, University of Manchester, England.

Part I
Introduction

1 On Appropriate Models for Transformation in Eastern Europe

Jeffrey Henderson

The historical rupture of 1989–91 in Eastern Europe, occasioned by the collapse of state socialism, placed on the agenda of those societies the possibility of capitalist forms of economic transformation and development. In societies that become abruptly disconnected from the relative certainties of their past – usually through war or revolution – it has often been the case that attempts to re-cast the future have involved a collective search for models of political and economic organization that promise liberation from the strictures of the past. The influence of the US political settlement subsequent to the War of Independence on the French Revolution is well known, as is the influence of the latter on liberation movements and nation-building in nineteenth century Europe, Latin America and elsewhere. For much of our own century it has been the Leninist model and the various Stalinist forms of state socialism which it engendered that has provided the guidelines for political and economic reconstruction in parts of what used to be called the 'third world', as well as, of course, Eastern Europe. Given their experience of state socialism, however, it was no surprise that the preferred pathway to the future for the vast majority of the post-socialist societies of Europe, involved, as fundamental components, capitalist economies and liberal-democratic state forms. From the vantage point of over a hundred years of mature industrial capitalism what was surprising, perhaps, was that the release from state socialism seems not to have been accompanied by serious reflection on the fact that capitalism, economically and politically, is far from monadic. Rather, viewed globally and comparatively, it is clear that the world economy is now composed – at national and occasionally sub-national levels – of a number of mutations whose common elements consist of little more than 'a mode of production in which formally free labour is recruited for regular employment by ongoing enterprises competing in the market for profit' (Runciman 1995: 33). Beyond that they have forms of economic and political organization that vary from the economically neo-liberal and politically democratic United States at one

3

polarity, to the 'market Stalinism' of the People's Republic of China at the other.

The release from state socialism, then, could have provided the opportunity to ask 'what sort of capitalism' might be appropriate for Eastern Europe and for the different societies that constitute the region. While that question has already been posed (for instance by Amsden *et al.* 1994 and Nolan 1995), it has yet to make a noticeable impact on intellectual and policy debates. In the belief that the new forms of economic organization in Eastern Europe have yet to solidify, the essays presented here, whatever their individual aims, have the collective aim of helping to push the question 'what sort of capitalism' to the forefront of debate. They do so, however, via a particular analytic lens: that of the developmental and transformational experiences of a number of the societies of the Asia-Pacific region. While we outline below the nature of each essay's contribution, we begin this introductory chapter by exploring why that question has yet to become a focus for debate. We subsequently outline the reasons why reflection on alternative forms of economic organization – and particularly some of those that emanate from East Asia – may well be a necessary prelude to building Eastern Europe as a mosaic of prosperous, egalitarian societies.

THE IDEOLOGY OF TRANSITION

Alice Amsden, Jacek Kochanowicz and Lance Taylor have argued that since 1989 much of Eastern Europe has been embroiled in a 'moral crusade of market fundamentalism' (Amsden *et al.* 1994: 4). While the consequences of that crusade have been uneven, as we indicate below, it has had the effect of imposing a particular discourse – particular ways of thinking and seeing – on the process of economic change. That process has become to be understood as one of 'transition'. *The Concise Oxford English Dictionary* defines transition as a 'passage, change, from one place or state or act or set of circumstances to another'. The sense the term conveys, then, is of a movement from a known starting-point to a known end-point. Putting to one side the dubious proposition that any aspect of human history can be conceived in this way, in the context of Eastern Europe the supposedly 'known' starting-point was the reality of state socialism; the 'reality' – it was assumed – that all the 'communist' countries of Europe were organized economically (and politically and socially) in essentially the same way. The 'known' end-point of the transition was assumed to be free-market capitalism and democratic state forms. As such it was taken for granted that 'free-markets' and 'capitalism' were synonymous and that the political reflex of capitalism was indeed liberal democracy.

These assumptions, together with the conviction that the key macroeconomic elements of change had to be rapidly instituted, came to form the bedrock of 'transition theory' and its practical corollary, 'shock therapy'. While not the most ideological of its proponents, it was Jeffrey Sachs who became the best-known advocate of this route to industrial capitalism in Eastern Europe. Formerly economic adviser to the Governments of Poland, the former Yugoslavia and Russia, Sachs (1995: 51) regards the main precepts of post-war capitalism as:

(1) open international trade; (2) currency convertability; (3) private ownership as the main engine of economic growth; (4) corporate ownership as the dominant organizational form for large enterprises; (5) openness to foreign investment; and (6) membership in key international economic institutions . . .

Though he recognizes that the world economy contains alternative 'models' of capitalism, these differ for him on only two main dimensions: 'the extent of the welfare state and the nature of corporate ownership' (Sachs 1995: 52). Differences in industrial policy, state ownership and the degree economic openness he dismisses as having been 'exaggerated by some analysts' (Sachs 1995: 52).

Thus while Sachs admits that capitalism is a variable commodity, he insists that its supposed common core – enshrined, presumably, in neoclassical economic theory – is the only 'version' that can be allowed to guide the transition in Eastern Europe. Acknowledging the differences, then, between 'Swedish-style social democracy [and] Thatcherite liberalism', he rejects the significance of these differences because 'for [Eastern Europe] the alternative models of Western Europe are almost identical' (Sachs 1990: 23).

Irrespective of Sachs' role as the principal proselytizer for 'shock therapy' it seems to have been the institutions of global economic power that have been primarily responsible for submerging the possibilities for reflection on alternative routes to industrial capitalism by government and other agencies in Eastern Europe. Peter Gowan (1995) argues that though alternative routes were on the agenda in 1989–90 – thanks to the French Government – they were effectively displaced as a result of pressure from the IMF and World Bank. Irrespective of one's assessment of Gowan's analysis of the reasons for this strategy (see his subsequent debate with John Lloyd: Lloyd 1996, Gowan 1996), it seems clear enough that these institutions have sought to impose the 'structural adjustment' policies they have applied in Latin America, Africa and other parts of the developing world, and with them to encourage the emergence of their version of free-market capitalism.

It is important not to underestimate the significance of the pressures that international economic agencies have exerted on the governments of the respective Eastern European countries and the way these pressures have circumscribed their possibilities for relatively autonomous policy-making (unlike many of the Asia-Pacific countries). Indeed, in the case of Hungary, a former Minister of Finance in the first post-socialist government reports (interview with Jeffrey Henderson, Richard Whitley and Laszlo Czaban, May 1995) that 'We had no choice but to institute IMF policy' and the former IMF Representative there is now Vice President of the National Bank!

Whatever the *political* project on which the international economic agencies may be engaged in Eastern Europe, the 'ideology of transition' has been informed by a particular *intellectual* project – a version of neoclassical economic theory – which among the social sciences is now a very peculiar beast. Firstly, given its scientistic pretentions, it purports to be universalistic and thus denies the possibility that variations in history, culture and institutional arrangements might suggest that the same policy will have different consequences in different contexts, or obversely, that different contexts might demand different types of policy. Conceptually and in terms of its policy prescriptions the more extreme versions of neoclassical theory are rather like a toolkit: standardized instruments that supposedly can be applied to solve problems irrespective of time and place. Secondly, on the part of its practitioners it seems to be accompanied by a supreme arrogance and lack of self-doubt. While Sachs himself seems to be an example of this, for Nobel Laureate, George Stigler, economics under the hegemony of the neoclassical paradigm has become *the* 'imperial science', subsuming and transcending all other attempts to explain human behaviour and its products (Stigler 1984). Thirdly, leading neoclassical economists now speak to governments and public alike with an authority that surpasses that of all other social scientists, and often matches that of natural scientists. Indeed, like natural science, some seem to claim a monopoly of truth that is unsustainable both epistemologically and in the practice of their science. As Chalmers Johnson (the United States' leading authority on the political economy of modern Japan) has remarked about Milton Friedman's claim – pertinent to this book – that Japanese economic success has nothing to do with state industrial policy (Johnson 1988: 80):

Friedman does not read Japanese and has made no study of the Japanese economy. He does not have to because he is speaking as one of the world's most eminent economic theorists.

While the course of economic change in Eastern Europe, as many are beginning to observe (for instance, Grabher 1995, Whitley and Henderson 1995 and a number of contributors to this volume), is still far from approximating the neoclassical ideal, it is that ideal that continues to legitimate the actions of international economic agencies and inform the policy advice proffered by many – and probably most – independent consultants both from within and from outside the respective countries themselves. Given that very few, if any, national economies – historically or today – have approximated the neoclassical ideal, it seems highly unlikely that the countries of Eastern Europe will do much better. Even though this might be the outcome of what is beginning to look like a long period of economic and social change in the region, it remains important to engage with the ideologies that inform and constrain that process. Such engagement is necessary in order to create the intellectual space within which alternative economic senarios can be evaluated, rather than being dismissed *a priori*, as has often been the case in the recent past. Creating such an intellectual space, as I argue below, involves attempts to shift the prevailing discourse of transition onto the terrain of *transformation*. This book represents a step in that direction.

TOWARDS A DISCOURSE OF TRANSFORMATION

The Concise Oxford English Dictionary defines the verb 'to transform' as to 'Make (esp. considerable) change in the form, outward appearance, character, disposition etc.' of the element in question. While economic and social transformation must include change in content as well as form, it seems clear that, at least in English, the term 'transformation' implies a process without a pre-defined end-point. Engaging in a discourse of transformation, then, opens up the possibility for serious reflection upon alternative forms of industrial capitalism in Eastern Europe, as well as – perhaps – experimentation with an array of trajectories towards those alternative forms. As Runciman (1995) has argued, it is incorrect to conceive of the history of capitalism as a unilinear, incremental progression. Rather the analogy of a tree with numerous branches is more apt. Some of the branches develop and prosper while others constrict and die; none of the branches, however, take the same form. For Runciman the form that a given capitalism ultimately might take depends upon the *practices* from which it originates, and these practices – if we interpret him correctly – are often historical caprices.

Historical caprice or not, attempts to envision the process of economic change in Eastern Europe through the lens of transformation, not only allows for, but indeed legitimates efforts to innovate on the institutions and practices of capitalism alike. Viewed through the lens of transition, however, the supposed end-point of the process of change pre-determines what institutions and practices can be allowed (or at least taken seriously) if that end-point is to be reached.

Though some and perhaps many of the social practices associated with economic organization and related matters of scientific and technological endeavour may have originated, across time, as caprices, it is clear that at key moments those practices have been manipulated if not dramatically changed by powerful institutional actors pursuing their own particular interests. For Gowan (1995, 1996) it is precisely because the economic practices of state socialism, under pressure from Western financial and geo-political interests, have been changed too quickly that the societies of Eastern Europe now find themselves in the economic, social and political demise that he and others (for example, Nolan 1995) have documented. Furthermore, a wealth of scholarship has shown that across centuries, if not millennia, of all the institutions that have acted on economic practices in their own interests, it has been the national state that has been most significant. Castells (1996: 7–10), drawing on the work of Qian (1985) and Mokyr (1990), argues that for ancient China, for instance, the downturn in its technological and thus economic fortunes can be traced to changes in state policy associated with the rise of the Ming and subsequently the Qing dynasties from the beginning the fifteenth century onwards (see also Seagrave 1996: Chapter 7). From being the richest and most technologically sophisticated society in the world, as a result of state directives restricting key techological developments (for instance construction of ocean-going vessels) and trading practices, lest they disrupt social stability, China's fortunes began to spiral downwards making it vulnerable to colonial incursion and consigning it for five hundred years to the relative economic oblivion from which it is just beginning to emerge.

Similarly – though with the opposite economic consequences – Supple (1973) has argued that it is impossible to conceive of European industrialization prior to 1914 without according a decisive role to state policy. Dean (1975) has made a similar point though with particular regard to economic development as a byproduct of the state's interests in preparing for, and making war. Harris (1992) and Harris and Lockwood in this volume, extend and deepen the state–war–economic development connection for contemporary societies in Asia, Europe and indeed around the globe.

Irrespective of the particular role one might accord to the state in the process of economic change – and in East Asia, since 1945, it has been decisive (among many contributions see, for instance, the essays collected in Appelbaum and Henderson 1992) – it is clear, as we have indicated above, that it is possible to construct successful capitalism on the basis of a wide variety of historical experiences, value systems and institutional structures. From the European examples of Germany, Austria, Switzerland and the Scandinavian economies, to the neo-liberal United States, to the 'collective capitalisms' of parts of East Asia we now know that dynamic, prosperous (and sometimes relatively egalitarian) capitalisms can incorporate vastly different forms of corporate and economic governance, different investment priorities and relations between finance and industrial capital, different capacities for, and orientations to, state economic planning, different welfare regimes etc. (among others, see Pfaller *et al.* 1991, Porter 1992, Whitley 1992, Albert 1993, Henderson 1993, Pollin 1995, Vartiainen 1995). We also know, partly from the example of Britain (Hutton 1995), that capitalisms constructed more or less on the basis of the neoclassical model can fail to deliver the dynamism and generalized prosperity that the model promises.

The crux of the argument here is that pressures that seek to push the variant societies and economies of Eastern Europe into the uniform straightjacket of neo-liberal 'free market' capitalism need to be resisted. Given the variety of successful forms of industrial capitalism that exist in the world economy, reflection – at the very least – on the extent to which aspects of their experience might constitute 'models' to help guide development in Eastern Europe, seems warranted. The essays collected here explore in detail the experiences of one part of the world – Pacific Asia – that provides fertile ground for reflection by those concerned with East European development. They do so, however, not in the interests of constructing another supposedly universalistic model that can then be counterposed to the neo-liberal one. That, as we have argued above, is epistemologically unsustainable and economically counterproductive. Rather they assess the developmental experiences of parts of East Asia (particularly the newly industrialized countries and China), sometimes in direct comparison to their counterparts in Eastern Europe, in the interests of extending knowledge of the range of experience that potentially could be used to inform the reconstruction of the former state socialist societies. In so doing, though by implication, they challenge the truth claims of the neo-liberal model and relocate it to its correct position as merely one other perspective which could inform East European development.

EAST ASIAN EXPERIENCE, EAST EUROPEAN COMPARISONS

Our substantive investigation of the relevance of East Asian economic experiences for Eastern Europe begins, in Part II, with five chapters which make direct comparisons of aspects of transformation in both regions. In Chapter 2, Jeffrey Henderson and Richard Whitley discuss the social and institutional contexts which have influenced the courses of industrialization and development in the two regions. Focusing predominantly on South Korea and Taiwan or the one hand, and the 'Visegrad' countries of Poland, Hungary and the Czech and Slovak Republics on the other, they argue that while there appear to be important similarities between the two regions, in terms of the significance of the state, the muted role of secondary associations (trade unions, business groups, etc.), the strong commitments to education and training among others, on closer examination, it is the differences that seem more significant. In this regard they stress, for instance, that while the state remains central to economic progress in Eastern Europe, unlike its counterparts in Pacific Asia, its economic bureaucracies are fragmented and generally lack the institutional capacity to orchestrate expansion and prosperity. Additionally, they point to the different nature of kinship structures in the two regions and hence to the differing implications that these have had for industrialization. Most importantly, however, they highlight the differences in the geo-political contexts of transformation in both cases and stress that while in East Asia economic modernization proceeded on the basis of stable state forms (albeit authoritarian, and in some cases military in nature), in Eastern Europe political reform is developing simultaneously with economic change and hence producing superimposed sets of contradictions, and potentially, conflicts. Recognizing these difficulties, Henderson and Whitley's broad conclusion is that if for no other reason, the East Asian experience is centrally important for Eastern Europe because it shows that in the struggle to build successful industrial capitalist economies under current world circumstances, a decisive role for the state – whatever the difficulties – remains inescapable.

In Chapter 3, Wladimir Andreff points out that the logic of 'transition theory' from the perspective of orthodox economics is that once the state has dismantled the institutional apparatus of state socialism, as far as the economy is concerned, it should 'wither away'. Against the orthodoxy, however, he points out that for the high-performing economies of East Asia, the state has not only been central to the process of industrialization and development, but has continued to be central – albeit in differing ways – to subsequent restructuring and transformation. Drawing on the East Asian experiences, he insists that an effective industrial policy is

not possess greater structural possibilities to improve economic performance than did Russia. Given the significant differences in performance that the two economies have subsequently recorded he concludes, therefore, that the explanation for these differences must be sought in the different policy regimes adopted by the respective governments.

Nolan argues that while the USSR had huge advantages over China in terms of natural resources, scientific and technical personnel, and so on, it failed to exploit them. For him the Stalinist system in the USSR and China had equivalent growth potential, but whereas these were released in China, they were not in the Soviet Union. The principal reason for this, he suggests, was that whereas Stalinism was reformed – and 'marketized' – in China, it remained intact there, while in the Soviet Union it collapsed. As a consequence the state in China has remained relatively coherent and capable of guiding economic growth and development (cf. Andreff's argument in Chapter 3 of this volume) whereas its disintegration in Russia has led to economic decline, growing poverty, social dislocation and the rest.

Echoing some of Peter Gowan's (1995, 1996) arguments, Nolan suggests that from Gorbachev onwards, leaders of the Soviet and Russian states have allowed their economic policies to be reconstructed on the basis of neoclassical principles, and particularly its 'shock therapy' variants, and the political system to be democratized. The consequence has been a superimposition of contradictions and conflicts from within both realms (cf. Henderson and Whitley, Chapter 2 in this volume) and with it the destruction of the Party and the state. In China, on the other hand, political leaders have shunned democratization, resisted economic liberalization but opened the economy to the benefits of foreign capital and expertise. Herein, then, lies the secret of the divergent economic trajectories of the two countries.

Exploring in detail some of the issues broached in his earlier book on Russia and China (Nolan 1995), in Chapter 5, Peter Nolan presents a provocative thesis. In effect he is arguing that the best political shell for developing industrial capitalism from a context of state socialism, may well be 'market Stalinism'.

In the final chapter of Part II, Dic Lo and Hugo Radice move the discussion from the macro level to that of the enterprise. Rejecting the simplistic plan–market dichotomy, which they see as being justified by the experience of the newly industrialized economies of East Asia, they use that experience to assess the course of economic transformation in Eastern Europe and China.

They begin by pointing out that for economic growth and development to take place, a capacity for technological and structural change at the level of the enterprise, is essential. This, however, can only be ach- ieved where there are institutional arrangements in the societies in ques- tion which encourage both coordinated industrial progress and subject enterprises to market disciplines. As institutions capable of performing both these functions do not emerge 'naturally' from market relations, they have to be socially constructed. As a consequence, the state has a central role to play in these developments and it is in this context, they suggest, that the East Asian NIC experience is a relevant guide to trans- formation in China and the former state socialist societies of Europe. The chapter proceeds by examining the detail of enterprise change in both cases.

With regard to Eastern Europe (principally the 'Visegrad' countries) Lo and Radice point out that the principles of shock therapy, which initially guided the transformation process, have been significantly modi- fied. Far from there having been a simple transfer of assets to private owners, ownership has taken diverse forms, and within these state par- ticipation – either directly or through various institutional intermediaries – remains significant. Specifying the contours of this generalization in the Czech Republic, Hungary and Poland, Lo and Radice conclude that while there are important similarities been Eastern Europe and East Asia, movement towards better economic performance, dynamism and pros- perity requires a thorough application of state-developmentalist strat- egies.

Switching their focus to examine enterprise development in China, Lo and Radice point out that state-owned enterprises remain a central part of the economy, and in spite of neo-liberal assumptions to the contrary, are beginning to perform well on most of the market-related criteria. While ex- ploring the reasons for this in relation to the state sector in Eastern Europe, Lo and Radice also point out that one of the most dynamic components of the Chinese economy – the township and village enterprises – does not con- sist of capitalist firms in any simple sense, but rather are public-community operations (cf. Nee and Su in this volume). For Lo and Radice, then, the Chinese experience goes right against the grain of neo-liberal orthodoxy and has substantial elements akin to the nature of the development project in the East Asian NICs.

While emphasizing that the East Asian 'model' highlights the need for the state to mediate technology transfer and foreign direct investment, and promote dynamic sectors irrespective of concern about supposed lack of 'comparative advantage', Lo and Radice conclude that successful late in- dustrialization rests on state promotion of organizational innovation and collective learning. The superior economic performance of China, *vis-à-*

vis Eastern Europe, they suggest, may have more to do with the former's *de facto* emulation of the East Asian 'model' than it does with the relative spread of market forces.

Part III of the book collects together four chapters which explore various aspects of development and transformation in East Asia or Eastern Europe, without any systematic attempts to compare the two regions. In the first of these – Chapter 7 – Victor Nee and Sijin Su explore the significance of the township and village enterprises for Chinese development.

Like Lo and Radice in the previous chapter, Nee and Su begin by pointing out that China's economic growth confounds the expectations of orthodox economists. Unlike in Eastern Europe, privatization of state assets in China has not been implemented, the state is not a neutral enforcer of contracts, law enforcement is often arbitrary and the intertwining of political with economic interests has led to widespread rent-seeking and corruption. Their chapter, at one level, explores a major reason for China's dramatic economic growth under these supposed unpropitious circumstances: the significance of rural industrialization.

Arguing against both state-centred and more orthodox conceptions for reforming state socialist economies, Nee and Su suggest that adequate explanations of China's recent economic development must focus on the changing incentives for both political and economic actors. With regard to rural industrialization – the growth of township and village enterprises – accounts which place the weight of explanation on one or the other, they suggest, are misinterpretations of reality. Rather they argue that it has been economic actors in the firms, supported by corporatist local governments, that have been responsible for the dynamism of China's rural industry.

Echoing the literature on Post-Fordist industrial districts (see, for instance, some of the essays in Amin 1994), Nee and Su argue that, in China's rural areas, spatial proximity and shared interests between political and economic actors have been galvanized by local corporatist governance structures with the effect that flexible adaptation to changing institutional environments (domestically and internationally) has been sustained. In the context of macroeconomic state policies favourable to market-oriented growth, Nee and Su claim in their chapter that it has been local corporatism that has been central to the Chinese strategy of economic growth. Having established this position, the chapter continues with a data-rich account of the rise of local corporatism and its contribution to Chinese economic development. It concludes by emphasizing that local corporatism, while partly a response to the central state's declining commitment to redistribution, has produced the networks of solidarity and trust and the context for the dissemination of market-relevant information that has enabled local economic actors to respond quickly to changing market circumstances. By exploring the sources of local economic dynamism, in this way, Nee and Su by implication point to an important structural weakness in the former state socialist economies of Eastern Europe.

In Chapter 8, Eun Mee Kim looks at the 'developmental alliance' between the state and business which many have argued has been the key to economic growth and prosperity in Japan and the newly industrialized countries of East Asia. Focusing on South Korea and Taiwan, Kim argues that the export-oriented industrialization strategy that has been so central to their economic success could not have been effectively implemented without the appropriate institutional framework that emerged from the nature of state–business relations.

The chapter begins by discussing the structure and dynamic of the developmental states of South Korea and Taiwan and how they were able to influence business strategy. Kim shows that partly for historical reasons there were key differences in the way the economic policy and influence of the state evolved in both cases, with the former being more directly interventionist than the latter. In subsequent sections Kim moves on to discuss the corporate structure in both countries and the nature of their respective 'developmental alliances'. She points out that in the Korean case the economy became dominated by a few (state-encouraged) family-owned conglomerates – *chaebol* – and the state worked through these to orchestrate the course of economic development. In Taiwan, where the economy was organized largely on the basis of networks of small and medium-sized companies, the state worked through its own or Kuo Min Tang (the ruling political party)-owned large enterprises that were involved in upstream processing, as well as through larger mainlander (as opposed to Taiwanese)-owned manufacturing companies.

In the final sections of the chapter Kim turns to examine some of the consequences of this form of 'alliance' capitalism. In particular, she suggests, it has led to significant constraints on individual liberties (including labour repression) and on the development of democratic state forms. In spite of significant conflagrations between the state, labour and other social movements – most recently in Korea in 1996 – democracy there remains essentially cosmetic (cf. Henderson 1993), though perhaps less so in Taiwan. As a consequence the 'developmental alliance' probably remains as significant to South Korea's economic future as it has to its past, though in Taiwan she suspects that further democratization will begin to change its nature there.

In the penultimate chapter, Sarah Vickerstaff, John Thirkell and Richard Scase re-focus our attention on Eastern Europe and at the enterprise level. Drawing on their research on changing patterns of labour relations in the former state socialist societies, their concern in this chapter is to illustrate the contested and contingent nature of ownership change and enterprise strategies with particular reference to labour relations.

Vickerstaff, Thirkell and Scase begin by arguing that while the command economy under state socialism severely constrained enterprise autonomy, particularly in areas of strategy formulation and implementation, it is not clear that privatization *per se* has been responsible for changes in managerial and employee behaviour as had been assumed (cf. Whitley *et al.* 1996). Indeed, echoing a number of other contributors to this volume (and Stark 1996), they point out that a mixture of ownership forms have developed in the region and the privatization of state assets there has had different meanings and different implications from its supposed equivalents in Western Europe and elsewhere. As a consequence of this their hypothesis is that other changes both at enterprise level and in society more generally have had greater implications for the development of labour relations than have changes in enterprise ownership.

Working through case studies of particular enterprises in Poland, Bulgaria and Slovakia, Vickerstaff, Thirkell and Scase show that the changing role of managers (particularly middle managers), developments in trade union organization, the changing significance of the economic bureaucracies of the state and their relation to the enterprises (cf. Henderson *et al.* 1995) are all more central to understanding the changing role of enterprises, and industrial relations as part of that, than is privatization. Thus once again, though by implication in this chapter, one of the central planks of orthodox economic policy on Eastern Europe – private ownership – has been shown to be less significant for economic development than had been assumed.

In the final chapter of the book, Laszlo Czaban seeks to explain the reasons why the economic development of Hungary from the 1960s through to the present day has been characterized by cycles of expansion and reversal. He suggests that the key to the explanation is to be found in the changing bases of competition between factions of the political and economic elites in a context where the options for economic policy were becoming increasingly circumscribed by the intervention of the IMF and other international agencies.

He begins by arguing that in state socialist societies, central planning was always a contested process, involving bargaining between ministries, trade unions and other interest groups such as chambers of commerce. By the

1960s in the Hungarian case, the government's attempts to respond – in policy terms – to whichever faction of the elite had the upper hand at the time, had resulted in an economy which regularly switched from periods of expansion to periods of contraction. The competition of elite interests underlying this cyclical process was exacerbated as foreign indebtedness grew.

Czaban suggests that the economic reforms beginning with the 'New Economic Mechanism' in 1968 signalled the beginning of the end of the elite's belief in state economic management and regulation, and its replacement with a belief in market rationality as a panacea for dealing with Hungary's economic problems. Elite competition and policy responses to it continued during the 1970s and 1980s, compounding the cyclical and destructive pattern of economic development and with it increasing problems of foreign indebtedness. The consequence, Czaban suggests, was an increasing IMF influence to the extent that as early as 1979, Hungarian economic policy had become 'IMF-conforming'. With this, the government's commitments to economic redistristribution became increasingly difficult to pursue, and eventually this in turn began to fuel the disintegration of the political elite. By the late 1980s the disintegration of the old elite had provided the context for the emergence of a new, reformed elite who increasingly began to see their interests as associated with a thoroughgoing capitalist transformation of the economy.

The beginnings of that transformation in 1989–90, however, did not resolve elite conflicts but rather, as Czaban shows, they became focused around differing conceptions of how the country should be modernized. Some sought a 'nationalist' route with the state encouraging the growth of an indigenous bourgeoisie, while others recognized that instituting the 'programme of transnational capital', was the only way forward for the Hungarian economy. Tensions around these issues within the new elite were exacerbated, Czaban suggests, by shock therapy and its aftermath. As a consequence the cyclical process of development has continued in Hungary and in Czaban's view has constrained the speed of transformation and restricted the prospects for economic growth and generalized prosperity.

Embedded in Czaban's contribution is an argument that a positive – though contested – process of organic development had begun in Hungary in the 1960s and that this was increasingly thrown off course and finally interrupted by the events of 1989–90 and their aftermath. Given the underdevelopment of a national bourgeoisie capable of delivering industrial capitalism in Hungary via the 'classic' route of Western Europe, the United States and Japan (Henderson *et al.* 1995), Czaban concludes that the ultimate determinants of the country's future will inevitably be foreign capital and the international economic agencies.

CONCLUSION

The essays collected in this volume cover a wide range of issues and are driven by diverse theoretical and practical considerations. Behind these diversities, however, lie two convictions. The first is that the models that have informed, and continue to inform, the course of economic transformation in Eastern Europe are not only inappropriate, but have helped fuel economic and social dislocation, and in places political instability may yet plunge parts of the region into catastrophe. The second is that there are among the diverse forms of industrial capitalism models which may well be more appropriate to Eastern European conditions. Among these are a number from the Asia-Pacific region which in various ways have informed highly successful industrial transformation there, and in the more mature economies, the creation of generalized prosperity.

While none of the contributors to this book would seek to elevate East Asian experience – or any other experience of development and transformation – to a universal truth, they have written in the belief that there are many aspects of this experience that could be recovered and used in the interests of re-directing East European development. Such re-direction, at the very least, should have a better than even chance of producing far greater material gains for the vast majority of the region's population than looks likely should current policy regimes continue to be applied.

REFERENCES

Albert, M. (1993), *Capitalism Against Capitalism*. London: Whurr.

Amsden, A.H., J. Kochanowicz and L. Taylor (1994), *The Market Meets its Match: Restructuring the Economies of Eastern Europe*. Cambridge, Mass., Harvard University Press.

Appelbaum, R.P. and J. Henderson (eds) (1992), *States and Development in the Asian Pacific Rim*. Newbury Park: Sage Publications.

Castells, M. (1996), *The Rise of the Network Society*. Oxford: Blackwell.

Dean, P. (1975), 'War and industrialisation' in J.M. Winter (ed.), *War and Economic Development: Essays in Memory of David Joslin*. Cambridge: Cambridge University Press: 91–102.

Gowan, P. (1995), 'Neo-liberal theory and practice for Eastern Europe'. *New Left Review*, 213: 3–60.

Gowan, P. (1996), ' Eastern Europe, Western power and neo-liberalism'. *New Left Review*, 216: 129–140.

Grabher, G. (1995), 'The elegance of incoherence: economic transformation in East Germany and Hungary' in E. Dittrich, G. Schmidt and R. Whitley (eds), *Industrial Transformation in Europe*. London: Sage Publications: 33–53.

Harris, N. (1992), 'States, economic development and the Asian Pacific rim' in R.P. Appelbaum and J. Henderson (eds), *States and Development in the Asian Pacific Rim*. Newbury Park: Sage Publications: 71–84.

Henderson, J. (1993), 'The role of the state in the economic transformation of East Asia' in C. Dixon and D. Drakakis–Smith (eds), *Economic and Social Development in Pacific Asia*. London: Routledge: 85–114.

Henderson, J. R. Whitley, G. Lengyel and L. Czaban (1995), 'Contention and confusion in industrial transformation: dilemmas of state economic management' in E. Dittrich, G. Schmidt and R. Whitley (eds), *Industrial Transformation in Europe*. London: Sage Publications: 79–108.

Hutton, W. (1995), *The State We're In*. London: Jonathan Cape.

Johnson, C. (1988), 'The Japanese political economy: a crisis in theory'. *Ethics and International Affairs*, 2: 79–97.

Lloyd, J. (1996), 'Eastern reformers and neo-marxist reviewers'. *New Left Review*, 216: 119–128.

Mokyr, J. (1990), *The Lever of Riches: Technological Creativity and Economic Progress*. New York: Oxford University Press.

Nolan, P. (1995), *China's Rise, Russia's Fall: Politics, Economics and Planning in the Transition from Stalinism*. London: Macmillan.

Pfaller, A., I. Gough and G. Therborn (eds) (1991), *Can the Welfare State Compete?* London: Macmillan.

Pollin, R. (1995), 'Financial structures and egalitarian economic policy'. *New Left Review*, 214: 26–61.

Porter, M.E. (1992), 'Capital disadvantage: America's failing capital investment system'. *Harvard Business Review*, September/October: 65–82.

Qian, W.Y. (1985), *The Great Inertia: Scientific Stagnation in Traditional China*. London: Croom Helm.

Runciman, W.G. (1995), 'The "triumph" of capitalism as a topic in the theory of social selection'. *New Left Review*, 210: 33–47.

Sachs, J.D. (1990), ' What is to be done?'. *The Economist*, January 13: 23–8.

Sachs, J.D. (1995), 'Consolidating capitalism'. *Foreign Policy*, 98: 50–64.

Sachs, J.D. and W.T. Woo (1994), 'Structural factors in the economic reforms of China, Eastern Europe and the former Soviet Union'. *Economic Policy: A European Forum*, 18: 101–31.

Seagrave, S. (1996), *Lords of the Rim: The Invisible Empire of the Overseas Chinese*. London: Corgi Books.

Stark, D. (1996), 'Recombinant property in East European capitalism'. *American Journal of Sociology*, 101(4): 993–1027.

Stigler, G. (1984), 'Economics – the imperial science?'. *Scandinavian Journal of Economics*, 86(3): 301–13.

Supple, B. (1973), 'The state and the industrial revolution 1700–1914' in C.M. Cipolla (ed), *The Fontana Economic History of Europe Vol. III: The Industrial Revolution*. London: Fontana: 301–57.

Vartiainen, J. (1995), 'The state and structural change: what can be learned from the successful late industrializers?' in H.J. Chang and R. Rowthorn (eds), *The Role of the State in Economic Change*. Oxford: Clarendon Press: 137–89

Whitley, R. (1992), *Business Systems in East Asia: Firms, Markets and Societies*. London: Sage Publications.

Whitley, R. and J. Henderson (1995), 'Emergent capitalism: ownership, control and change in Hungarian enterprises' in H. Rudolf (ed.), *WZB Jahrbuch 1995*. Berlin: Edition Sigma: 285–306.

Whitley, R., J. Henderson, G. Lengyel and L. Czaban (1996), 'Continuity and change in an emergent market economy: the limited transformation of large enterprises in Europe' in R. Whitley and P.H. Kristensen (eds), *The Changing European Firm*. London: Routledge: 210–37.

Note: I am grateful to the Economic and Social Research Council for funding the project *The Development of Firms and Markets in Hungary* (grant R234422) and the European Commission's ACE Programme for funding the project *The Development of Firms, Markets and Management in Slovenia* (grant 940751R). This chapter is informed by work done in connection with those projects.

Part II

Transformation in Comparative Perspective

2 Social and Political Dimensions of Economic Transformation: Eastern Europe and Pacific Asia

Jeffrey Henderson and Richard Whitley

The extent to which one experience of development can be seen as capable of providing a model for others is associated not merely with questions of formal policy, but with the historical, social and institutional contexts within which the various experiences arise. Consequently in this chapter we identify and discuss the significance of a number of processes and institutional arenas through which the political economies of Eastern Europe and Pacific Asia can be compared. At the territorial level our focus is not these regions in their entirety. Rather our concerns are with the smaller economies of East-Central Europe – essentially the Visegrad group (Poland, the Czech and Slovak Republics and Hungary) – on the one hand, and the newly industrialized countries of Pacific Asia – particularly South Korea and Taiwan – on the other. The chapter consists of an identification of five arenas in which the East-Central European societies appear, at first sight, to be similar to their East Asian counterparts. This is followed by a discussion of six other arenas in which there appear to be significant differences. Finally we assess the implications which these similarities and differences have for the mobilization of aspects of the East Asian experience in the interests of Eastern European development.

DIMENSIONS OF TRANSFORMATION: SIMILARITIES

In comparing East-Central Europe with Pacific Asia it is important to be aware that, just as there are significant historical and structural differences between the Central European societies themselves and between them and those in Eastern Europe, so too there are major variations in the patterns of industrialization and dominant institutions in Japan, the newly industrialized countries of East Asia (South Korea – hereafter Korea – Taiwan, Hong

Kong and Singapore), and for the purposes of this chapter, also Malaysia (Appelbaum and Henderson 1992, Whitley 1992a). Although as Wade (1990), Castells (1992), Henderson (1993), Amsden *et al.* (1994) among others have emphasized, the state has been the primary collective actor in the industrial development of these societies since 1945, its organization, policy interventions, business alliances etc., have differed considerably over time and between them. Similarly, the significance of market coordination to their development trajectories has differed – with Hong Kong being the only one of them to rely substantially on this mechanism – as has the role of foreign direct investment (FDI). In the latter case, only in Singapore and Malaysia – of the societies pertinent to this chapter – has FDI been decisive. When one takes into account additionally that the East Asian societies under scrutiny here also differ in terms of the varying legacies of colonialism, and that only one of them – Malaysia – is multi-racial and retains a significant agricultural sector (cf. Henderson and Appelbaum 1992, Henderson 1993, Lubeck 1992), then clearly to posit a single East Asian approach to industrialization is misleading. For the purposes of this chapter our solution is to follow Amsden *et al.* (1994) in their focus on Korea and Taiwan as instances of state-led industrialization in societies with weak secondary associations and low levels of institutional pluralism, but with supplementary reference to the other societies where relevant.

At first sight there appear to be five major structural and institutional similarities between the former state socialist societies of East-Central Europe and post-war Korea and Taiwan. These are: the role of the state in economic transformation; the weakness of secondary institutions; educational provision and levels of attainment; the role of formal institutions in regulating economic relations; and levels of income inequality.

The Role of the State

The continuing ideological dogmatism of certain neoclassical economists and the World Bank notwithstanding, it is now widely accepted that the state dominated post-war economic development in Korea and Taiwan and was decisive also in Hong Kong, Singapore and Malaysia (on the latter three see Lim 1983, Rodan 1989, Castells *et al.* 1990, Schiffer 1991, Jomo 1990). While Taiwan was the only one (with the partial exception of Singapore) to develop a significant state-owned industrial presence, both governments (Taiwan from the early 1950s, Korea from the early 1960s) operated as collective capitalists in the sense that they induced entire industries through their associations with privately owned big business, which in some cases they themselves were responsible for creating. Rather like the origins of the Japanese *zaibatsu* in the last decades of the nineteenth century, so the Korean *chaebol* after 1961 were products of state policy (Amsden 1989, Koo and Kim 1992). In the case of Taiwan, state-owned companies were complemented by enterprises owned by the ruling party, the Kuo Min Tang (KMT), and by mainlander capitalists, beholden to the KMT, that had fled China in the late 1940s. Such companies were the principal beneficiaries of the government's import-substitution industrialization strategies from the early 1950s and, in moderated form, through to the present day (Hsiao 1995).

More specifically, in both cases the use of capital market-generated investment has been discouraged, and cheap credit has been delivered to favoured big businesses through state-owned banks (until 1987 in Korea, but still heavily regulated). In the circumstances of the Korean *chaebol*, which were deliberately structured by the state with significant debt–equity ratios, controlling the source of finance in this way has given government economic planners substantial leverage over corporate strategy (Cumings 1987, Woo 1991). Additionally the respective governments have controlled access to foreign exchange, technology and other inputs, and have manipulated the activities of TNCs within their borders in the interests of national economic gain. In both cases the respective governments have operated a 'plan rational' approach to economic development and as such have been able and willing to discipline business (as well as labour – see below) in the interests of state-generated national economic goals (Henderson 1993). While the relation between the state and big business in Korea and Taiwan, consequent in part to globalization and the growing economic power of some of the companies, is undoubtedly changing (Hsiao 1995, Jung 1995), it remains the case that centralized authoritarian states with considerable political and bureaucratic autonomy from civil society have been a *sine qua non* of their economic development and transformation.

Similarly, of course, the national states of East-Central Europe still dominate their respective economies. However, for reasons which we explore below, their capacity to control the course of economic transformation, is ebbing. Rather than constituting 'strong' states capable of orchestrating and controlling their paths to the future, in some cases their attempts at economic management have been confused and contradictory, associated with institutional fragmentation and riven by the clash of vested interests (on the Hungarian case, see Henderson *et al.* 1995). In such circumstances they are beginning to approximate Migdal's (1988) notion of 'weak' states and as such their capacity to exert strong, consistent and long-term control over economic actors seems considerably less than their Pacific Asian counterparts.

Secondary Associations

This relative dominance of the state over economic actors in both East Asia and East-Central Europe has been accompanied by a lack of strong secondary associations independent of the state and/or the ruling party. In the Korean and Taiwanese cases this was a legacy of the structures of pre-industrial society and of their subjection to Japanese colonialism prior to 1945. This lack of strong, independent secondary associations has been compounded by the authoritarian, militaristic state forms developed by the KMT in Taiwan and the Park regime in Korea after 1961. In the former case, the relationship between the state, the KMT (synonymous to all intents and purposes) and business associations, for instance, has constituted an 'authoritarian corporatism' with elaborate systems of surveillance and control over potential alternative sources of institutional power. This is an element of state–society relations in Taiwan that has led the noted Taiwanese sociologist, H.H. Michael Hsiao, to describe the state there as 'Leninist' (Hsaio 1995: 77).

Labour unions in particular have been firmly controlled throughout the East Asian region (Frenkel 1993). In Korea and Taiwan this has been achieved on occasion by brutal suppression (Deyo 1989, Park 1994). Although independent unions have emerged in recent years in both countries, helping to improve wage rates in Korea (Asia Monitor Resources Center 1988, Deyo 1989) and contributing to the gradual democratization process in Taiwan (Ho 1990), they are unlikely to be able to influence the course of economic transformation to even the minimal extent now possible for their counterparts in such neo-liberal economies as Britain and the United States.

In East-Central Europe business associations, while not quasi-state or party institutions as in Taiwan, are fragmented and weak and, rather like their equivalents in Hong Kong and Malaysia for instance, are more vehicles for personal ambition than disciplined, cohesive peak associations in the West European mode. Trade unions, on the other hand, continuing as they do to organize substantial sections of the industrial working class, potentially have a major role to play in the transformation processes of the Central European region, and in some cases, with the advent of socialist-dominated governments, are already involved in the management of transformation (Dittrich and Haferkemper 1995, Tatur 1995).

Education and Training

The transformation processes of both the East Asian and Central European economies have benefited from high levels of investment in education by the state, and in some Asian countries by families. In both cases this has resulted in educated labour forces at relatively early stages of industrialization and restructuring. Many East-Central European economies in addition developed quite elaborate vocational and technical training systems and as a consequence have large numbers of skilled workers, albeit in areas which are less appropriate for market-oriented firms. Compared to the economies of Western Europe and North America, which industrialized in the nineteenth century, the prospects for development and transformation in East Asia and Central Europe have arguably been enhanced by their ability to draw upon reservoirs of skilled, technically trained workers, and in some case on highly skilled engineers and scientists.

Economic Coordination

In addition to the role of the state in economic coordination in both regions, at a more micro level – and other than in Japan – high levels of distrust in formal institutions and legal frameworks are evident. In Korea and Taiwan this has resulted from the legacy of Japanese colonialism, the imposition of an alien KMT government in the latter, the Korean War in the former, and military-backed regimes and the residues of pre-industrial cultural and political patterns in both cases (Gold 1986, Jacobs 1985, Pye 1985, Whitley 1992a).

In East-Central Europe the distrust – indeed cynicism – has been a consequence largely of the Stalinist experience. The result of all this has been a preference in both regions for informal and personal ways of organizing, maintaining and policing economic relations and transactions, as opposed to formal, public and impersonal ones. The likelihood of contractual, 'arms' length' forms of economic governance becoming established in East-Central Europe seems slim, just as they have not become established in Pacific Asia (Bruszt 1989, Mares *et al.* 1994, Numazaki 1992, Redding 1990).

Income Inequality

Land reforms in Japan, Korea and Taiwan prior to industrialization, together with relatively open educational systems in the post-war period, have helped produce lower degrees of income inequality than other societies at similar stages of development (Haggard 1990: 225–50). The redistribution policies pursued since 1970 by the Malaysian Government has had a similar effect there (Jomo 1990), while the overtly egalitarian commitments of the European state socialist societies has resulted also in a relative equality of incomes and life chances.

Although inequalities are growing in many East-Central European countries as neo-liberal policies pursued under the aegis of the IMF and World Bank take effect and as capitalist uneven development becomes the order of the day, they remain relatively low and generally are not regarded as a legitimate consequence of transformation by political elites or the population at large. As a consequence, there seems at least a possibility that economic transformation in East-Central Europe (assuming it can deliver benefits sooner rather than later) will proceed without substantial grassroots disruption, rather as in most of the East Asian economies, but unlike many of the industrializing economies of Latin America (Gereffi and Wyman 1990).

DIMENSIONS OF TRANSFORMATION: DIFFERENCES

While the structural and institutional dimensions sketched above appear at first sight to be similar with regard to the background and course of transformation in Pacific Asia and Central Europe, on closer examination some of them turn out to be more differences than similarities. In this section of the chapter we identify a number of dimensions around which the societies of East-Central Europe and Pacific Asia seem to diverge. Inevitably this partly involves revisiting some of the issues already discussed.

The State and the Economic Bureaucracy

In Central Europe the low legitimacy of the various national states and their dependence on Soviet military and economic support during the state socialist period, together with the burden of foreign indebtedness in many – though not all – of these countries (of which more below), arguably make them less able to perform the strong developmentalist role of their Korean and Taiwanese counterparts (cf. Midgal 1988). This is especially so with regard to the direction of enterprise strategies and imposition of penalties for failure to meet state targets which are obviously difficult to accomplish in liberal democracies built on the ruins of state socialism. Furthermore, the cohesion and integration of state bureaucracies in many of these societies declined during the 1970s and 1980s as the state became more fragmented and subject to pressures from special interest groups (Carroll *et al.* 1988, Henderson *et al.* 1995). Together with the widespread ignorance of how firms operate in market economies, and increasing separation of planing Ministries from enterprise activities as the economic system became more complex and differentiated, the technical ability of bureaucrats to coordinate and steer economic development in East Europe in a similar way to those in East Asia is clearly questionable.

Additionally, the bulk of the bureaucratic personnel in these former state socialist societies, as Amsden *et al.* (1994) point out, was not selected according to their intellectual abilities (cf. Los 1993), and their low prestige and payment over the past few decades have meant that many of the more capable people left for more lucrative and higher-status posts after 1989. Thus a key component of successful East Asian industrialization, namely a cohesive, well paid, highly educated and selected bureaucracy which has high social prestige, is lacking in most post-socialist countries. Overall, then, the preconditions for long-term and effective state coordination of the reindustrialization of Eastern Europe in the East Asian mode are only weakly present as far as the state itself is concerned.

Secondary Associations and Rule of Law

Although the impact of labour unions on the course of transformation has thus far been limited in East Asia and post-1989 East-Central Europe, in the latter case they are distinguished from the former in the sense that they have a substantial numerical presence in terms of the proportion of the workforce they organize, are typically organized around industrial branches (though somewhat fragmented by political divisions) and, importantly, have a considerable degree of legitimacy. Both the 'transmission belt', formerly party-controlled unions and the dissident, worker-based collective movements of Bulgaria and Poland for instance, retain and/or have recovered a substantial amount of popular support and participate in tripartite councils with the state and employers' groups (Tatur, 1995). Thus the labour movement in general is more organized, successful in mobilizing loyalties and formally involved in managing the transformation process in many East European countries than in Korea and Taiwan. While not replicating the post-war Austrian or German forms of corporatism, this role of the unions is more akin to continental European forms of capitalism than East Asian ones.

Despite the corruption and systematic subordination of the legal system to party and personal interests during the state socialist period, and its variable institutionalization across East Europe before the World War II, it seems reasonable to suggest that the ideal of the rule of law and general commitment to formal legal procedures remain more significant in this region than in East Asia (Sajo 1989, Hankiss 1989). As Jacobs (1985), and others (for example Pye 1985), have emphasized, the traditional 'virtuocracies' of China and Korea entrenched the rule of virtuous men as the preferable foundation of the political system, and the idea of the state and its leaders being subject to an independent formal legal system has not found much favour in post-war Korea and Taiwan. As the actions of the Constitutional Court in Hungary during the first post-communist government have shown, the ability of the new democracies to establish effective formal legal institutions is not negligible, and clearly differentiates some of these countries from their East Asian counterparts.

Similarly, despite the state socialist regimes' attempts to destroy organized religion, the enforced secularization of beliefs and values seems to have been only partially successful, with both the Roman Catholic and Orthodox churches still able to mobilize commitments, especially in Poland and in rural communities (Podgorecki 1993). Whether the bulk of the population in East Europe still adheres strongly to the Christian doctrine, it has clearly been important in effecting the development of distinctive ethical norms which differ significantly from those dominating East Asian societies (Berger and Hsiao 1988, Redding 1990, Rozman 1991, Wolferen, 1989). Relatedly, where the Church has been able to retain or renew its organizational powers it can be expected to encourage more associational pluralism and contribute to the strengthening of civil society to a greater extent than religious groups in Korea or Taiwan.

Family and Kinship

The final institutional feature impinging upon economic development which varies between most East European societies and those in East Asia is the cohesion and social priority of the family and kinship connections. As Pye (1985), among others (for example, Greenhalgh 1988, Pelzel, 1970, Redding 1990, Wong 1985), has emphasized, the family and lineage are crucial sources of social identity and foci of loyalty in Chinese, Korean and Japanese societies, as is manifested in the importance of family names and ancestor veneration. Individual interests and rights are subordinated to those of the family, with resources typically being pooled and invested for collective family objectives. Additionally, families have been, and usually still are, dominated by the father with male children being privileged over female ones and patrilocal residence patterns firmly established. In East Europe, the significance of the family as a social unit and source of identity varies between countries, religious groups and ethnic membership but seems rather less marked than in East Asia, not least as a result of the fragmentation of traditional communities during the phase of enforced industrialization and subsequent growth of 'consumerism' to mitigate political dissent (Csepeli and Orkeny, 1992). While families and kinship networks were, and remain, important for obtaining favours, mobilizing resources and developing trust in a hostile and untrustworthy world, individual achievement and development seem to be more important values than family success in many East European countries (Mares *et al.*, 1994). As Hankiss (1989: 42) suggests on the basis of a European value systems study: 'Hungarians turned out to be surprisingly more egoistic than their (West) European counterparts' and more Hungarians (44 per cent) than respondents from nine West European countries agreed with the statement that 'people have their own lives; they should not sacrifice themselves for their children'.

In addition to these institutional differences between many of the societies of East-Central Europe and their East Asian counterparts, there are a number of general features of their economies and the contexts of their transformation that raise further questions about the direct applicability of East Asian experiences.

Development or Restructuring?

The newly industrialized countries of Pacific Asia have reached that status through a process of development from a predominantly agricultural base. Unlike their counterparts in Latin America, however, they industrialized without the deadweight of feudal landlords and an inefficient agricultural system holding them back (because of the land reforms begun by the Japanese in Korea and Taiwan and completed by the post-war Rhee and Chiang regimes respectively). Partly for this reason and partly because of their suppression of other sources of power (urban middle classes and workers), they emerged with states that had a high degree of autonomy from civil society and with economic bureaucracies with a high degree of autonomy from the political process. In these circumstances they were able to plan the course of industrialization relatively unencumbered and more or less from scratch.

The societies of East-Central Europe, however, already boast economies that are at least semi-industrialized. Consequently their transformation is not so much a process of 'development' but more one of 'restructuring'. They already have industrial bases with particular enterprise cultures, sets of custom and practice, managerial and worker norms. They are staffed by workers geared largely to the individual wage as the source of household income, unlike their East Asian counterparts who, with the primary exception Singapore, tend to be 'semi-proletarianized' and hence have household incomes which perhaps can be more reliably subsidized by informal economic activities (see Henderson 1991, Cheng and Gereffi 1994, and more generally and theoretically, Wallerstein 1983). In other words the East-Central European societies may be more 'path dependent' and hence more constrained in the transformational choices available to them.

Geo-politics and the World Economy

The contemporary economies of Korea, Taiwan and Japan were as much products of the origins of the Cold War as the post-communist societies of Central Europe were of its termination. They were built consciously as bulwarks against communism and were recipients of billions of dollars in war contracts and military and civil aid from the US government. Additionally, their room for policy manoeuvre was not disabled by foreign indebtedness and consequently they were not subject to significant interference by the IMF and the World Bank in their attempts to formulate and apply *dirigiste* development strategies. Thirdly, their move to export-oriented strategies coincided with an unprecedented expansion in world trade in manufactured commodities, in a period when the world's major markets were much more open than they are today (Wade 1990, Woo 1991).

In contrast, much of East-Central Europe has had relatively little foreign aid, is heavily burdened by servicing foreign debts, has been urged by the World Bank to privatize state enterprises rapidly before restructuring them, to liberalize imports and severely reduce the economic role of the state, and has had only limited tariff-free access to the European Union and other Western markets. Consequently they have had little time to adjust to international competition and have been much more dependent on direct foreign investment and ownership of enterprises than most of their East Asian counterparts (with the major exceptions of Singapore and Malaysia). The sorts of autarkic, state-dominated policies pursued successfully by some of these latter states are not nearly as feasible, therefore, for most East European ones in the 1990s.

Systemic Change

The final issue for the purposes of this discussion is the fact that the societies of East-Central Europe are attempting a total systemic transformation of a sort unprecedented in the twentieth century with the exception of the Bolshevik revolution itself. The societies of Pacific Asia embarked on their routes to the modern world under circumstances in which they already had market economies and where their political systems were relatively stable – if not secure – and, importantly, were centralized and authoritarian. Even in the contemporary cases of China and Vietnam, capitalism and industrialization have proceeded – for the moment – along with the retention of Stalinist authoritarianism at the level of the state. In as far as the East-Central European societies are attempting to become capitalist, more thoroughly industrial and democratic at the same time, they are engaged on a multiplicity of superimposed transformations – with all the attendant contradictions and conflicts that this implies – of which the outcome at best is highly uncertain. It is a transformational project which was perhaps historically inevitable but it is one with whose mixed blessings the East Asian societies did not have to deal.

CONCLUSIONS

In relation to the experience of the East Asian countries discussed here, the particular institutional features of the East-Central European societies, their varied inheritances from state socialism, and their distinct patterns of economic development since 1989, allow two broad conclusions to be drawn. The first concerns the role of the state. Whether one agrees with Amsden *et al.* (1994) and others on the ubiquitous significance of the state in coordinating industrial development and developing large scale capitalism or not, and this obviously depends on how the state is understood in different countries at different times, and on how capitalist development is conceived and analysed, it seems clear that there is no alternative collective agent in East Europe to manage the transformation of these societies to democratic capitalism. Since markets coordinating widespread, long-term and diverse economic activities do not develop 'naturally' from pre-capitalist societies but, on the contrary, require specific institutions and social structural features to function effectively, and these did not exist in East Europe in 1989, they have to be consciously established. As the East Asian examples have indicated, such direct development of market-supporting institutions can be successfully undertaken in particular circumstances by the state. Given the lack of alternative collective agents in the former state socialist countries, it has to be the state which carries out this function.

However, as we have seen, this does not mean that the present states of East Europe are ideally equipped for this task. Fragmented by competing interest groups, lacking broadly based legitimacy for pursuing state-coordinated development as well as a well-paid, prestigious highly selected and educated bureaucracy, and under external pressure to follow inappropriate models of capitalist development, many states are in a weak position to manage the transformation process effectively. Additionally, the successful establishment of democracy means that in much of Easten Europe authoritarian development paths are not possible. Commitment to the transformation process, and to managing the difficulties involved, has to be elicited by politicians. Equally, social discipline needs to be developed through the internalization and legitimation of appropriate norms, rather than being imposed by authoritarian means. Given the legacies of absolutism and state socialism in the region, these tasks will indeed be a major challenge to political parties, bureaucrats and the intelligentsia.

The second broad conclusion concerns the forms of capitalism that are emerging in Eastern Europe. As Stark (1992) and others (for example, Cirtautus 1994, Grabher, 1995) have emphasized, there were significant differences between the regimes of post-war Eastern Europe, just as there were variations in the sort of political economy they inherited. Additionally, the past five years have witnessed contrasting developmental patterns in the reform of major institutions, notably the state, trade unions and the banking system, and in the economic transformation policies followed. While, then, they have undoubtedly shared important common features that differentiate them from both 'Western' societies and East Asian ones, they also differ among themselves in certain respects which can be expected to have an effect on the sorts of capitalism that eventually become established. These include: the nature of the political system, particularly the structure and roles of parliamentary parties and the political executive; the nature and significance of religious and ethnic identities within and between nation states; the degree of Western cultural and institutional influence, especially on the legal and political systems; the length and depth of state socialist rule; the extent to which the former *nomenklatura* has faded away or transformed itself into the new business elite; the significance of corruption and 'bandit capitalism'; and finally, the feasibility of, and determination to, pursue autarkic economic policies and exert international political and military influence. In these last two respects, Russia is clearly quite different from the smaller states.

In terms of the policies pursued thus far, the extent of 'shock therapy', levels of unemployment, modes and degrees of privatization of state enterprises, openness to foreign investment of different kinds and banking system reforms all vary across these countries, and are likely to diverge further as changes become irreversible and develop distinctive transformation trajectories. In the medium term, then, Eastern Europe will manifest a variety of forms of economic organization, just as Western Europe does (Whitley 1992b, Whitley and Kristensen 1996), probably sharing some characteristics with other continental European societies and possibly some with certain East Asian ones. To understand how and why these different sorts of economic organization become established, and to offer more informed policy advice, the comparative analysis of capitalist economies and their institutional contexts is invaluable. It is in the context of this comparative evaluation that we would insist on the relevance of the Pacific Asian experiences of industrialization for the former state socialist societies of Europe.

REFERENCES

Amsden, A.H. (1989), *Asia's Next Giant: South Korea and Late Industrialization.* New York: Oxford University Press.

Amsden, A.H., J. Kochanowicz and L. Taylor (1994), *The Market Meets Its Match: Restructuring the Economies of Eastern Europe.* Cambridge, Mass: Harvard University Press.

Appelbaum, R.P. and J. Henderson (eds) (1992), *States and Development in the Asian Pacific Rim.* Newbury Park: Sage Publications.

Asia Monitor Resources Center (1988), *Min-Ju No-Jo: South Korea's New Trade Unions.* Hong Kong: Asia Monitor Resources Center.

Berger, P. and H.H.M. Hsiao (eds) (1988), *In Search of an East Asian Development Model.* New Brunswick, NJ: Transaction Books.

Bruszt, L. (1989), '"Without us but for us"? Political orientation in Hungary in the period of late paternalism' in P. Somlai (ed.), *Changing Values in Hungarian Society.* Budapest: Coordinating Council of Research Programme TS-3.

Carroll, G.R., J. Goodstein and A. Gyenes (1988), 'Organisations and the state: effects of the institutional environment on agricultural cooperatives in Hungary'. *Administrative Science Quarterly,* 33: 233–56.

Castells, M. (1992), 'Four Asian tigers with a dragon head: a comparative analysis of the state, economy and society in the Asian Pacific Rim' in R.P. Appelbaum and J. Henderson (eds), *States and Development in the Asian Pacific Rim.* Newbury Park: Sage Publications: 33–70.

Castells, M., L. Goh and R.Y. Kwok, (1990), *The Shek Kip Mei Syndrome: Economic Development and Public Housing in Hong Kong and Singapore.* London: Pion.

Cirtautus, A.M. (1994), 'In pursuit of the democratic interest: the institutionalization of parties and interests in Eastern Europe' in C.G.A. Bryant and E. Mokrzycki (eds), *The New Great Transformation.* Routledge: London.

Csepeli, G. and A. Orkeny (1992), *Ideology and Political Beliefs in Hungary.* London: Pinter

Cumings, B. (1987), 'The origins and development of the Northeast Asian political economy' in F.C. Deyo (ed.), *The Political Economy of the New Asian Industrialism.* Ithaca: Cornell University Press.

Deyo, F.C. (1989), *Beneath the Miracle: Labor Subordination in the New Asian Industrialism.* Berkeley: University of California Press.

Dittrich, E. and M. Haferkemper (1995), 'Labour relations in the making: Bulgaria, Hungary, Poland and the Czech Republic' in E. Dittrich, G. Schmidt and R. Whitley (eds), *Industrial Transformation in Europe.* London: Sage Publications.

Frenkel, S. (ed.) (1993), *Organized Labor in the Asia-Pacific Region* Ithaca: Cornell International Industrial and Labor Relations Reports.

Gereffi, G. and D. Wyman (eds) (1990), *Manufacturing Miracles: Paths to Industrialization in Latin American and East Asia.* Princeton: Princeton University Press.

Gold, T.B. (1986), *State and Society in the Taiwan Miracle.* Armonk, NY: M.E. Sharpe.

Grabher, G. (1995), 'The elegance of incoherence: economic transformation in East Germany and Hungary' in E. Dittrich, G. Schmidt and R. Whitley (eds.), *Industrial Transformation in Europe.* London: Sage Publications.

Greenhalgh, S. (1988), 'Families and networks in Taiwan's economic development' in E.A. Winckler and S. Greenhalgh (eds), *Contending Approaches to the Political Economy of Taiwan.* Armonk, NY: M.E. Sharpe.

Haggard, S. (1990), *Pathways from the Periphery: the Politics of Growth in the Newly Industrializing Countries.* Ithaca: Cornell University Press.

Hankiss, E. (1989). 'Between two worlds' in P. Somlai (ed.) *Changing Values in Hungarian Society.* Budapest: Coordinating Council of Research Program TS-3.

Henderson, J. (1991), 'Urbanisation in the Hong Kong–South China region: an introduction to dynamics and dilemmas'. *International Journal of Urban and Regional Research*, 15(2): 169–79.

Henderson, J. (1993), 'The role of the state in the economic transformation in East Asia' in C. Dixon and D. Drakakis-Smith (eds), *Economic and Social Development in Pacific Asia.* London: Routledge: 85–114.

Henderson, J. and R.P. Appelbaum (1992), 'Situating the state in the East Asian development process' in R.P. Appelbaum and J. Henderson (eds), *States and Development in the Asian Pacific Rim.* Newbury Park: Sage Publications: 1–26.

Henderson, J., R. Whitley, G. Lengyel and L. Czaban (1995), 'Contention and confusion in industrial transformation: dilemmas of state economic management' in E. Dittrich, G. Schmidt and R. Whitley (eds), *Industrial Transformation in Europe.* London: Sage Publications.

Ho, S.Y. (1990), *Taiwan – After a Long Silence.* Hong Kong: Asia Monitor Resources Center.

Hsiao, H.H.M. (1995), 'The state and business relations in Taiwan', *Journal of Far Eastern Business*, 1(3): 76–97.

Jacobs, N. (1985), *The Korean Road to Modernization and Development.* Urbana: University of Illinois Press.

Jomo, K.S. (1990), *Growth and Structural Change in the Malaysian Economy.* London: Macmillan.

Jung, K.H. (1995), 'Changing business–government relations in Korea'. *Journal of Far Eastern Business*, 1(3): 98–112.

Koo, H. and E.M. Kim (1992), 'The developmental state and capital accumulation in South Korea' in R.P. Applebaum and J. Henderson (eds), *States and Development in the Asian Pacific Rim.* Newbury Park: Sage Publications.

Lim, L.Y.C. (1983), 'Singapore's success: the myth of the free market economy'. *Asian Survey*, 23(6): 752–64.

Los, M. (1993), 'Crimes of the functionaries: bribery, extortion and favouritism' in M. Marnyama (ed.), *Management Reform in Eastern and Central Europe.* Aldershot: Dartmouth Press.

Lubeck, P. (1992), 'Malaysian industrialization, ethnic divisions and the NIC model: the limits to replication' in R.P. Appelbaum and J. Henderson (eds), *States and Development in the Asian Pacific Rim*. Newbury Park: Sage Publications: 176–98.

Mares, P., L. Musil and L. Rabusic (1994), 'Values and the welfare state in Czechoslovakia' in C.G.A. Bryant and E. Mokrzycki (eds), *The New Great Transformation*. London: Routledge.

Migdal, J.S. (1988), *Strong Societies and Weak States: State–Society Relations and State Capabilities in the Third World*. Princeton: Princeton University Press.

Numazaki, I. (1992), *Networks and Partnerships: the Social Organisation of the Chinese Business Elite in Taiwan*. Unpublished PhD Dissertation, Department of Anthropology, Michigan State University.

Park, Y.G. (1994), 'State regulation, the labour market and economic development: the Republic of Korea' in G. Rodgers (ed.), *Workers, Institutions and Economic Growth in Asia*. Geneva: International Labour Office.

Pelzel, J.C. (1970), 'Japanese kinship: a comparison' in M. Freedman (ed.), *Family and Kinship in Chinese Society*. Stanford: Stanford University Press.

Podgorecki, A. (1993), 'Polish traditions and perspectives of post-socialist reform' in M. Maruyama (ed.), *Management Reform in Eastern and Central Europe*. Aldershot: Dartmouth Press.

Pye, L.W. (1985), *Asian Power and Politics: The Cultural Dimensions of Authority*. Cambridge, Mass: Harvard University Press.

Redding, S.G. (1990), *The Spirit of Chinese Capitalism*. Berlin: de Gruyter.

Rodan, G. (1989), *The Political Economy of Singapore's Industrialisation: National State and International Capital*. London: Macmillan.

Rozman, G. (ed.) (1991), *The East Asian Region: Confucian Heritage and its Modern Adaptation*. Princeton: Princeton University Press.

Sajo, A. (1989), 'Rights-awareness in Hungary' in P. Samlai (ed.), *Changing Values in Hungarian Society*. Budapest: Coordinating Council of Research Program TS-3.

Schiffer, J. (1991), 'State policy and economic growth: a note on the Hong Kong model'. *International Journal of Urban and Regional Research*, 15(2): 180–96.

Stark, D. (1992), 'Path dependence and privatisation strategies in East-Central Europe'. *East European Politics and Societies*, 6: 17–51.

Tatur, M. (1995), 'Towards corporatism? the transformation of interest policy and interest regulation in Eastern Europe' in E. Dittrich, G. Schmidt and R. Whitley (eds), *Industrial Transformation in Europe*. London: Sage Publications.

Wade, R. (1990), *Governing the Market: Economic Theory and the Role of Government in East Asian Industrialization*. Princeton: Princeton University Press.

Wallerstein, I. (1983), *Historical Capitalism*. London: Verso.

Whitley, R. (1992a), *Business Systems in East Asia: Firms, Markets and Societies*. London: Sage Publications.

Whitley, R. (ed.) (1992b), *European Business Systems: Firms and Markets in Their National Contexts*. London: Sage Publications.

Whitley, R. and P.H. Kristensen (eds) (1996), *The Changing European Firm*. London: Routledge.

Wolferen, K. van (1989), *The Enigma of Japanese Power*. London: Macmillan.

Wong, S.L. (1985), 'The Chinese family firm: a model'. *British Journal of Sociology*, 36: 58–72.

Woo, J.E. (1991), *Race to the Swift: State and Finance in South Korean Industrialization*. New York: Columbia University Press.

Note: We are grateful to the Economic and Social Research Council for funding the project *The Development of Firms and Markets in Hungary* (grant R234422) on which this chapter draws.

3 Industrial Transformation in East-Central Europe and East Asia: Should the State Wither Away?

Wladimir Andreff

In the 1960s, the rate of economic growth was already higher, on average, in the East Asian countries (EACs) than in the Central-Eastern European (CEECs) members of former Comecon. Later on, the gap between the two areas grew. While economic growth was hardly affected by crisis in the EACs during the 1970s and 1980s, it slowed down in the CEECs, dramatically so in the 1980s. The break-up of the communist system first worsened this economic crisis in the latter region in the early 1990s and since then only a few former socialist countries have recovered a positive, though rather low, rate of economic growth: Poland, Romania, Slovenia, Hungary and the Czech Republic. On the other hand, after a period of slower economic growth in 1985–90, the newly industrialized countries (NICs) of East Asia enjoyed a nice recovery, with growth rates ranging between 5.5 and 9.9 per cent in 1993.

Let us now assess the economic performance of the two areas relying on a second index measuring their 'international attractiveness', namely their capability to attract foreign direct investment. In 1991–3, among our sampled countries, the most attractive were Singapore and Malaysia. Then comes a second group of significant host countries led by Thailand and South Korea. Hungary was the best performer among CEECs. Except for Hungary, the Czech Republic, Russia and Poland, all the other CEECs were capable only of attracting 'peanuts' (lower than $120 million a year), as far as foreign direct investment is concerned. The attractiveness of Singapore, Malaysia and Thailand has increased in recent years while on average the East Asian countries performed considerably better than the CEECs.

Many sets of variables can explain the gap between the East Asian countries' and the CEECs' economic performance, but we focus here only on one of them, which is the role of the state in the process of industrial transformation. At first glance, two features common to both areas are: a rather

41

limited influence of the state on industrial activity, and a political (ideo-logical?) desire to push the state away from all business. The liberal econ-omic view about this process is that the state must shrink with transition to a fully-fledged market economy and, at the end of the day, it should 'wither away'. Unfortunately the whole story has not been that simple in East Asia as the World Bank (1993) has now admitted, highlighting industrial policy as a crucial component in the region's success story. Our point here goes even further: the success story of most Asian NICs has been achieved *not in spite of* state intervention in the economy, but on the contrary has been due to a straightforward state policy of influencing and, sometimes, levering market forces in order to gear them towards industrial transformation. The logical consequence of this point is that the transition strategy in the first years of the CEECs post-communist regimes, in as far as it attempted to make the state as absent from industrial business as possible (through liber-alization, privatization and the like), has been misconceived. We therefore advocate that a state-run and state-oriented policy of industrial restructur-ing is badly needed due to the legacy of a distorted industrial structure in-herited from years of centrally planned priorities to heavy (and polluting) industries. Sooner (as the German *Treuhandanstalt*) or later (as the Czech government led by Vaclav Klaus), all CEECs have discovered, after a few years of transition, how much an industrial policy is unavoidable and how limited it could be without the state as its conductor.

INDUSTRIAL POLICY IN EAST ASIA: THE STATE DID NOT WITHER AWAY

State Leadership of Industrial Policy

It must be recalled that a kind of planning, though not a mandatory one, was regulating economic activity in several East Asian countries. In Korea, the Economic Planning Board not only planned industrial development, but heavily influenced the state budget up to the mid-1980s, when it supervised all loans and investments. President Park strengthened the hierarchical position of the Economic Planning Board in promoting its head to the rank of deputy Prime Minister. In addition, the Ministry of Trade and Industry was connected with Korean tycoons and businessmen while the Ministry's sectoral divisions were cooperating with specific employers' associ-ations. Although Korean commercial banks were privatized in 1987, credit allocation still remained tightly linked to state economic and industrial programmes.

Despite its seeming economic liberalism, Malaysia is the ASEAN member country in which the state's economic weight is the highest (the state budget is about 40 per cent of GNP). The economy is orientated by the means of an indicative planning system. So far, six five-year plans have been worked out by the Economic Planning Unit, which is part of the Prime Minister's secretariat. The Economic Planning Unit consults with Ministries, the Central Bank and, since the beginning of the 1980s, business partners. The Malaysian Industrial Development Authority was created in 1965 for promoting industrial development while an Investment Incentives Act defined financial incentives provided to priority sectors. In Thailand, the National Economic and Social Development Board has been less concerned with providing incentives to industrialists than with defining general guidelines for industrial development. There, the most significant roles in determining industrial policy have been played by the Board of Investment and the Ministry of Industry.

As to Singapore, a strong state succeeded in fighting against corruption, cheating, bribery, rackets and mafias. Moreover, the state share of GDP is about 40 per cent; a high figure compared to many developing countries. In spite of the publicized image of a 'liberal' Singaporian economy, the state industrial sector, for instance, employed over 11 per cent of the total labour force in 1986. Additionally, we should not forget that the People's Action Party, in power from the late 1950s, developed a socialist (though 'reformist') programme of economic development. A state development plan was worked out for 1961–64, but the main plan target was to trigger an increase of private investment (Margolin 1989). Planning in Singapore is something like indicative planning *à la française*: the state suggests and foresees, businessmen make decisions.

In 1961 the Economic Development Board replaced the Singapore Industrial Promotion Board created in 1957. One of its main tasks was to supply infrastructure and public utilities to industry. Between 1967 and 1969, several statutory boards emerged in Singapore. They were both profitable and were utilized as the spearheads of state industrial policy. Expenditures of the seven biggest statutory boards – Housing Development Board, Jurong Town Corporation, Public Utilities Board, Port of Singapore Authority, Telecoms, Urban Redevelopment Authority, Sentosa Development Corporation – reached one-third of the total amount spent for industry in 1986. The privatization drive, since 1986, mostly transferred only a minority share of state assets into private hands so that the state kept its monitoring power on 'partially privatized' public corporations.

Thus it appears, to say the least, that state bodies have monitored industrial transformation, to some extent, in all sampled East Asian countries, although nobody contends that they are not market economies. This must be kept in mind as the first lesson from the East Asian experience, when discussing industrial strategies for post-communist economies. The state of course did not 'wither away' from economic activity. On the contrary, it strengthened its influence on business (except after 1985 in some East Asian countries) by channelling and influencing market development though not hindering it. Sometimes the state determined priority projects or sectors, sometimes it picked the winners, sometimes it contracted out production to private entrepreneurs in a kind of renewed 'putting out' system as in Taiwan. The state usually did not support a single 'champion'; it submitted several domestic enterprises to mutual competition and to the challenge of world markets. Such a state, however, had to be a strong one, capable of enforcing its decisions, resisting lobby pressures, and clarifying the rules of the economic game .

This so-called 'Capitalist Developmental State' (Johnson 1987) in East Asia rapidly appeared as a much more effective set of institutions than in the European state socialist societies. Even though the state is becoming less influential in the sampled East Asian countries in recent years, it has actively contributed to the East Asian economic 'miracle'. This can be explained in looking at the relationships between state bodies and policies on the one hand, and private business strategies on the other, which were – and still are – rather specific and, at any rate, very different from the centrally planned, top-down relations of the former state socialist societies.

Industrial Networks Between the State and Private Business

'Korea Inc.' or 'Malaysia Inc.' (for Incorporated) is the frequent label associated with the outcome of relations between the state and private business in East Asia. The three pillars of the 'Inc.' model are administrative guidance, public-private networks and what may be called 'industrial targeting'.

Administrative guidance refers to measures and recommendations taken by the state, without legal or coercive enforcement, which are supposed to encourage a cluster of enterprises to behave in such a way as to reach targets fixed by administrative authorities. Those enterprises which respond to state recommendations are rewarded with various (primarily fiscal) benefits. We have to stress that such recommendations are not backed by law. They are usually informal and are rarely written down. They are all the more efficient in that they are geared towards a homogeneous and well-structured group of enterprises, instead of being addressed to firms with conflicting stakes. The result is a positive role for the state and an efficient intervention in the market economy; quite the opposite of mandatory planning by former socialist states. In East Asian countries the state is a producer (although not the main or unique one), and to some extent a protector, a planner, a prospector. First and foremost, however, it is a trusted guide.

Administrative guidance thus lays the ground for a state–private enterprise dialogue, mutual consultations and, finally, common networks. These latter are strengthened in South Korea by various informal networks which stem from the local origins of businessmen, common school and academic curricula, and encompass the whole society. Some networks are nevertheless formal, such as the Joint Export Development Committee established in 1965 to gather together civil servants and private businessmen with the aim of managing export incentives. Korean employers' associations usually participated in programmes of industrial modernization launched by the state and then, in compensation, retained the capacity of allocating export quotas among their members (Rhee *et al.* 1984). For seventeen years, General Park chaired a monthly meeting of major ministers, employers' associations and heads of some of the big conglomerates (*chaebols*). Employers' associations still consider themselves as useful links between the state and the enterprises. It is not however, the mere fact that the state and enterprises colluded which characterises Korean industrial policy; what is more specific is that the state remained capable of autonomous decisions *vis-à-vis* enterprises and of imposing performance requirements on them. Some institutionalist economists (for example, Lee 1992) see Korean industrial development as a consequence of the links between the government and business, while others refer to the 'economic general staff' (Wade 1990) managing the country, an idea which fits well with the 'Inc.' model.

In Malaysia, the concept of 'Malaysia Inc.' has even been defined by the Prime Minister in the early 1980s as a cooperation between the government and private sector which enables the latter to increase its contribution to nationwide economic development. The network system is less homogeneous in Malaysia in so far as civil servants are mainly ethnically Malay and a majority of businessmen, mostly Chinese. We find here the reason why the government attempted to clarify what 'Malaysia Inc.' was supposed to be and why it included into the definition an improvement of the dialogue between ethnic groups, that is, between a Malay-dominated state and a Chinese dominated economy. It seems that, as a result of the 'Malaysia Inc.' watchword, increased consultation and better cooperation started between the state and business. The peak of this kind of relationship is, each year, a week devoted to a meeting of all employers' associations and all divisions of the Ministry of Industry.

The power structure in Thailand is triangular: the royal family, the army and Sino-Thai business groups, with tight links relating the army to business. The Thai regime evolved toward a kind of liberal corporatism where the state remains prominent and private economic agents have a very significant role. Since the early 1970s employers' associations strengthened their bargaining power with the state. By the end of the 1970s a Joint Public–Private Committee had been created, supported by the Prime Minister (Rojanastien), a fan of the 'Thai Inc.' idea. The Joint Committee associates the Chambers of Commerce, the Association of Thai industrialists and banks; it is chaired by the Prime Minister and deals with 'red tape' and regulation issues. Committee members are so prestigious that all the decisions they make are then implemented by different Ministries. Meetings of the Committee were convened every month up to 1985 but have since become less frequent.

In the city-state of Singapore, due to limited space, administrative guidance is well known for minimizing red tape and focusing on land allocation; industrial policy is to a large extent similar to a policy of local (regional) development. The main policy tool is state ownership of land from which are derived long-term leasing arrangements. Industrial concentration is located and relocated for the sake of the 'public interest' within the city-state borders. Networking between local authorities and business is quite natural, given their close geographic proximity.

The Economic Development Board was created in 1959 to coordinate local political leaders (former trade unionists) and open-minded industrialists. Its task was to provide technical assistance to the latter, to work out development planning, to supply credit to industry and to set up joint ventures with private capital. Although they backed nationalization, as a principle, Singaporian leaders usually preferred to support well-managed private enterprises than state-owned lame ducks, even though the state was conceived of as the guide towards a higher stage of economic development. Singapore is thus a twofold mixed economy which connects public and private stakes, and (see below) domestic and foreign capital.

'Industrial targeting' means that industrial policy measures and incentives consist in favouring one sector or one subset of all enterprises (taken as the policy 'target'). There are only a few state-owned enterprises in Korea (with a state share of over 50 per cent of total capital), of which about 75 seem to be rather efficient (Park 1987). They are used as a tool for starting up new production or activity and sometimes they are privatized at a later date. The limited economic weight of Korean public enterprises (accounting for less than 3 per cent of total employment in industry) restricts their capacity to be the principal agents of industrial policy. Industrial policy, however, was nevertheless tightly 'targeted'. Korean enterprises, either public or private, were protected (see below) from both imports and foreign investors. Contrary to many developing countries, such protection did not give rise to 'white elephants'. Why?: because the 'targets' of industrial policy were picked according to their potential for penetrating world markets and then were immersed by the state into fierce competition among themselves. Since 1980 Korea has adopted a more standard 'horizontal' industrial policy, but something remains of the former targeting, particularly in the electronic components and car industries.

Industrial policy is implemented in Malaysia through state Economic Development Corporations which have created, in each Malaysian state, public enterprises or public–private joint ventures. The number of non-financial public enterprises increased from 22 in the 1970s to 354 in 1985, the year when the privatization programme began (with 77 public industrial enterprises concerned). The state also created a holding company, HICOM, at the end of the 1970s, which invested in many projects (in cars, steel and cement) with too small a production capacity compared with the size of international competitors. Most of these projects started producing just before the slump year of 1985 and at that time were regarded as 'white elephants', including the Proton car project which benefited from a significantly lower VAT rating than (foreign) competitors. Such circumstances paved the way for the 1986 privatization programme. Proton gave up its management to its foreign partner (Mitsubishi) and, with the help of economic recovery in Malaysia, was able to sell over 500 000 cars between 1985 and 1994, 100 000 of which were exported.

EAT (electricity) and Thai Airways, together with paper and textile plants and sugar refineries are among the few public enterprises in Thailand. In the 1950s Sino-Thai owned enterprises started to recruit army generals to their staff, and this sealed a non-competition pact between the state and the private sector. The Thai state remained, nevertheless, rather reluctant to embark on industrial targeting, but it sponsored anyway some targeted projects, such as joint ventures with foreign investors for car-assembly lines in 1961. In 1969, the Ministry of Industry launched consultations with the Association of Thai Industrialists which was lobbying to limit the number of car assemblers in the country. Car assembly capacity reached six times domestic sales in 1975, while imported cars still dominated the domestic market. Since 1978, Thai industrial policy has been activated. Import of foreign cars was prohibited and the proportion of local content was raised to 50 per cent for cars assembled in the country. Today, the Thai car market is the most important in ASEAN (456 000 cars sold in 1993), and the number of subcontractors, backed by the state, has increased. The Thai automotive parts industry now appears strong enough to attract investment from Japanese auto-component producers.

In Singapore, reduced taxation on fixed capital, and fiscal 'holidays' on reinvested profits were provided to 'pioneer' industries. In addition, in the 1960s, the Economic Development Board undertook the building of flatted factories (three floors high) for the purpose of welcoming, at low cost, small and dynamic enterprises (expected to grow rapidly). Flatted factories were built close to housing estates by Singapore Factory Development Ltd, an Economic Development Board affiliate. In the 1980s, Singapore switched these forms of industrial targeting from manufacturing to international services based on new information technologies. For example, the state created in 1980 two National Boards charged with circulating knowledge and products of the computer industry in the whole economy. The privatization programme, launched in 1985, is state-managed (by a Public Sector Divestment Committee), is rather slow, and does not dampen state support for the most risky and promising enterprises.

All sampled East Asian countries obviously are neither planned economies nor fully fledged market economies; they stand somewhere in between. They range among the variety of capitalist mixed economies, although they are of course very different, for instance, from the French mixed economy. The specific and crucial feature of the East Asian 'Inc.' model can be grasped by stressing the relationship between the state and (private and public) enterprises. In the space between plan and market, and among mixed economies, there is a place for a kind of network economy exemplified by the NICs of East Asia. The economies of East-Central Europe have already abandoned mandatory planning and muddle through to reach a market economy. They are thus embarked on the same path as that crossed by East Asia from the 1960s to 1980s. A network economy could be a relevant model for the whole transformation period, especially if we remember the significance of networks in the former state socialist system, not all of which have been dismantled (see Andreff 1995a, 1996; Rizopoulos 1995).

In a network economy, the problem of maintaining competition has to be tackled particularly when the economy is hyper-concentrated on a dozen big trusts as in the case of the Korean *chaebol*. Many Korean markets are oligopolistic or even (in 21 reported cases) monopolistic but, paradoxically, fierce competition prevails. In other words, markets are contestable, because all *chaebol* are involved in almost all the same industries. For instance, liberalization of the petro-chemical industry in 1987 opened the opportunity for Samsung and Hyundai to enter, what was for them, new business. In Malaysia, the concentration ratio for the four biggest firms was higher than 40 per cent in 80 per cent of industrial sectors in 1993. The market power captured by a few enterprises seems to be higher in Malaysia than even in Korea and the issue of competition there remains a tricky one. The Thai economy is known to be much less concentrated, though Singapore exhibits quite high concentrations.

Foreign Trade Protection and Foreign Investment Regulation

Exports have been promoted in all East Asian countries (EACs), but the transition to export-led growth has been achieved without reducing – sometimes even by strengthening – protectionist policies started in the 1950s. South Korean reforms of the 1960s generated a favourable economic context for exports: taxes on import revenues were cut by 50 per cent, fiscal amortization of the fixed capital used for producing export goods was accelerated, imported inputs for export-products benefited from tariff holidays, and export credit was subsidized. In other words, Korean comparative advantage and export competitiveness relied on 'a little help' from the state (Amsden 1989). In the longer term, Korean success was due to linking import substitution to export promotion on the one hand (Benabou 1982) and enterprise protection to their export performance on the other. Nothing like the invisible hand of the international market, but on the contrary the visible hand of the Korean state was handling the whole strategy. The above-mentioned reforms opened up a new avenue for free trade on the import side (for inputs) for Korean exporters while they did not open the domestic market to any foreign competitor. By the mid-1960s, the state had adopted a limited list of prohibited imports (non-tariff barriers) superseding previous fluctuating and arbitrary prohibitions. Heavy tariffs on luxury goods were maintained until 1983.

Tariff policy was primarily concerned with fiscal issues in Malaysia, and not with industrial policy purposes in the 1950s. The World Bank advised the government in 1955 to raise tariff protection of 'pioneer' industries, calculated as the difference between local production costs and import costs (Young *et al.* 1980). On the basis of its average tariffs, Malaysia is the second least protectionist state in the ASEAN region, after Singapore. However, the differentiation between tariffs on intermediary goods and final goods results in an increased effective protection estimated at a rate of about 55 per cent (compared with an average nominal rate of 22 per cent) in the late 1970s. The privileged Proton car is protected with an effective rate of 170 per cent over imported cars. Singapore meanwhile switched definitively from import substitution to export promotion in 1966.

In Thailand, contrary to many developing countries, export success has been achieved by small and medium enterprises in spite of tariff protection. The transition towards export promotion was initiated by the state under pressure of the Association of Thai Industries. Those sectors which emerged during the import substitution stage became exporters such as textile, clothing and, more recently, electronics industries. Thailand does not apply quotas significantly, and the average tariff is rather low (11.5 per cent). The car industry is nevertheless the most protected, with a 450 per cent rate of effective protection; the current government has lowered tariffs on cars and computers in so far as international competitive standards are now almost met by these industries.

The EACs' coordination of industrial policy and trade protection for new industries are examples, in some respects, of a strategy initially advocated by Friedrich List under the label of 'infant industry protection'. Their experience also demonstrates that industrial policy cannot be designed independently from a foreign trade policy (Brasseul 1993).

Foreign direct investment (FDI) has always been integrated in the EACs' industrial policy, though this does not mean that it was welcomed without any restriction. In 1987–92, the ratio between FDI inflows and gross domestic investment was 1.1 per cent in Korea, 4.2 per cent in Thailand and 15.7 per cent in Malaysia. In 1992, it was 0.5 per cent in Korea and 30.6 per cent in Singapore. FDI was not allowed in the 1950s in Korea. In 1962, a former Foreign Capital Inducement Law was liberalized and the Economic Planning Board had to implement it and to supervise foreign investment projects: only 12 of them were approved from 1962 to 1965. A new tendency started in 1969 when the government opened two free-trade zones which attracted foreign – mainly Japanese – enterprises. A 1973 law gave priority to joint ventures (with a maximum 50 per cent share allowed to foreign capital in several sectors) and licence agreements, in order to increase control over Japanese capital inflows. Foreign investors were submitted to TRIMS – trade related investment measures – pertaining to technology transfer, export performance and to local content of production. In the early 1980s, the Korean government revised its position and the number of sectors open to FDI has risen to 521 out of 855 classified sectors. On the other hand, the Monopoly Regulation and Fair Trade Act was utilized for supervising foreign investors' activity. After 1984, FDI regulation was further liberalized step by step.

After Singapore, Malaysia is the most open EAC as regards FDI. The Pioneer Industries Act passed in 1958 has been the main tool for promoting investment, either domestic or foreign, in as much as no industry was closed to foreign investment (including petroleum, mining, etc.). In 1968 a new Investment Incentives Act offered a trade-off to foreign investors between fiscal holidays and tax credits depending on location, local content and export performance. After 1970, the state attitude to FDI changed and restrictive clauses were introduced in the Investment Code compelling foreign investors to develop partnerships with Malaysian enterprises. A slowdown in FDI inflows in 1981 followed by an economic recession in 1985 triggered a new mood among state decision-makers who suppressed the most constraining restrictions and, in 1990, adopted the most interesting fiscal exemptions in the whole of ASEAN.

In Thailand, a 1959 law promoted FDI and since the 1972 Alien Business Law, foreign investors have been welcomed in almost all industries but restricted to a minority share – sometimes lower than 40 per cent in any venture. The Investment Board was used to impose performance clauses on foreign multinational corporations. After 1988, the foreign share was regulated according to the export potential of each project. Despite its liberal image, Thailand has attracted significant FDI only since 1985.

Singapore, since 1959, has been the most open EAC to multinational penetration. The Economic Development Board (a state agency) has even supplied credit to joint ventures with foreign investors. Combining state guidance and multinational involvement is the peculiar recipe for Singapore's success story.

Concluding from the East Asian experience, and looking beyond national specificities, we can summarize the main factors in their success stories in developing and transforming industries as follows:

- the state exercised industrial leadership, had intervention capabilities and, sometimes, engaged in indicative planning;
- state bodies appear to have monitored industrial transformation within the framework of market economies;
- states were strong enough to resist and to curb lobbies, smugglers, mafias and so forth, and to orchestrate market forces in some circumstances;
- state and business enterprises were linked together by a network of rather confident and regular economic relations channelling accurate information, within the so-called 'Inc.' model (a specific vintage of a mixed economy characterised as a network economy);
- efficient state intervention was based on administrative guidance of well-identified clusters of enterprises;
- industrial policy and incentives usually favoured a specific 'target' – one sector or one cluster of enterprises – and were often based on fiscal and financial benefits, but sometimes prohibitions superseded incentives;

- regarded as tools for industrial policy, both import substitution and export promotion were implemented for the purpose of protecting infant industries and, after the latter had met international competitiveness standards, they were used for propelling local products onto world markets;
- relatively liberal attitudes to foreign direct investment have been an active part of the EACs industrial policy, though states have steadily maintained a foot in the door with clear and stable regulations (rules of the game for foreign investors), including some trade-related investment controls.

INDUSTRIAL TRANSFORMATION IN CENTRAL-EASTERN EUROPE NEEDS TIME AND THE STATE

Liberalization and Privatization: Weak Tools for Industrial Restructuring

Six years after the beginning of economic transition in the CEECs, the results can be briefly sketched as follows. The economies in transition are now more or less stabilized (Andreff 1994a) and liberalized except for the CIS and the Balkans. Though some market forces are at work (Andreff 1993a), the privatization drive has a sluggish momentum (Andreff 1993b). The other side of the coin, however, is that there has been a recovery from a deep recession, a tentative economic restructuring, and a weak and somewhat fragmented state which is not actually capable of promoting a clear and consistent policy of industrial transformation (Andreff 1995a).

Trade and price liberalization have been achieved in the CEECs on the one hand as a means of breaking-up with the former planned economy, and on the other as a possible (or 'efficient' according to the assumption of liberal economics) lever for economic restructuring. New trade relationships and a new flexible market price system were supposed to eliminate the 'lame ducks' from heavy industry (producing for a negative value-added) and to screen the winners (profitable enterprises). In other words, it was assumed that the market as such was capable of restructuring and transforming industry. Such an assumption does not pay enough attention to the above-mentioned East Asian experience or to Western European restructuring of obsolete industries either. Industrial transformation in East Asia took decades and was not the result of market forces in isolation from state intervention. A long time-span (about 25 to 30 years) was necessary to restructure Western European outdated industries such as steel, textiles, shipbuilding, coal mining and so on, precisely because the market failed to do it and hence this paved the way for massive state expenditures. In addition, in the CEECs, emerging markets are all but pure and perfect, or contestable, at least in industries to be restructured. Trade and price liberalization often transformed state monopolies into private rent-seeking monopolies more eager to maintain their monopoly position and thereby reap extra profits than to restructure and split themselves into competing firms (for elaboration see Andreff 1992, 1993a, 1993b, 1994c, 1994d, 1995b, 1996) Moreover, it is well known from economic analysis that private monopolies do not yield more economic efficiency than state monopolies. In cases such as the CEECs, which so urgently need to modernize industry and agriculture and to develop external services for enterprises, short-term microeconomic profitability clashes with the long-term macroeconomic costs of not restructuring.

The dream of a therapy based on a kind of nineteenth-century *laissez-faire* soon dwindled and vanished in the CEECs. Why not then keep monopolies in state hands for a while with the explicit target of dismantling them and fuelling competition among new enterprises emerging from their dismantlement? The East Asian experience, in particular the Korean one, shows that the state can behave as a stick and/or a carrot, pushing enterprises to compete. From the French experience we draw the lesson that the state can be capable of a dramatic restructuring of public enterprises such that they can be turned around financially, become internationally competitive (and some of them now belong to the finest jewels of the world oligopoly in their industry) and then be made ready for further and successful privatization (Andreff 1992, 1994d).

The lack of restructuring in the state sector is clearly one of the many obstacles to swift and efficient privatization in the CEECs (Andreff 1993b). On the other hand, a slow privatization process logically compels state officials to tackle the problem of upgrading a vast public sector which they cannot quickly divest. This point is significant and supports the need for a state-coordinated industrial policy. Restructuring the enterprises that are still state-run is probably more urgent than rushing into mass privatization programmes with debatable results (Andreff 1994c) or postponing a genuine and deep implementation of the privatization policy, as in many CIS countries, Romania and Bulgaria. In the countries most advanced in the transformation process (Hungary, Poland and the Czech Republic), the public sector share remains at nearly 50 per cent of GNP (a nice definition of a mixed economy!) This share has few chances of decreasing as rapidly in the coming years as it has decreased in the first years of transition in so far as the easiest privatization deals have now been achieved. The remaining state enterprises should be upgraded and restructured before finding potential rescuers or buyers interested in their privatization. The East Asian experience demonstrates that privatization programmes were launched in the 1980s when public enterprises were already strong enough (and some of them even profitable) to compete on world and domestic markets.

Recalling now a train of thought we developed over some years (Andreff 1992, 1994d), successful privatization techniques can only rely on sales of public assets. The CEECs lack almost all the preconditions for successful privatization based on asset sales, and consequently suffer from shortfalls in savings and a low marginal utility of shares compared with basic needs, consumer goods and services; elements, in other words, which contrast with the East Asian experience.

The lack of a vast and dynamic stock market, of a banking system unencumbered with bad loans, of enough market-related personnel such as skilled bookkeepers, accountants, experienced lawyers, fiscal advisers, brokers, institutional investors (insurance companies, financial intermediaries) and of a social class (though emerging) of entrepreneurs and capitalist tycoons, has already been stressed in the economic literature on transitional societies as obstacles to the privatization process. Thus, if large-scale privatization should have been a main road to restructuring, it seems that, on the contrary, it has actually shrunk into a tiny path except in those CEECs which have implemented 'voucher' and mass privatization programmes. These latter ones have barely triggered, until now, a deep restructuring of heavy industry and agriculture, as we can see primarily from the Czech and Russian experiences (Andreff 1994c).

The main unsolved problem with the distribution of cheap vouchers to the population, then redeemed into shares, is that of corporate governance (Andreff 1994b, Frydman and Rapaczynski 1994). About 75 per cent of the 15 000 enterprises privatized up to July 1994 in Russia have chosen this second variant of privatization (which gives insiders 51 per cent of total share ownership) and are now under the control and monitoring of former managers or worker's collectives, or a coalition of both of them. Under such circumstances, why would they wish to restructure newly privatized enterprises with the consequent reduction of overmanning, followed with lay-offs of redundant employees and increased discipline at the workplace? In the Czech Republic, during the first wave of mass privatization, 88 per cent of the privatization projects were initiated by managers of state enterprises themselves who, in most cases, kept control over the newly privatized enterprises. Again the pressure for restructuring is rather low and as a result the Czech unemployment rate remains the lowest among CEECs.

We can thus wonder whether, if strong enough, the state in a transitional economy could have adopted another way of muddling through towards restructuring, other than privatization for its own sake. In this respect, the East Asian experience matters. Industrial transformation there relied on the state fighting against corruption, bribery, cheating, smuggling, the local mafias and so forth. It appears today, especially in Russia and the CIS countries, though to a lesser degree in other CEECs, that the main winners in the privatization process have been mafia members, former *nomenklatura* and Communist Party hardliners converted into new businessmen and, more generally, people eager to earn easy money in the shortest span of time possible. What chance is there of these people investing in long-term projects or in restructuring industry and agriculture when they are used to investing in (useful) services, but also in speculative (useless) businesses, in laundering 'dirty' money and in transferring funds to hard-currency accounts abroad? Repressing such economic behaviour (the stick) needs a strong, trusted state, while providing incentives (the carrot) needs increased economic and political stability which, again, can only rely on strengthening the state instead of letting it wither away. Otherwise – and this can be observed in the CIS countries – relationships between the state and private businessmen degenerate into a very collusive and corrupted network aimed at the preservation of vested interests.

A new and delicate balance must be found between private action and state administration (Frydman and Rapaczynski 1994) so that an East Asian-style industrial policy becomes workable with the state being both a player and a rule-maker. In this respect, the image of the 'three C's' – coordination, cooperation and competition – seems appealing for economic governance (van Brabant 1994). The case for industrial policy in the transition period is not only based on market failures, but it is one based also on the non-existence of markets or at best only rudimentary market responses. In such conditions, the crucial point is not whether the state should or should not intervene, it is rather a question of what are the state coordination and cooperation measures which can increase the response rate of economic agents (Landesmann 1993). State industrial policies have been an integrated and central feature of most successful 'catching-up' processes in Western Europe and East Asia. These have usually required decades: similarly industrial transformation in the CEECs must be thought of as a long-term process and industrial policy must accordingly be designed for a time horizon of between 15 and 30 years depending on the countries and industries concerned. The de-industrialization which was a product of stabilization policies should be halted as soon as possible as a first step towards industrial transformation.

The Return of State Industrial Policy

In recent OECD publications, the emphasis is on the nationwide economic efficiency of member countries as a consequence of efficiency in both public and private sectors. Although pertaining to developed market economies, this statement could well apply to the East Asian countries. On the other hand, it could not fit well with the economic situation in the CEECs where efficiency is not high enough in both sectors. There is probably no better starting-point for supporting the idea of a state industrial policy relying on incentives and still-existing public enterprises, instead of striving to extend privatization to big trusts with a somewhat dubious outcome. In the CEECs it is worth attempting to implement state incentives to private enterprises of the same kind as those (fiscal and financial) developed in the EACs. This suggestion is sometimes rejected (as by Dabrowski 1994) saying that 'this [the EACs'] experience has little relevance to the Central and East European reality, mainly because of completely different economic, social and cultural backgrounds'; but this criticism is almost entirely nullified by the fact that it is put to the fore by the very economists who have attempted to 'import' the Reaganite–Thatcherite recipes into the CEECs in spite of their 'different economic, social and cultural backgrounds' compared with the US and the UK. The state as a conductor should guide the whole industrial transformation instead of bargaining with former industrial lobbies or with newly developed collusive networks. Such an industrial policy can only be effective if the state does not have to mobilize too many means of sustaining and subsidizing public enterprises; in other words, state intervention and finance geared towards the private sector can only exist in the CEECs if the state starts with improving economic efficiency in the public sector, namely in state-run or public enterprises. A prerequisite for restructuring public enterprises and banks and for using them as a tool for industrial policy, is cleaning their balance sheets of payment arrears and bad loans (see Andreff 1995a).

Once financially rehabilitated, public enterprises in the CEECs should focus on two targets: the restructuring of their own physical assets and 'privatization' (improvement or 'commercialization') of their own management (Andreff 1995a). These two targets, once achieved, would pave the way for public enterprises to compete with private domestic and even foreign firms, as has been the case in a number of East Asian countries.

The first aim of industrial restructuring is to trigger a steady supply response to the demand generated by the beginnings of economic recovery; this will require a 'flexible' production system. A new flexibility can obviously be reached through new activities in the private sector but also through a better resource allocation among and within remaining public enterprises. This means sometimes that particular public enterprises will need to be dismantled. The process of dismantling them, however, must involve the maintenance of efficient technical interdependencies or economies of scale when they exist. In other cases, though rare in formerly centralized economies, several public enterprises need to be merged, or at least, some common functions (finance, marketing, and so on.) may be worth amalgamation. In all these respects, state institutions have to learn how to use new instruments designed to interact with (private or public) firms which are increasingly guided by outlets and markets. This learning process will involve, in the CEECs, a shift towards the use of indirect policy instruments such as tax incentives, credit support, infrastructure, Research and Development – financed by the state, as in East Asia – as well as provision for training and marketing.

There is a trade-off open to the state between so-called reactive and active industrial policies (Landesmann 1993). A reactive policy is the one which is set into motion in response to social and political pressures emerging from any attempt at structural adjustment; it had already been tried – unsuccessfully – in some of the CEECs during the state socialist period. An active industrial policy involves running-down obsolete plants and enterprises as well as building-up new ones (sometimes associated with a kind of non-spontaneous 'creative destruction' process).

The issue of state industrial policy is now discussed in increasing detail in the economic literature (see, for instance, van Brabant 1993, Hare 1995, Landesmann 1993, Lindpere 1994, Socha and Sztanderska 1994, Török 1994, Zeman 1994). It has now been admitted by numerous CEEC political leaders that such a policy is a normal component of a transition strategy, along with stabilization, trade liberalization, privatization and adjustment policies. Very often, however, the devil is in the detail and the discussion embarks on the list of industries and targets which has to be privileged by industrial policy. As Cowling (1990) remarks:

> The role of the state should be limited to the strategic oversight of development, rather than getting involved with the operational detail, and that strategic oversight is only essential in the case of a limited array of key industries, many sectors being left to market processes without strategic guidance. The role of the state has to be seen as catalytic; proactive rather than reactive.

Cowling's comment implicitly underlines the difference between the sorts of industrial policy discussed here and former central planning and sectoral tutelage. His comment also sounds very much like the EACs' practice of industrial policy.

For the last decade of the communist regimes, investment had been partly neglected in a deepening economic crisis (Andreff 1993c). Industrial restructuring, in particular restructuring public enterprises, obviously needs a large-scale investment to 'rationalize', to rehabilitate and to modernize the obsolete physical assets used as the means of production. Such investment must not be confused with bailing out obsolete large trusts as seemingly has been the case in Poland with URSUS, STAR and others (Bouin and Grosfeld 1995), or with the DIMAG steel works in Hungary and ZETOR, TATRA and SKODA PLZEN in the Czech Republic. Investment is also necessary for switching from the former extensive growth to intensive growth based on radical productivity increases. Even efficient resource allocation usually requires substantial investment flows which must be added to investment triggered by the development of new production capacities. Investment decision-making hence arises as one of the crucial issues in the management of the remaining public enterprises.

A second aim in restructuring public enterprises is to 'privatize' their management inasmuch as it is not yet possible to transfer their assets to the private sector. This means at first that the public enterprise must adopt market (or 'commercial') management criteria and, in particular, must cover its expenses with its receipts and, as far as possible, make a profit. Public enterprise management consequently has to be autonomous, in administrative and economic terms, from any state body (including state banks). Managers must be stimulated with monetary and stock-equity incentives to run the enterprise in such a way as to be profitable, competitive and efficient. Incentives must depend on economic performance, just as in the EACs, and managers must pay for any loss or be immediately fired. Already restructured enterprises have to be managed in the same way as private enterprises (the issue of privatizing restructured firms then appears secondary on economic grounds, and turns into a question of political – and not merely economic – choice). On the other hand, a substantial stimulation can fix managers in public enterprises and then partly counteract the current brain-drain of managers to the private sector observed in CEECs.

A state industrial policy has obviously a strong impact on unemployment. We do not propose to deal with the unemployment issue within the limits of this chapter, but we just stress that the magnitude of industrial transformation in the CEECs calls for something more elaborate than the IMF-sponsored 'safety nets'; namely, a significant (and expensive) social policy is required. This is probably the main difference between the EACs' experience and what would be necessary for the CEECs and reflecting the difference between industrial transformation in developing countries and restructuring a developed, but distorted, industrial structure.

Regulating Foreign Trade and Investment

Policy-makers concerned with industrial restructuring should keep in mind such medium and long-term objectives as specialization in the national economy for international markets, as has been the case in the EACs. Relevant initiatives here should include measures pertaining to foreign trade and foreign direct investment. Foreign trade liberalization in the CEECs has triggered trade diversion and even disruption with their former CMEA partners and trade creation with Western markets (van Brabant 1994). In the first two years of trade liberalization, enterprises adjusted to new market conditions and, in some countries such as Poland, public enterprises turned out to be a basic factor sustaining the foreign trade balance (Dudzinski 1995). The private sector in Poland, on the other hand, had a harmful effect on foreign trade by creating a \$3.8 billion deficit in 1991 (Hausner and Owsiak 1992). More recently, however, all the CEECs have been swamped by competing imports and their exports to the West (in particular to EU countries) have met tariff and non-tariff barriers. As a consequence, their hard currency trade balances have continued to record annual deficits. Export orientation towards the West was nevertheless advisable in so far as it has been a distinguishing characteristic of successful catching-up processes, including in East Asia. In the CEECs, hard currency shortages and the heavy burdens of foreign debt servicing make export orientations all the more important.

In the first years of stabilization exports were fuelled by currency devaluations. In a longer run, however, devaluation is insufficient to sustain an export orientation unless it is complemented with a sharp international product re-specialization which could only be the outcome of a pre-existing successful restructuring. Such restructuring should be considered as badly needed for balancing foreign trade in the long run. Moreover, an important by-product of this will be the development of product capabilities which will allow competition with imported goods. A sustained export effort can thus yield beneficial results in recapturing domestic markets which have been flooded by imports.

The view that opening CEEC markets was too costly a process has also been expressed (Hausner and Owsiak 1992). On the one hand, each CEEC has abandoned foreign trade planning and has introduced rather low tariffs. On the other hand, EU countries which are new major trading partners for the CEECs, have not opened their markets significantly to CEEC products in spite of association agreements having been signed between the EU and the CEECs. An export orientation is a sensible strategy for a country if, and only if, its major partners are not putting a brake on export flows through their own import protection. If Eastern European calls for opening Western markets are not listened to, then pressure for protectionism could spread throughout the transitional economies. There is already some evidence of such developments in Poland and Hungary.

Liberalization and protection should not be taken for basic values as such: the East Asian experience reminds us that export promotion, import substitution, selective protection of infant and open door policies can be combined. They should be combined in transitional economies, even though some economists find it 'unthinkable' that protection of domestic markets should be on the agenda in the CEECs (Socha 1994). 'Unthinkable' or not, the practical issue is whether it is 'workable': why not test it?

Foreign direct investment in the CEECs has remained limited, except in Hungary, and has not yet reached the required magnitude for providing significant help for industrial restructuring and economic recovery. The CEECs are not booming economies as the EACs were, and still are; some of them have not even recovered their economic growth. The attractiveness of a country for FDI usually relies on four factors: comparative economic advantage (including the size of the domestic market), economic stability, the financial risk linked to the past and current foreign debt management, and state policy towards foreign investors together with political stability. Although Russia, and to a lesser degree Poland, have rather obvious comparative advantages in terms of natural resources, labour endowments and market size, only Hungary has been able to attract an FDI inflow higher than $1 billion a year. The possibilities for economic growth are greater in Poland than Russia, partly because the former ranks among the least destabilized of the CEEC economies (together with Hungary, the Czech Republic, Estonia and Slovenia). Investment risk is assessed by international bankers (see for instance *Euromoney* in 1994) in such a way that the CEECs are ranked in ascending order as follows: 1) Czech Republic, 2) Hungary, 3) Slovenia, 4) Slovakia, 5) Poland, 6) Romania, etc. (Russia is ranked 19th among the CEECs). The countries ranked as having the least risk have either rather low foreign debt indicators or have trusted debt management with regular debt servicing, no renegotiation or rescheduling. In addition, all of them are assessed as the best political risks. This leads us to political stability, which as far as FDI is concerned means stable rules of the game for foreign investors. Regarding the latter criterion, economic policy has steadily emphasized the role of FDI in China since 1978 and in Hungary since 1986 and in both cases FDI inflows have benefited from an image of political stability (based on a kind of political consensus in Hungary and a single-party dictatorship in China). As some businessmen have put it, foreign capital is a shy deer which needs trust and stability to be tamed. State policy must encourage FDI with no reversals as in Russia and no hindrances as in many CEECs. As the CEECs are competing with one another, and with the rest of the world, to attract FDI, it will not suffice to declare an 'open door policy' for FDI and then change the regulations as many of the EACs have done for some decades. In marked contrast to the EACs, the CEECs will have to stick to a stable and consistently attractive policy.

CONCLUSIONS

We derive from this chapter two basic conclusions. Firstly, industrial transformation in Central-Eastern Europe needs state intervention and this in turn requires that the state retain a significant position within the economy: it should not wither away. Secondly, the East Asian experience is of interest for designing industrial policies in the CEECs, once their national specificities are taken into account. In other words, such policies will need to adapt East Asian experiences to local CEEC circumstances. We have indicated some of the ways in which that could be done.

REFERENCES

Amsden A. (1989), *Asia's Next Giant: South Korea and Late Industrialization*. New York: Oxford University Press.

Andreff, W. (1989), 'Testing the Soviet-type industrialisation model in socialist-orientated developing countries' in S. Gomulka, Y.C. Ha and C.O. Kim (eds), *Economic Reforms in the Socialist World*. London: Macmillan.

Andreff, W. (1992), 'French privatization techniques and experience: a model for Central-Eastern Europe?' in F. Targetti (ed.), *Privatization in Europe: West and East Experiences*. Aldershot: Dartmouth.

Andreff, W. (1993a), 'The West's experience and the East' in J. van Brabant (ed.), *The New Eastern Europe and the World Economy*. Boulder: Westview Press.

Andreff, W. (1993b), 'Internal and external constraints on privatization in Eastern Europe', *History of European Ideas*, 17(6).

Andreff, W. (1993c), *La Crise des Economies Socialistes: La Rupture d'un Systeme*. Grenoble: Presses Universitaires de Genoble.

Andreff, W. (1994a), 'Quand la stabilisation dure ... L'hypothese d'une inflation inertielle en Europe centrale et orientale'. *Revue Economique*, 45(3).

Andreff, W. (1994b), 'Economic disintegration and privatization in Central and Eastern Europe' in L. Csaba (ed.) *Privatization, Liberalisation and Destruction: Recreating the Market in Eastern Europe*. Aldershot: Dartmouth.

Andreff, W. (1994c), 'Planning private ownership: is the Czechoslovak solution a model?'. *Privatization in the Transition Process: Recent Experiences in Eastern Europe*, UNCTAD and Kopint-Datorg.

Andreff, W. (1994d), 'East European privatization in the light of Western experience'. *Ergo: Journal of Transforming Economies and Societies*, 1(1).

Andreff, W. (ed.) (1995a), *Le Secteur Public à l'Est: Restructuration Industrielle et Financiere*. Paris: L'Harmattan.

Andreff, W. (1995b), 'Le contrôl des entreprises privatisées dans les économies en transition: une approch théorique'. *Revue Economique*, 46(3).

Andreff, W. (1996), 'Corporate governance of privatized enterprises in transforming economies: a theoretical approach'. *MOCT-MOST*, 6(2).

Benabou, R. (1982), 'La Corée du Sud ou l'industrialisation planifiée'. *Economie Prospective Internationale*, 10.

Bouin, O. and I. Grosfield (1995), 'La dynamique de restructuration des entreprises Polonaises et Tcheques'. *Revue Economique*, 46(3).

Brasseul, J. (1993), *Les Nouveaux Pays Industrialisés*. Armand Colin.

Cowling, K. (1990), 'A new industrial strategy: preparing Europe for the turn of the century'. *International Journal of Industrial Organisation*, 8.

Dabrowski, M. (1994) 'The role of the government in postcommunist economies'. in L. Csaba (ed.), *Privatization, Liberalisation and Destruction: Recreating the Market in Eastern Europe*. Aldershot: Dartmouth.

Dudzinski, A. (1995), 'Les mutations du secteur public' in W. Andreff (ed.), *Le Secteur Public à l'Est: Restructuration Industrielle et Financière*. Paris, L'Harmattan.

Frydman, R. and A. Rapaczynski (1994), *Privatization in Eastern Europe: Is the State Withering Away?* Central European University Press.

Hare, P. (1995), 'Industrial policy in Eastern Europe: the Hungarian example', *MOCT-MOST*, 5(1).

Hausner, J. and S. Owsiak (1992), 'Financial crisis of a state in transformation: the Polish case'. *Economic and Social Policy Series*, 26, Friedrich Ebert Stiftung.

Johnson, C. (1987) 'Political institutions and economic performance: the government-business relationship in Japan, South Korea and Taiwan' in F. Deyo (ed.), *The Political Economy of the New Asian Industrialism*. Ithaca: Cornell University Press.

Judet, P. (1981), *Les Nouveaux Pays Industriels*. Paris: Les Editions Ouvrières.

Landesmann, M.A. (1993), 'Industrial policy and the transition in East-Central Europe'. *Discussion Papers on Economic Transition*, No. DPET 9204, University of Cambridge, January.

Lee, C.H. (1992) 'The government, financial system, and large private enterprises in the economic development of South Korea'. *World Development*, 20(2).

Lindpere, H. (1994), 'The role of the state in industrial restructuring: the Estonian case'. *Working Papers*, 7, Cracow: University Council for Economic and Management Education Transfer.

Margolin, J.L. (1989), *Singapour 1959–1987: Genèse d'un Nouveau Pays Industriel*. Paris: L'Harmattan.

Park, Y.C. (1987) 'Evaluation de la performance des entreprises à capitaux publics en Corée'. *Finances et Développement*, 24(2).

Rhee, Y.W., R. Larsen and G. Purcell (1984), *Korea's Competitive Edge*. Baltimore: John Hopkins University Press.

Rizopoulos Y. (1995), 'Groupes d'intérêt, action publique et dynamique industrielle' in W. Andreff (ed.), *Le Secteur Public à l'Est: Restructuration Industrielle et Financière*. Paris: L'Harmattan.

Smigielska, G. (1992), 'The role of the state during the transformation process'. *Seminar Papers* 8, Friedrich Ebert Stiftung and Cracow Academy of Economics, February.

Socha, M.W. and U. Sztanderska (1994), 'Restructuring and industrial policy in Poland'. *MOCT-MOST*, 4(2).

Török, A. (1994), 'A one-sided restructuring process: challenges for Hungary's industrial policy in the nineties'. *MOCT-MOST*, 4(2).

van Brabant, J.M. (1993), *Industrial Policy in Eastern Europe. Governing the Transition*. Kluwer.

van Brabant, J.M. (1994), 'Privatization, industrial policy and governing the transitions'. *MOCT-MOST*, 4(1).

Voszka, E. (1994), 'Centralization, renationalization, redistribution: the role of the government in changing the ownership structure in Hungary, 1989–1993'. Centre for Economic Policy Research, *Discussion Papers Series*, 916, Centre for Economic Policy Research, February.

Wade, R. (1990), *Governing the Market: Economic Theory and the Role of Government in East Asian Industrialization*. Princeton, Princeton University Press.

Young, K., W. Bussink and P. Hassan (1980), *Malaysia: Growth and Equity in a Multiracial Society*. Baltimore: Johns Hopkins University Press.

Zeman, K. (1994), 'Industry-related policies in the first phase of the transition towards a market economy in the Czech and Slovak Republics'. *MOCT-MOST*, 4(2).

4 Privatization and the State: Russia, Eastern Europe, East Asia

Nigel Harris and David Lockwood

A comparison of the economic transformation of the Soviet Union and East Asia (for the purposes of this chapter, the newly industrialized countries – excluding Hong Kong – China and Vietnam) produces an impression of clear similarity and radical contrast. The aim of transformation seems to have been similar in both sets of cases: the transformation of a militarily inspired, state-run economy into a market-oriented one. The outcomes of the process have been vastly different – an 'economic miracle' on the one hand, decline and collapse on the other.

The process of national development has historically involved a considerable degree of economic intervention by the state. The global process of structural adjustment on the other hand, involves (among other things) disentangling economic forces from state political intervention. The former process has characterized the East Asian economies (the newly industrialized countries – NICs – in the past, China and Vietnam today); the latter is the task facing the former Soviet bloc (and now the NICs). Comparative studies which produce prescriptions derived from the process of development in East Asia are, therefore, not particularly appropriate for the process of structural adjustment in Eastern Europe and the former Soviet Union.

A more relevant comparison can be made between the former Centrally Planned Economies (CPEs) of the two areas if we start out from what characterized them all: a strong state which sought to preserve and defend itself through control of the national economy. Why that control came (or is coming) to an end and the effect of its demise on the CPE states is the subject of this chapter. It seeks to examine the reaction of the CPE states to structural adjustment and development (especially with regard to privatization) in the context of global economic development.

THE WAR-MAKING STATE

The State Develops Capitalism

The preparation and periodic waging of war is the predominant motif in the history of states. Economic development, from the viewpoint of the ruler, is a by-product of the state's pursuit of war – from Britain in the eighteenth century to Japan in the twentieth (and South Korea and Taiwan in the 1960s and 1970s ; see Harris 1992: 27–39). Between wars, the struggle of princes to pay for their preparations for the next war and the cumulative costs of past wars dominated public finance and the political relationships between governments, taxpayers and the mass of those who generated society's income.

The competition between states, and the military needs that it engendered, in certain circumstances created beneficial conditions for the emergence of capitalism. This would be 'unintelligible', writes Hintze, 'without an insight into how it was conditioned by the course of nation-building . . . during the last four centuries.' (Hintze in Gilbert 1975: 427). It is important to note, however, that the state did not set out to 'create' capitalism. Its emergence was a by-product of the need of states 'to maximize both their military investments and the efficiency of these investments.' (Brenner 1986: 32). Harris concludes (1994: 4):

> Capitalism owes much to the patronage of rulers searching for the revenues that would ensure the capacity to fight – rather than that patronage indicating the control of the State by capital.

Instead of simply seizing the wealth of the emerging capitalist classes, states found it more effective to protect property rights and tax property-owners. States, therefore, had an interest in promoting and protecting the first shoots of capitalism. In establishing its supremacy over a national territory, the state at the same time marked out and defended a wider, national market than had hitherto been possible. This was indispensable for the further development of capitalism (Amsden, 1985: 172). The role of the state in sponsoring capitalism became even more direct, and perhaps, in cases of late industrialization, as the importance of capitalism for economic development became clearer, more conscious.

War preparation provides the rationale for a public interest in the performance of the economy – and the development of a formal discipline, economics, to inform policy-making – and for public intervention. It provides the reason for extending the perimeter of the 'nation' to include all (or most) of the inhabitants of the territory the state holds, to seek to create a secure social foundation for war-making, and as a by-product, the basis for populist politics. In the welfare state, the material survival of the population, the basis for the quality of the citizen-army, is lifted from its fluctuating fortunes in the labour market; market demand can no longer be permitted to determine the size and quality of the labour force, and thereby the strength of the army. Of course, in some cases, the central rationale disappears; in Sweden, for instance, the drive to sustain the 'socialized nation' became remote from the original purpose of a war-making state.

In some of the best-known cases – Frederick's Prussia was famous in its time – the war-making state entirely absorbs civil society. Civilians become auxiliaries to the army, the 'administrative tail'. Soviet 'War Communism' and China's 'Great Leap Forward' were even more extreme cases. The workforce was entirely subject to direction of labour, to orders, housed in barracks and fed in communal cookhouses on a rationed diet determined by what the planners considered sufficient for material survival. This essentially military regime became identified – in the minds of Lenin and Mao – as the prototype of socialism; of collective self-sacrifice for common ends. All sectors now became subordinate to supplying war; agriculture was no longer an economic activity, but a matter of providing the war-making state with resources and a means to keep the population alive to supply the army, the fuel for a military machine.

In the war-making state, the government has a paramount interest in not being dependent on supplies from the domains, or dependent upon the goodwill, of any other government. It needs therefore, first and foremost, to develop under its direct control the means to meet its needs for weaponry and equipment. For more than a century this has meant, for those powers which could afford it, developing their own capacity to make steel, heavy capital goods and the final products: weaponry.

In the relevant theory of economic development, heavy industry was to be developed in order that the supposed historical development from light industry, could be bypassed, moving straight to the development of the capacity to 'make the machines that make the machines', despite the punishing sacrifices this capital-intensive development imposed upon capital-scarce economies. The argument in terms of economic development warrants scepticism, and the 1920s debate within the Soviet Communist Party between Bukharin and Preobrazhensky was slightly beside the point. The proper rationale for the disproportionate growth of heavy industry in the Soviet Five Year Plans was provided, not by the theoreticians, but by Stalin's estimation of the urgent and overriding priority for the Soviet Union to be as militarily prepared as its nearest rivals.

The heavy industrial bias in the priority part of the economy (combined with labour-intensive activity in the low-priority sectors) was bequeathed not only to all centrally planned economies, but to all other autarkic or mercantilist developing countries (the same approach had governed West European policy in the 1930s and 1940s). It became, again quite spuriously in terms of the tradition of thought, identified as peculiarly socialist. The same was true of the general tendency to identify economic development as a quasi-military campaign, a war on backwardness, replete with assaults, attacks, the seizure of the 'commanding heights' of the economy, along with the idea of 'strategic industries', 'a concept that is so elusive', according to Little *et al.* (1993: 311) 'as to be of doubtful validity'.

In this century, the phenomenal social stresses and strains of industrialization in a militarily competitive context have required closure against spiritual pollution of foreigners, most starkly in the case of Stalin's Russia, Eastern Europe in the 1950s, Mao's China, North Korea and North Vietnam. In the case of Albania, the price of isolationism, of 'ultra-Stalinism', was an extraordinary degree of economic backwardness, leaving in the early 1990s 'a grim picture of economic decline and poverty not seen in Europe this century' (World Bank 1994a: 6). The speedy collapse of the closed societies – once they began to open up – vindicates the fears of their former rulers.

A military drive to expand production has historically had some striking successes, not least in the performance of the German and Japanese economies in the 1930s. But the expansion by military order tends to be effective only extensively, for an output of fairly crude quality; coal output is, for a short period, easier to expand than computers, let alone computer software. The more sophisticated the quality of output, the less subject to sheer *blitzkrieg* (even if backed by ferocious punishments) the targets of the national plan. It becomes necessary to engage psychological incentives, the willingly volunteered skills of the worker in sustaining and improving quality.

State and Capital

Within the capitalist mode of production there are a number of central relationships in operation. One such system of relations is that of capital itself. Another is the system of states. Both 'relation systems' are circumscribed and determined by the level of development of the productive forces. But despite this common determination, they are separate, and driven by different material motives.

What are the differences between the two systems? On the one hand, capital is (as soon as it is able) driven to internationalize – to seek the largest markets and achieve the greatest concentration. On the other hand, the state is wedded to a national territory, locked into actual or potential military conflict with rival states, and therefore dependent on national economic development. While capitalists compete, in the main, commercially, states compete with each other (in fact, are forced to do so) by means of physical power. War is the prerogative of states.

The degree to which the state is able to exercise its power over, and in spite of, capitalists is determined by both the global economy (the power of states relative to that of capital within it) and the particular domestic class context. Were a state to be capable of autonomous (from external sources) economic direction, and relatively untrammelled by a domestic capitalist class, we would expect its policies to be militarily oriented and tending towards autarky. This, we would suggest, was precisely the case in the Soviet bloc and in South Korea and Taiwan (at least until the collapse of the former and until the 1960s in the latter).

In the century after 1870 – the year of the onset of the nineteenth century's long drawn out Great Depression – the world order was dominated by the global rivalries of the Great Powers, culminating in two World Wars of unprecedented destructiveness, and the Great Depression of the inter-war years which inaugurated in policy the most extreme scale of economic nationalism and economic warfare – what we have identified here as mercantilism and economic autarky. The ferocity of the rivalries reshaped all significant political forces and options, forced the complete alignment of business and the national state (thus destroying the basis for the further development of the cosmopolitan business class emerging in the period 1840 to 1870; see Jones 1987), and the creation of centralized all-powerful states, dominating society and economy, founded often in large public sectors and, a necessary adjunct of this, central planning. The process was long and not at all related simply to the immediate occurrence of war. Indeed, the final creation of predominant public sectors and a panoply of welfare protection came after World War II in Europe – now not so much to prepare for World War III as to secure social stability in anticipation of long-term high unemployment, as followed 1919. But through all the vicissitudes, the continuing centralization of social power on the state and expansion of the public domain had an apparently inexorable character. Open collisions or the sudden increase in the fear of war expanded public expenditure; but after the end of hostilities or the fears, there was no complete return to the *status quo ante* – that is, until the 1980s. It seemed as if public spending was on a ratchet which constantly encouraged upward movement, never downward.

The fateful decision of the Soviet state around 1923 to re-enter the contest between the dominant states and do so as a Great Power (albeit an economically backward one) transformed the options facing Soviet society. Without the significant role of entrenched interests – wiped out in the 1917 Revolution and the Civil War – it was possible for the Soviet state to reshape society in a much more purified manner than that attempted in other Great Powers (where, at most, a softer corporatism paralleled Soviet military society). The precepts of Fordism, of the Taylorist organization of large-scale assembly manufacturing – so welcomed by Lenin and so parallel to the organization of the large field army – intensified the drive to turn society into one gigantic military factory. The residue of a socialist discourse – the 'self-emancipation of the working-class' – was hijacked to offer an opaque screen for this extraordinary tyranny.

So powerful and pervasive was the intellectual climate of national competition and militarism that it became treasonable even to discuss, let alone question, either of them. Furthermore, to some degree, the opposition itself acquired the same coloration. Consider Otto Hintze's observation of the German Social Democrats before World War I (Hintze 1906: 211):

> Social Democracy, which in principle is against everything connected with militarism, not only owes to it the discipline on which its party organisation largely rests, but also in its ideology for the future it has unconsciously adopted a good measure of the coercion of the individual by the community which comes from the Prussian military State.

Sixty years later, the historian of the Latin American Left in the 1960s notes its fascination with militarism, elements both substantive and shallow (like forms of dress): 'For more than a decade the urban middle class, university-educated, politicized youth of an entire continent was mesmerized by the armed struggle' (Castaneda, 1994: 16). The same observation was true in Asia and Africa.

The material basis for this fascination – the interest of states in developing capitalism (the real project of much of the Left) – lasted from the phase of classical imperialism through to the 1960s. While the development of capitalism necessitated a national market and a national base, the state was a welcome ally. The fact that they represented two systems only became apparent, as Block (1980: 341) put it, 'in those periods in which the modus vivendi breaks down'. According to Offe, the breakdown would not occur 'if [the state] can equate the needs of capital with the national interest' (Offe in Jessop 1977: 366).

GLOBALIZATION

Macroeconomic reform has become a global fashion, and each national programme has tended to converge on an agenda of surprising uniformity. Why, in the past two decades, have governments moved to open their economies to a technical integration in a global pattern of specialization? On the face of it, it would seem an unlikely change that those directing the state should relinquish those powers of patronage and influence which in part secure the political means to perpetuate their rule. In practice, the commitment of governments has often been hesitant and ambiguous, driven most often only by economic crisis rather than intellectual conviction.

Global economic integration has diluted the nationality of capital and along with it the bonds between particular companies and particular states. Capital discovered that states all over the world were willing to provide infrastructure, and even defence. Capital definitely needs a state; but not a particular state. The relationship between the two is contingent.

For the developed countries, the process of unwinding the mercantilist structures put in place in the 1930s and 1940s (in response to slump and war) was spread over a long period of time, but even so the two world recessions of the 1970s (roughly 1973–5 and 1979–81) forced radical reform in the 1980s at just the time when the processes of global integration had moved on from trade to capital flows. For the developing countries, many of the mercantilist structures were only put in place in the 1960s and 1970s (for the former colonies, part of the mercantilism was something they inherited from the colonial period). Latin America, however, followed the European model, except that the phase of mercantilism persisted much later – until the early 1980s for Mexico, Brazil and Argentina, when financial crisis forced reform in the most painful circumstances. In Sub-Saharan Africa, elements of economic autarky were put in place in the 1960s when overall growth was sustained by buoyant demand for Africa's raw material exports; the decline in raw material prices was offset by borrowing in the 1970s, but terminated in severe recession with the second global downturn and the round of oil price increases in the late 1970s.

East and South-east Asia were engaged in a headlong process of growth, led by the export of manufactured goods, and this growth itself, as well as the pressure of trading partners to open domestic markets, impelled reform – but without pain. Even so, the last of the old sort of heavy industrial drives – in South Korea and Taiwan in the 1970s – severely destabilized them with the onset of the second round of oil price increases and world recession. The murder of the Korean President in 1979 interwove a major political crisis with slump. Nonetheless, high-growth economies based upon manufactured exports seem to possess a degree of great flexibility – the macro-economic performance returned to high growth with extraordinary speed (and absorbed without strain the upsurge of worker and democratic militancy from 1987, leading to major increases in wages).

However, while dismantling structures which have been in place for a long time is one thread in the story, the behaviour of the governments of developing countries in the short term – in the 1970s – was a key element in undermining older structures in the 1980s. Many governments endeavoured to accelerate out of the slump (and the increase in oil prices) of the early 1970s. They did so through increased external borrowing (gaining access to the now easily available recycled petrodollars), and – like the governments in Europe and North America in the 1930s – a major expansion in state investment. On the then-current prognostications for world growth, it made sense, and many governments felt vindicated by an acceleration in growth. The second round of oil price increases and a world recession brought this to a sharp close with a rapid end to the possibility of borrowing and a major debt crisis – which, this time round, forced structural reform.

The short-term crisis was embodied in two insupportable deficits – on external payments (trade and capital) and the government budget, often made much worse by high inflation (in Bolivia, 2500 per cent; in Poland in late 1989, 3000 per cent) as the result of high levels of government deficit. But the long-term problem was a degree of rigidity in the economy which prevented governments responding to unanticipated economic shocks with adequate flexibility.

Left to its own devices, advanced capital is both able and obliged to move beyond national boundaries if it is to be competitive. Capital can thus free itself from the encumbrances of the war-making state. In the process, it forces the state into a new role: as a provider of infrastructure and a transmitter of global economic demands, rather than an economic actor with its own interests (defence, military/heavy industry).

This change renders redundant a major part of the old establishment – from part of the armed forces to part of the 'military-industrial complex' (MIC). Simultaneously, the logic of global economic integration is rendering increasingly expensive the maintenance of the old self-sufficient economy, capable of meeting all defence needs from within national boundaries. The fate of the steel industry in Europe and North America is a commentary on this change. Thus, the market encroaches upon the old MIC, turning the state's needs for defence supplies to the global market. The same may become true of the military labour force, and lead to the end of the citizen-army. The market equivalent of a professional citizen-army is an army of mercenaries, recruited from wherever they are available and paid the

rate for the job. The market distortions of military conscription and re-
served monopoly defence suppliers, whether within or without the public
domain, is also under threat in a globally integrated economy (this is not entirely a theoretical question; ageing in the future will severely reduce the
availability of young men and women in the developed countries).

However, there are no smooth transitions. Institutions do not gently
fade from one mode of operation to another. The interests in the employment of the old state, its armed forces and the MIC, do not quietly accept
their liquidation as the war-making state moves into being a market-
facilitating state. With enough political leverage these interests can indeed
halt or delay this evolution at an intermediate stage, the 'rent-seeking
state'.

The three prototype forms of state suggested here – war-making, rent-
seeking and market-facilitating – in practice are not mutually exclusive. In
practice, rent-seeking occurs in the other two, so does war-making, and in
some cases, market-facilitation. Furthermore, on the basis of these three
functions, many other roles are acquired which immensely confuse the picture. However, it is useful to retain a set of exclusive categories to highlight
the changes taking place.

Structural adjustment takes on a different significance. All important
states in the last period were obliged, as a condition of defending their survival, to seek to create an independent war-making capacity. That implied
a particular type of domestic economic regime. These structures, however,
now impede the growth of the world economy, and macroeconomic reform
is the means to ease the transition from war-making to market-facilitation.
In this context, the countries formerly identified as centrally planned were
no more than the most extreme versions of war-making states, a model
governing to different degrees both East and West. However, that extrem-
ity created a structure with great political power to frustrate the transition,
to trap society in the intermediate phase of a rent-seeking state.

THE CENTRALLY PLANNED ECONOMIES

Socialist industrialization and particularly very rapid industrialization
which was necessary. . . . in the Soviet Union, as a political requirement of
national defence and of the solution of all kinds of political and social
problems, due to backwardness, requires centralized disposal of resources. . . . Economic incentives are in this period replaced by moral and
political appeals to the workers, by appeals to their patriotism and socialist consciousness. This is, so to speak, a highly politicized economy,

both with regard to the means of planning and management and the incentives it utilizes. I think that essentially it can be described as a *sui generis* war economy (Lange 1957: 15–16).

If we are to capture faithfully the aims of the Soviet elite, then we must accord first place to military defence, and derivatively to heavy industry, as the aim of economic development . . . the military and heavy industrial attainments of the advanced capitalist countries are the principal goal towards which development has been directed (Berliner. 1988: 61–2).

Are there any parallels between structural adjustment and what occurred in the former centrally planned economies? There are some, particularly in the similarities within the East Asian group. But reform in economies with strong elements of private ownership and domestic markets was inevitably different. 'Instead of transferring individual enterprises (largely commercialized) from a public into an existing private-dominated domain', Brus writes (in UNCTAD 1994: 49), 'with operating market institutions long habituated to such operations by the society, the process of transformation in post-communist countries consists of privatization of the entire economy accompanied by its marketization' – a major institutional transformation and change in social behaviour, often in conditions of severe economic instability.

These were economies of peculiar rigidity, characterized by complete political direction, without mechanisms of self-adjustment, with, by modern standards, a high degree of inward orientation. Most importantly of all, they were economic structures (production relations) dominated by the state – and the state (physically manifested in the leaderships of the Communist Parties) resisted changes to the economic structure.

War Economies: Eastern Europe and the Soviet Union

In the Soviet Union, all activities were subordinate services to sustain the military-industrial complex (MIC), and in time of real war – as in World War II – the system worked. However, it required that the minimum standard of living be sustained and improved outside of periods of war and it was here the maldistribution of investment undermined the system. Agriculture, the most extreme victim of Stalin's creation of a war economy, in due course wrought its revenge. With its impoverished capital base and demoralized workforce, it changed from being a minimally competent servicing sector to being dependent, a prodigious consumer of capital without adequate improvement in supply.

The size of the Soviet MIC, the heart simultaneously of the Warsaw Pact and the CMEA, is difficult to estimate. Brown *et al.* (1992) calculate the direct military employment at 9.3 million, and the associated civilian workforce at 13.8 million, Winiecki (1992) estimates another four million were employed here but not acknowledged in official figures. He also argues that 80 per cent of national spending upon research and development was for military or military-related purposes. Defence spending in the Soviet Union, according to Easterly and Fischer (1994), rose from some 2 per cent of gross domestic product in 1928 to between 15 and 16 per cent in the late 1980s (in the 1980s, they calculate, spending rose from 12 to 16 per cent). A defender of the old order argued that Western estimates of Soviet expenditure could not be true since they would involve economic collapse – at rates of spending at 15 per cent or more of gross domestic product,

> a modern State is not able to secure economic growth, is compelled to eat away at the accumulation of national wealth or to live at the expense of the credits of other countries. Fortunately, we are not yet observing such a picture in the USSR (Ludin 1989: 50 [trans. Lockwood]).

It now seems the author was wrong in estimating the scale of Soviet spending, but correct in his inference of the likely results.

The ramifications of the scale of expenditure were wider still. The MIC had priority in the distribution of scarce resources, the most scarce skilled labour, domestic inputs, foreign exchange and imports. Virtually all sectors of the economy were involved in some way. Lopatin (1990: 6 [trans. Lockwood]) writes:

> In practice the economy has been militarised to such an extent that perhaps you do not find branches of the national economy which would not work for military needs. Even enterprises which are producing equipment for civilian needs, do it with regard to military utilisation.

Indeed, the Soviet MIC also produced an important share of output for the civil economy. In 1980, military industries produced 30 per cent of bicycles for the civilian market, 60 per cent of trams, 10 per cent of passenger cars, all motor scooters, television sets, radios and cameras (Hewett 1988: 174). By mid-1990, they produced 83 per cent of medical, 92 per cent of light industrial and 76 per cent of agricultural processing equipment (Gonchov 1991).

However, the problems of improving productivity were steadily increasing. Poland, Hungary and Yugoslavia, facing comparable problems, had tried to employ in the 1970s the import of foreign technology to improve productivity, but debts increased faster than the stream of exports from the new capacity. The Soviet Union attempted something similar, paying for the imports with expanded exports of oil and other raw materials. Weakening oil prices, however, obliged the regime to promote manufactured exports, but again, attaining the quality required for sale in open markets required domestic reform. In any case, such a tactic could affect only a small part of the giant Soviet economy, and only then if the matching inputs – and the relations of production – were available to exploit the innovations. The remedy flouted the central rationale of the Soviet system, self-sufficiency.

By the 1980s, Moscow was finding it increasingly difficult to sustain military spending to match the scale and quality of the defence output of the United States and its allies without radical improvement in the civil economy, a general increase in productivity. The composition of output was changing and no longer driven by the old imperatives of the command economy. The rate of growth of the world economy provided a less hospitable environment for Soviet exports, and domestic demand for oil constantly threatened exports. The regime was moved slowly to accepting that self-sufficiency must be qualified, but the movement was not fast enough to offset the emerging social crisis, the rebellion against a poor and deteriorating quality of life.

Furthermore, the quality of even military output was beginning to decline (Kagarlitsky, 1990: 342). To make up for this, the military increased its demand for resources, and there were no policy mechanisms to control this – as Brezhnev once put it: 'As much will be spent on defence as is necessary' (cited in Ludin 1989). It seemed the MIC had slipped out of control. Simultaneously, Reagan's Strategic Defence Initiative – Star Wars – opened up an entirely new and economically impossible scale of military competition. The Afghan War sucked the Soviet army into a military débâcle as demoralizing as that of the US army in Vietnam, and very much more devastating for the Soviet economy. The structure appeared to be immobile, its leadership paralysed by the structures they were supposed to direct. It was the role of Gorbachev to recognize that domestic paralysis was held in place by the external military threat – détente became the precondition of economic reform.

If the MIC was a great burden during the years of development, if in the end it precipitated the collapse of the economy – and with it CMEA and the Soviet Union – it was only appropriate that it should be the MIC which was most devastated by the crisis. The effect was magnified in much smaller economies where the specific gravity of military and heavy industrial production was greater. Over half the industrial assets of the Ukraine were designed to produce heavy and military equipment. With the end of the networks of which it was a part and the decline in military procurement (among other factors), the Ukraine experienced, between 1991 and 1994, a 40 per cent decline in its official output (McCarthy *et al.* 1994). At this stage, in Russia, the civil output which military factories had produced became a saviour (Vasiliev 1994).

The loss of direction of the regime was even more destructive. The great federal Ministries which directed from Moscow vast centralized industrial baronies across the constituent territories of the Soviet Union, collapsed with as much speed as the centralized network of the Communist Party. The military itself shared in this disintegration as it lost both its forward defence line in Eastern Europe, and its inner defence line in the Soviet Union. The symbol of the decay was illustrated by the disintegration of the military conscription system – in 1994, 84 per cent of those eligible for the draft evaded it (against 48 per cent in 1989); the rate for 1995 was put at 80 per cent (and 90 per cent in Moscow). Efforts to restore the role of the military within the CIS and in Chechnya; the role of the Ministry of Defence in protecting or seeking to reclaim from privatization its erstwhile industries; efforts to expand the military budget (taking, on press accounts, a third of current spending); all suggest the restoration of the role of the armed forces is, so far as the current leadership is concerned, still a key part of the central story of restoring the Russian state.

The initial reform process in Eastern Europe and the Soviet Union seemed to precipitate extraordinary declines in gross output: −12.5 and −9 per cent in Poland; −10.2 and −26.0 in Bulgaria; −3.5 and −16.4 in Czechoslovakia; and despite a much longer reform period, −6.5 and −7.8 in Hungary (all 1990 and 1991; Solimano 1992). In three years, the Ukraine experienced a 40 per cent decline (McCarthy *et al.*,1994). The data are unsound – compared to inflated estimates before reform, biased towards heavy industry, and under-recording the new private and servicing activities – yet a decline there almost certainly was.

The declines in output were, however, more the result of a series of extraordinary shocks which, in part, preceded reform and made for emergency responses – 'more a generalized recession than a shake out of the economy associated with structural reforms' (Commander *et al.* 1991: 8). What were the shocks?

- The collapse of the central planning system unwound the linkages of the economies with alarming speed, without there existing either market or monetary mechanisms to establish alternative means to distribute the output.

- This disaster was associated with the reaction of the Soviet Union to the failure of its East European trade partners to deliver goods to cover Soviet exports to them; Moscow suspended or cut its export deliveries, leading to the disintegration of the network, particularly important for trade in capital and military goods, for material-intensive products. The collapse of the CMEA hit Czechoslovakia and Bulgaria particularly hard; 60 per cent of Czech exports to CMEA were machinery and equipment (particularly from what was to become Slovakia), much of it technically tied to specific patterns of consumption in the CMEA group and not saleable elsewhere. In the first quarter of 1990, Romania's exports to non-convertible currency areas declined by 62 per cent.

- Of particular importance to CMEA buyers of Soviet exports was the supply of oil. Very cheap oil (by world standards) had created an industrial structure in the Soviet Union and Eastern Europe which was heavily dependent upon continued supply – the Soviet steel industry, for example, utilized 50 per cent more energy per tonne than the Japanese. And the capacity could not easily or swiftly be converted either to economize or utilize other forms of energy. Oil prices were, for example, for wholesale industrial consumers 26.3 per cent of world market prices in 1989, 19.4 per cent in 1990 – and gas prices were 32.7 and 21.4 per cent respectively (IMF *et al.* 1990). The problems particularly affected the Urals, the Ukraine, Slovakia and other components of the CMEA heavy industry network.

- The break-up of the Soviet Union was even more economically destructive for the constituent parts of the USSR, completed by the disintegration of the Rubel zone in 1993. Political and military instability compounded the disasters, leading to some of the most severe output declines : Armenia –52.0 and –28.0 (1992 and 1993); Azerbaijan –26.8 and –14.4; Georgia –20.6 (1991), –45.6 and –30.0; Tajikistan –30.0 and –30.0 (Havrylyshyn and Tarr 1994).

- With the break-up of both CMEA and the Soviet Union, Russia endeavoured to move export prices for oil towards world market levels and to demand hard currency payments – thus Ukrainian imports (from Russia and Turkmenistan) were 19 per cent of world market prices in 1992, 37 per cent in the first quarter of 1993. If Russian prices had reached world levels, the Ukraine would have been obliged to transfer to Russia revenue equal to 30 per cent of its gross domestic product (Dabrowski 1994). As the Ukraine's hard currency exports fell by two-thirds (1992–3), import costs soared, and the government was able to meet only half the cost of its daily energy imports of, at then-exchange rates, US$15 million. The Ukrainian problem was vastly exaggerated since the government endeavoured to hold down the domestic price of oil to well below the world market level.

- If the heart of the crisis of output was heavy and military industry within both the CMEA and the Soviet Union, the problems were exacerbated by changing government policy priorities. The cutting of state purchases of output and the decline in investment was crucial here, as was the attempt by the Russian government to cut military procurement by 80 per cent in 1992.

- Furthermore, conversion of exports to hard currency markets was made much more difficult by the onset of recession in the OECD group, as well as the muddled protectionism which so often characterized Western trade policy.

- There were also the familiar symptoms of crisis – high inflation, high debt service problems, debts spreading through the economy and covered only by soft banking credits, capital flight, severe problems of basic supply. They made suddenly much more severe the long-term issues of an overproduction of unsaleable heavy industrial goods that went to stocks along with a gross shortage of consumer goods and an excess supply of money.

- Finally, there were the shocks specific to particular countries and moments – for example, the Gulf War severely affected Romanian oil imports and hence its export of refined products; the embargo on trade with Serbia affected Hungary, Bulgaria and Romania; the peasant seizure of lands in Romania led to a break-up of common services to agriculture, a disastrous decline in irrigation and fertilizer inputs and hence of agricultural output; a couple of years' drought exaggerated the problems.

It could hardly have been a worse time to undertake structural reforms. Yet the emergency character of the shocks as well as the political crisis severely limited government options; on the other hand, it gave a rare popular mandate for radical change, a moment of opportunity, a phase of 'extraordinary politics' (Balcerowicz and Gelb 1994). However, the crisis also fell upon a political and economic order that was demoralized and without direction, that had in some cases pursued reform for a decade or more without success.

War Economies: China and Vietnam

China was protected by backwardness from achieving the consistency of the Soviet alignment between the MIC and the rest of the economy. The regime adopted the same principles – between 1953 and 1985, 45 per cent of state investment was devoted to heavy industry, and much of the 'other' category in government expenditure (worker housing, infrastructure, etc.); at its peak, heavy industry took 54 per cent of state investment. Agriculture, on which three-quarters of the population depended, received 10 per cent of state investment (peaking in the years following famine, 1963–5, at 17.6 per cent). Essentially, agriculture was a servicing sector to supply cheap food for the industrial labour force and, as in the Soviet Union in the 1930s, a share of exports (for China, 60 per cent of total exports in the 1950s if we include processed agricultural goods). But China's backwardness, its incapacity to absorb the major part of the economy into the state sector, saved it from the Soviet débâcle. In the late 1970s, the state opted to concentrate on what it held and give free rein to the rural sector and rural industrialization.

China began reforms without any conception of where they might lead. Despite the political upheavals of the Cultural Revolution, the economy was not in severe economic crisis in the late 1970s although the technical quality of the industrial output, particularly in the defence sector, was poor and there were shortages of supply in consumer goods. But, unlike the situation before reform in the Soviet Union and much of eastern Europe, there was no severe external payments problem, large cumulative debt, high rate of inflation, or large monetary overhang. The agricultural reforms which began the process were only half supported in Beijing, but they led on to *ad hoc* measures, culminating in the permission granted to an underindustrialized southern province to admit foreign investment. The rate of growth soared, and growth and reform were mutually reinforcing.

China, like Vietnam later and Laos later still (and possibly like Albania in the future) had the advantage of backwardness. A major part of China's economy was outside the state sector, and this, rather than the state sector itself, provided the foundation for a very rapid rate of growth based upon non-subsidized rural industrialization (the case is argued in several sources, but see Sachs and Woo 1994). In China, 71 per cent of the labour force was employed in agriculture and 15 per cent in industry in the late 1970s (when the reform programme began), whereas in Russia the comparable figures in the late 1980s were 14 and 32 per cent. Those employed in Chinese agriculture were very low-paid and received social services only to the degree which they could pay for them (real per capita rural consumption was a third of the urban level), while Russian agriculture was manned by those who were in effect state employees (with real per capita consumption levels 15 per cent below urban, without including income in kind from private plots, etc.). Chinese agriculture was taxed, Russian a major consumer of budgetary funds. Thus, China was able to exploit a comparative advantage in virtually unlimited supplies of cheap, albeit unskilled, labour, and build a major new economic sector, as it were, alongside the old; Russia could not.

Vietnam offers a striking case at both extremities of the equation; it was more militarized than Russia and more backward than China. There can rarely have been a more completely militarized society than the former North Vietnam. For nearly four decades, the regime was engaged in real war, as opposed to war-preparation, leading to the complete absorption of civil society in the war effort. Yet it was also continuous war which made impossible the creation of anything remotely comparable to the MIC which dominated the Soviet Union and China's state sector. There were very few large plants and none of the great industrial baronies of Moscow's Ministries. In the mid-1980s the share of gross domestic product of Vietnam's State Owned Enterprises (SOEs) was just over a fifth, much the same as in supposedly free-enterprise Malaysia – compared to 80 to 90 per cent in the Soviet Union, Poland, Czechoslovakia, the German Democratic Republic. North Vietnam was a client-state; its people did the fighting, but the industrial capacity was located in the Soviet Union and Eastern Europe (as South Vietnam's war-making capacity was located in the United States).Thus, once reform began, economic growth in the most militarized of the former Centrally Planned Economies (CPEs) took off, apparently as fast as it had done in China (World Bank 1993).

GLOBALIZATION AND THE STATE

The weakening of central control while political discretion remained powerful, even predominant, opened up great opportunities for corruption and nepotism. They were always present to some degree, flourishing in the hiatus between plan and market, but the end of the plan without effective markets vastly inflated opportunities. Rent-seeking of a significant kind is limited to the old elites, but those much larger sections of the population which were beneficiaries of public largesse (from pensioners to the employees of the MIC) constitute an obstacle to market reform. They can force the suspension of the process of change, leading to what Olsen (1982) sees as the tendency of society to sclerosis. Without the shock of plan-wrecking campaigns that Nove (1961: 288–306) identified as the dynamic of growth, the planned economy tends to inertia. The transition from war-making to market-facilitating halts in transition at rent-seeking.

However, the dichotomy between war-making and market-facilitating is too primitive to capture the differentia of the intermediate phase. There market competitiveness is finely interwoven with political discretion and favour; each is exploited to strengthen the other. This appears to be particularly true in certain armed forces as reductions in military spending occur or extraordinary opportunities arise, for private business, each with a different set of relationships to foreign governments and business. Different sections of the Chinese People's Liberation Army created some of the fastest growing and largest business groups in the country – the Poly Group (under the General Staff Department), Norinco (under the Commission for Science, Technology and Industry for National Defence), Xingxing Corporation (under the General Logistics Department), and a host of others (China Electronic Industrial Corporation, China Shipbuilding Trading Corporation, Great Wall Industries, China National Aero-Technical Import-Export Corporation, Huitong, Sanju or the 999 Group; see *Financial Times*, 29 November 1994). Hardly any modern sectors of the civil economy were unaffected by this very powerful group of enterprises with a foot in both the old and the new camps – and with perhaps a strong interest in preventing both a return to central *diktat* and a full transition to pure market operations (where they would lose political patronage). The public control of the armed forces is severely weakened in so far as they have access to funds beyond budgetary supervision – the expenditure of the People's Liberation Army is, on some estimates, two to three times larger than its officially budgeted revenue. On the other hand, the Party leadership rightly fears that the immersion of the army in money-making might profoundly reduce its capacity to fight.

On the other hand, increasing debt became an important means of evading the supposedly therapeutic logic of bankruptcy . The problems are exaggerated by the tradition of treating finance – like all other sectors supporting the war-making capacity – as a costless service-support, rather than another economic activity with a given rate of return. The collapse of central direction removed constraints on managers in this respect. Increasing bank credits, the accumulation of intercompany arrears, a failure to pay taxes and the workforce, all constitute means to escape the 'hard budget', while managers persisted in asset stripping and diverting profits to their own private companies (or 'cooperatives'). Privatization does not necessarily change this, unless it forces company reorganization and the formation of new managements. The cases of privatization briefly examined here each illustrate one or other theme in the resistance of the old state to relinquishing its entrenched position.

Privatization: Russia and the Ukraine

The SOEs of Russia, the heart of a social system of much greater longevity than anywhere else, were always likely to be most resistant to being launched on open markets. Yet it was Russia, with the Czech Republic and Slovakia, which made the most rapid progress in privatization and where there was probably 'the largest sale of assets ever conducted' (Lieberman *et al.* 1994: 10). By 1995, there were 500 private licensed commercial banks, 600 investment funds, 15 779 medium and large private corporations that had been SOEs, and 40 million shareholders (out of 140 million voucher holders). An estimated 62 per cent of the economy – and 86 per cent of the industrial labour force – were private, a transition achieved in little over 18 months. The editors of a World Bank volume on Russian privatization (Lieberman and Nellis 1994: 1) found the achievements 'border on the miraculous'; as with so many miracles, the closer the examination, the less the miraculousness.

First, the Russian SOEs secured their survival – and continued to do so after privatization – through not repaying bank credits, not paying suppliers, not meeting tax obligations, and sometimes not paying their workers. At its peak, intercorporate arrears equalled 40 to 45 per cent of the gross domestic product (a mechanism in which the inefficient destroyed the efficient). At one stage, in 1993, the Central Bank financed industry and agriculture, the federal budget and the successor states of the Soviet Union (to continue to purchase Russian exports). Second, three-quarters of the privatization in the first phase constituted 'closed subscriptions' in which managers and workers, Enterprise Councils of Labour Collectives (STKs), purchased 51 per cent of the shares. The Privatization Commission of each SOE was appointed by the Chief Executive of the SOE, and this body set the value of the SOE. The book value of the assets was accepted in July 1992 for sale purposes which in conditions of high inflation constituted 'a huge transfer of wealth from the State to insiders' (Lieberman *et al.* 1994: 13). On the basis of voucher auctions made by June 1993, Lieberman *et al.* (1994) estimate the value of all Russia's industry at $5 billion, or roughly the same as one of the Fortune 500 companies of the United States. For the open subscription, privileged access was given to existing managers; they could employ company welfare funds to buy shares, and special arrangements for them to obtain finance meant that very little of the personal funds of managers was employed. A survey cited in the same source suggests that, at the end, about 70 per cent of the equity of the former SOEs was in the hands of 'insiders', 16 per cent with local authorities, and the rest in various forms of outside investment, with 9.5 per cent with large shareholders. Other survey evidence suggests that it is management, not the workforce, which have been the beneficiaries. As Schleifer and Boycko (1994: 75) note:

Most enterprises continue to be run unchallenged by the old management teams . . . their management is principally dedicated to preserving
traditional product lines, which may have no markets, as their core activity. In many cases, enterprise managers have consolidated control by
buying shares in the aftermarket and are simply killing time, hoping for
a miracle (and credits).

The procedure followed is justified as a bribe to existing stake-holders to
accept the new deal – 'to ensure speedy privatization . . . breaking the ownership position of the branch Ministries was the overwhelming priority if
the irreversibility of the transition was to be ensured . . . the speed deemed
necessary could not be attained without "bribing the insiders"' (Sutela
1994: 418).

It might be expected that, sooner or later, companies would have to turn
to capital markets for loans, and borrowing might only be possible with
changes of ownership and management. However, the cheap credits of the
Central Bank or house banks offset this need. It seems still to be true that 'a
management team's most valuable asset may turn out to be its lobbying
connections and power'(Lieberman *et al.* 1994: 31). In sum, the process of
privatization has made it extremely difficult for outside interests to change
the operation of most of the companies.

Thirdly, the end of the control of central Ministries and the empower-
ment of local authorities – *oblast* or municipalities – to be the main representative of the state in privatization has enormously increased the speed of
the transition, but it has also encouraged the emergence of local ruling
groups, administration and former SOEs, to defend their interests against
outsiders. A study by Alexandra Vacroux (1994) of Primorsky Krai
vividly shows the emergence of a group of the largest former SOEs, PAKT
(Primosky Manufacturing Shareholders Corporation) as a cartel to defend
their interests; four of the leading members took over the regional administration (as Governor and three deputy Governors), using this position in
order – ultimately unsuccessfully – to block bids by investors from outside
so that managers could retain control. Vacroux (1994: 43) concludes that
'Widespread voucher privatization may actually inhibit progress towards a
competitive, decentralized Russian market by empowering large enterprises to recentralize the economy along geographical rather than industrial lines.'

Finally, the MIC was in general excluded from the transition, although
informally some companies have been privatized. Indeed, this sector of
industry is explicitly excluded from the process, and firms are not even to
be turned into joint-stock companies. They remain executive arms of the

Ministry concerned, funded entirely by the Central Bank. The exact numbers are not known, but they could be equal to the large and medium SOEs privatized: 12–14 000 in all. Thus, the important sectoral lobbies – energy, defence, heavy industry, agriculture – remained entrenched.

It could be that a major part of the MIC is, as some observers believe. unsaleable – there was too little to be salvaged in companies too big to be reformed (on the other hand, sheer size is of immense political strength in pressurising public authorities). In many cases, the net value-added at world market prices may be negative, particularly where existing managers – the so-called 'kleptocrats' – have stripped the assets and/or diverted profits to their own private or cooperative enterprises. 'For the director of such an enterprise', Burtin (1994: 7 [trans. Lockwood]) comments 'full ownership would mean rapid and inevitable bankruptcy. Why should he start digging his own grave?'.

Russia's 'managerial revolution' defied the former diagnosis – that the SOEs needed reorganization and new entrepreneurial management. The old bureaucratic officials of the SOEs, essentially civil servants, drilled through a lifetime of routine operations in obedience to their Ministerial directors, had none of the characteristics required of capitalists, risk-taking and innovation. So far, few of Russia's successful businessmen and women have been drawn from the ranks of the senior echelons of the *nomenklatura*, and few SOEs seem to become successful without a wholesale change of management (as for example with the much-lauded case of Uralmash – where, incidentally, the workforce shrank from 45 000 to 19 000). Indeed, privatization of the SOEs has immensely fortified the position of the old industrial *nomenklatura* against easy challenge. This makes the transformation of production relations immensely difficult.

Nor did the privatization of banks introduce more rigorous criteria governing credit. Frequently, large industrial groups set up house banks to act as a pipeline for Central Bank credit to companies in the group. Observers noted that many of the new banks, owned by their managers, were simply uncritical suppliers of credit to their shareholders and customers, rather than independent auditors assessing relative risk.

The real private sector was the mass of small competitive firms that had been started from scratch in those sectors of the economy formerly shunned by the SOEs: retail and wholesale trade, hotels and restaurants, other services. Within the ranks of the 215 000 'cooperatives' there were some of these, but others were no more than means for SOEs to hide profits through transfer pricing (Shatalov 1991). Beyond these two, the grey economy was said to encompass unrecorded activity equal to a quarter or more of the gross domestic product.

The Russian economy, whatever its legal structure, remained sociologically in the hands of the old order. It was still a state-dominated economy (whether this was federal, republican, regional or local government). The state continued to act as owner, regulator, partner and policeman. Even the privatized SOEs remained dependent upon public credits and contacts. The discretionary character of a politically directed economy remained strong – most notoriously with Viktor Chernomydin, creator of the giant energy corporation, Gazprom, one of its largest shareholders and the last Soviet Minister of Energy, who played the key role in ensuring the energy industry was taxed at only one-third of the level in comparable countries (as a percentage of gross domestic product).

The Ukraine is even more overburdened with the MIC. By 1995, the new republic had become mired in a self-paralysing condition of rent-seeking activity. With some 10 000 large and medium SOEs, the economy was dominated by an all-Soviet Union and all-CMEA military-industrial complex. Heavy industry supplied between 60 and 70 per cent of total output in 1991, and the direct military component of this was put at 10–15 per cent of industrial output. Furthermore, the structure of output was peculiarly energy-intensive (and energy-wasteful), so the continuation of a supply of cheap energy was a condition of survival.

The series of shocks sustained in the early 1990s and enumerated earlier, paralysed the political order of the new state up to at least late 1994, so there were few reforms. On the contrary, the government tried to react to the crises with intensified controls – the old formula of the directed economy.

The government deficit and bank credits were the primary mechanisms for keeping the economy afloat, reaching in value up to one-third of the official gross domestic product. They were also powerful factors in generating possibly the highest rate of inflation in the world for a peacetime economy. In 1992, for example, off-budget subsidies and capital transfers constituted 16 per cent of gross domestic product when there was a 62 per cent shortfall in planned VAT collections (producing a budget deficit equal to 28 per cent of GDP).

Increased administrative regulation has been the other arm of government policy. Yet the degree of regulation – without the support of a regime of institutionalized terror to induce obedience – has produced perverse results, increased unofficial activity: 'beyond a certain point', writes Kaufman (1994: 63), 'there appears to be an inverse relationship between the degree of central administrative controls and intervention over the official economy . . . and the degree of administrative control by the State over the overall economy.'

The unofficial economy has boomed, offsetting some of the disastrous implications of the official decline, from both spontaneous privatization of the SOEs – asset-stripping and decapitalization in favour of private operations – as well as the growth of new activities. A survey of 200 companies cited by Kaufman, implies 55 per cent of activity was unofficial; other estimates range from 25 to 75 per cent of the official economy (McCarthy *et al.* 1994; *Financial Times*, 28 November 1994). However, the persistence of the old economic system had one merit. While output officially declined by 40 per cent, unemployment remained officially low although possibly a third of the labour force was said to be on short time or unpaid leave (McCarthy *et al.* 1994). The SOE managers were said to be broadly opposed to any effective stabilization measures lest this reduce the credits sustaining industry and agriculture and rents available in trading in export licences (introduced to stop the outflow of raw materials to Russia), or access to heavily subsidized oil imports which SOEs could re-export to foreign markets or sell on the domestic black market.

The Ukraine – like the Urals, Slovakia, Manchuria and other areas – has an extreme form of the MIC syndrome. Collapse did not lead to an open private market but to generalized rent-seeking. However, both the Urals and Manchuria are part of much larger economies, so more complex social forces are available to press for continued reform. In the Ukraine, the alliance of government and SOEs exercises far too great a role to make easy reforms that might affect the position of the SOEs. Only the unofficial economy was – expensively, wastefully and messily – achieving part of the reform programme.

Privatization: China and Vietnam

The differences between Russia and China are immense, most strikingly in the low per capita income of China but also in the record of extraordinary growth through the 1980s – real per capita gross national product increased 7.2 per cent per year between 1978 and 1990, with average annual economic growth at over 10 per cent; in the 15 years to 1994 exports increased by 16 per cent per year. Furthermore, the institutional structure has for long been quite different. Chinese central Ministries never concentrated the degree of power seen in the Soviet Union (White 1993: 22). The break-up of the Moscow Ministries led to a high degree of decentralization, but this is very recent. In China decentralization to the provinces is very much older and the provinces are very much more powerful *vis-à-vis* the centre (and the 80 per cent of SOEs for which provincial authorities are responsible are much more dependent on them).

The reform programme, as noted earlier, had initially no clear agenda: it proceeded through adjustment or 'muddling through' (McMillan and Naughton 1992: 131). The SOEs were never scheduled for privatization, although there has been discussion of the sale of a minority of shares. Nonetheless, officially the regime has not revised its original conception – in the words of the director of the State Council research office, 'Privatization is not a model for us . . . (SOEs) still represent our country's general economic power and are the chief source of the State's budget and the main force for economic stability' (*The Economist* 18 March 1995).

The growth of the Chinese economy has come disproportionately from enterprises outside the ranks of the SOEs, the Town and Village Enterprises (TVEs) – under local authority direction – and the small private and foreign (or joint venture) sectors. However, a number of SOEs have also exploited the opportunities of a high-growth economy to transform themselves, if not into private corporations, into entrepreneurial and expansionist firms (keeping a foot both in profitable markets and political patronage). However, for many other SOEs, the growth of the new sectors and of imports – as well as the development of provincial protectionism, interrupting interprovincial trade flows – has imposed new burdens. Of the 108 000 SOEs (employing 108 million workers, three in four of the urban labour force), between a half and two-thirds were said to be losing money in 1994: intercorporate arrears reached 600 billion yuan (equivalent at the then-exchange rate to US$70 billion) or equal to 30 per cent of the value of industrial output. Bank credit financed 80 to 90 per cent of SOE current operations, and the SOEs took the bulk of bank credit (for example, 68 per cent of fixed investment funds in 1994), although their share of industrial output was down to 43 per cent (compared to 81 per cent in 1978).

The picture of SOE cumulative debt is as misleading in China as it is in Russia, since the framework of incentives guiding Chinese managers encourages allowing debt to increase in order to pursue other options. Fan and Woo (1993), on the basis of survey of 300 SOEs between 1984 and 1988, argue that decentralizing responsibility for SOEs to the provincial and local level allowed managers to realize their innate tendencies to over-consume and over-invest. Bank credit is seen as virtually a free public good, so the demand for it is infinite whatever the official price. Furthermore, local banks have a strong incentive to lend to important borrowers, and then seek to force the Central Bank to cover the resulting deficit. Local authorities, which are administratively responsible for local banks, also have an incentive to press the banks to finance their own industries. So far, the Central

Bank has proved reluctant to risk bankrupting the borrower or offending the provincial leadership.

The resulting credit – at least in the mid-1980s – may then flow into improving the incomes of workers (factory cadres of the party have an incentive to maintain their popularity, one of the elements in possible promotion), managerial perquisites, investment in other enterprises or in Hong Kong (for speculative purposes, or for re-entry to China now as private foreign investment to exploit the tax advantages for foreign investors). Simultaneously, tax payments and profit remittances decline. Between 1978 – when SOE profits and taxes supplied over 83 per cent of government revenue – and 1992, SOE profit rates declined from 15.5 to 2.7 per cent. The redistribution from public bank credit to private gain is summarized in the saying, 'The losses of SOEs are socialized, but the profits are privatized.'

SOE borrowing helps to expand the government deficit to possibly three or four times what is officially recorded, and is thus a powerful factor in promoting inflation. Furthermore, at low interest rates, SOEs have a strong incentive to on-lend funds to the non-SOE sectors. If SOEs can borrow at 11 per cent, they can sometimes on-lend at 40 per cent; Gang Fan (1994: 110 Note 4) estimates this diversion of credit covers some 30 per cent of state lending to SOEs. It is, as Lin *et al.* (1994: 28) put it, 'rampant rent-seeking', and they put the total leakage of funds as high as a fifth of the national income. The Central Bank appears captive to the process. In 1993, in an effort to curb the excessively high rate of growth the bank ordered the return of 220 billion yuan credit which had not been authorized; officially, only a third was returned (Blaho 1994). It follows that much of the banking system is technically insolvent. At least 30 per cent of the loan portfolios of three of the top four banks are credit extensions to SOEs, and are said to be equal to 70 per cent of the working capital of the banks.

While there are giant corporations operating nationally in China, the majority are closely related to provincial or local government, something which may in time also develop in Russia. In China, the richer provinces can afford to offer their SOEs soft loans or reduce their tax burden if they are large employers. On the other hand, some SOEs complain that they are heavily burdened by tax payments to local authorities – losing, some claim, up to 90 per cent of their net income; since SOEs are probably simultaneously indebted, the tax flow may represent only a means of transferring funds from the Central Bank to the local government.

Local authority finance is divided into budgetary and extra-budgetary, with the first being shared with the centre, the second not. SOE after-tax profits are one component in local authority extra-budgetary funds. These increased as a proportion of budgetary funds between 1978 and 1990 from 66 to 84 per cent, suggesting that local authorities are partly escaping from the financial tutelage of the centre. Simultaneously, local government gained *de facto* control of budgetary tax rates and tax bases, leading to an increased diversion of tax revenues and SOE profits away from the centre (and a tendency for local government to hide funds through reclassification). Between 1978 and 1992, total government revenue as a proportion of gross national product declined from 34 to 17 per cent, and the share of central government in total budgeted revenue declined from 57 to 41 per cent (Ma 1995, Fan 1994: 117).

The result has been seen as a clear shift in the balance of power between the centre and the provinces, producing a framework where, as the World Bank (1994b: xiii) notes, individual provinces are tending to behave like independent countries, 'with an increase in external (overseas) trade and a relative decline in trade flows with each other'. The SOEs play a crucial role here in forming the basis for independent local economic development and provincial authorities have a strong incentive to protect and advance the economic role of their SOEs.

The most remarkable feature of Chinese local government and the source of much of national economic growth, are the TVEs. They have grown from a 22 per cent share of gross industrial output in 1978 (with the SOE share at 78 per cent), to, in 1990, 35.6 per cent, with an annual rate of growth (1979–90) of 18.2 per cent (White 1993: 127). From 1981 to 1991, the average annual increase in the number of TVEs, the numbers employed and the value of output were respectively 26.6, 11.2 and 29.6 per cent (Lin *et al.* 1994). By contrast, the private sector share in 1990 was put at 5.4 per cent, and 'other' (mainly joint ventures with foreign partners) at 4.4 per cent.

Some argue that the TVEs are essentially market-oriented, and perhaps in comparison to many of the SOEs, they are. They have certainly been set up in response to market demand, unlike many of the SOEs (which are a response to government demand). But they are also public-sector operations. Local government obliges local banks to allocate investment funds by criteria other than profitability (Wong 1993). Political and administrative criteria shape TVE behaviour through local government control of finance, labour, management, land, material inputs and much of the marketing of the output. The constraints here may be tighter at a local level than those governing SOEs since municipalities have less access to resources than provinces, but TVEs are still instruments of public policy. In terms of private ownership, less than 10 per cent of the industrial sector of China is involved.

China is a market economy. Domestic economic activity is in the main determined by domestic and foreign market demand. Many of the SOEs have exploited the growth of the economy and become highly commercialized. The TVEs are similarly primarily focused upon markets. Given the high rate of growth of the economy, the MIC must be economically of declining significance. But China is not a private economy, and the process of growth has led to a redistribution of activity between two parts of the public sector, SOEs and TVEs. The private sector proper remains relatively small, although of great significance for exports. High economic growth has made this less problematic than in Russia and Eastern Europe – deficits in public finance and local favours to state industry are more tolerable with a buoyant income. The radical structural change is rather the creation of local-government-led competitive conglomerates in which SOEs and TVEs are arms of local government development strategies, operating in open markets. This is, at the level of the province, rather more like the South Korean and Taiwanese national development strategies than a simple free-market model – that is, industries, backed by cheap state finance, whether public or private are focused firmly on external markets rather than supplying state or domestic demand.

Vietnam provides a striking contrast to both Russia and China. On the official figures, it is one of the poorest countries in the world (with a per capita gross national product below US$200 per year), and devastated by decades of war and the economic imperatives of survival imposed upon a war-making state. It absorbed the shocks of both the end of Soviet and East European aid (equal to 9 per cent of gross domestic product in 1989) and the collapse of CMEA (supplying 57 per cent of imports in 1988, 5 per cent in 1991). It operated under a US trade embargo, and without external assistance in the 1990s. Yet Vietnam's gross domestic product registered the shocks only in a decline in the rate of growth to 5 per cent in 1990 and 6 per cent in 1991 (before rebounding to 8.3 per cent in 1993). Total investment and imports did not vary, although industrial output declined by 4 per cent in 1989.

The reform programme of 1989, *dong moi* (the first reforms date from 1986), returned agriculture to family farming, decontrolled prices, introduced positive interest rates, devalued the currency, introduced fiscal reform and cut the armed forces by half a million men. The country's good fortune arose from the coincidence of oil exports coming on-stream at the same time as the reforms made for an extraordinary increase in agricultural output – rice exports, zero in 1988, were 2 million tonnes in 1992. The broader reforms stimulated raw material and labour-intensive manufactured exports, so that by now, under half of exports are provided by oil and rice.

Vietnam combined the chronic deprivation of an extreme war-making state with the status, in terms of the supply of war equipment, of client-state (World Bank 1993). As a result, the government did not create what would have become a heavy burden in the present phase, a significant, self-sufficient and politically-directed heavy and military industry. There were some 12 000 SOEs in total in 1988, employing about 2.7 million workers or 7 per cent of the labour force (and 40 per cent of the industrial labour force), to produce 44 per cent of the official gross domestic product. A third of them were said to be making losses in 1990, the rate of return was below the rate of inflation and the cumulate SOE debt was put at the equivalent of US$800 million.

In 1989, direct subsidies to the SOEs were cut, the supply of imports at below cost ended in 1991, and subsidized credit ended in 1992 (some low-interest loans continued). Since 1990, 2000 SOEs have been closed, 3000 merged (with a reduction of employment of 1.7 million), leaving 7000 operative. Of these, 5000 are small. Of the rest, about 35 per cent were directly administered by the central government, most of them through the Ministries of Defence and of Agriculture. They include the largest and most capital-intensive factories. However, the state remained dependent upon the SOEs as a whole for current revenue (the 1994 taxes on sales and profit remittances made up about 60 per cent of government income).

The reform programme – including changes to strengthen the position of managers – has produced some familiar reactions: asset-stripping and the diversion of public resources to the private companies of SOE managers or to joint ventures with foreign firms. As in China, SOEs have disposed illegally of some of their extensive land-holdings, turning them to other uses, and converting company assets to commercial purposes – as the guesthouses of Ministries and other public agencies have been converted to unofficial tourist hotels. But intercorporate arrears and debts to the banking system have not loomed large – under 5 per cent of the gross domestic product (compared to 100 per cent in Russia in 1992, or 80 per cent in Romania in late 1991). Nor have the claims of workers on the social security funds of SOEs been an obstacle to changing jobs. Unlike Russia and China, there seem to be few welfare privileges attached to SOE employment in general, and with a buoyant demand for labour in the economy at large, lay-offs have been relatively easy to accomplish. Furthermore, an important share of worker income is linked to bonuses based upon profitability; in prosperous firms, the bonus can provide an addition to income equal to half a year's basic pay. Indebted firms cannot pay bonuses – so workers have a strong interest in forcing their employers to avoid debt (whereas in both Russia and China increasing bank credits have sometimes provided the basis for wage increases).

The government has not proposed privatization. By 1995, two-thirds of the Vietnamese gross domestic product was said to be derived from the private sector. But this had not been achieved by privatizing industry so much as permitting, in effect, private agriculture and the creation of new private firms. The figure is an heroic guess since so much of the economy is now below the threshold of statistical detection.

The dynamism of the Vietnamese economy is as great as that of China, although the economy starts from a much lower base point. The country is very much smaller and therefore more susceptible to central control. The government – perhaps in making hard budgets stick and minimizing rent-seeking in the SOEs, at the same time exercises very little control over the new private sector, legal and illegal. It seems possible that the combination of quasi-military discipline over the public sector with benign neglect of the private, may allow high growth without significant privatization – or that privatization can be postponed until, as the result of differential rates of growth, the SOEs are too small a proportion of the economy to be politically problematic. If this is so, Vietnam stands one of the better chances of making the transition to a market-facilitating state without getting caught en route in rent-seeking.

Commonalities

Each case of privatization is in important respects unique, turning upon the endowment (both in terms of the size and composition of output, and the involvement of the MIC, activities least commercially viable), the political order, the intensity of economic shocks experienced etc. But there were features in common:

*   As soon as central direction weakened, the use of debt, intercompany arrears, failure to pay taxes and spontaneous privatization, was used to evade reorganization or decline, and to enrich the managers. In Albania, by the end of 1992, gross arrears, including unpaid tax, reached 180 per cent of outstanding bank credit (World Bank 1994a). Everywhere governments, willingly or not, tolerated this effort to defeat their declared purposes and secure the survival of the old discredited economic order.

- The preservation or enhancement of the position of the old managers can also be seen in the mode of privatization, especially in the popularity of management or worker–management buy-outs, cooperatives and the voucher system employed in Russia (whereas the voucher system in the Czech Republic vested power in the state-controlled banks). On the face of it, the most popular forms of privatization made speedy reorganization and reform more difficult and postponed indefinitely creating structures which would lead to increased productivity.
- The state very often retained a predominant role. The figures of the proportion of the economy that had become private were entirely misleading if they were supposed to indicate the degree to which state and political dominance had declined and a market economy been introduced.
- Finally, the resistance to privatization – even in its most managerially privileged form – was strong and grew, the longer the process of reform took. Sometimes it was involved in fears of a foreign takeover.

Sometimes the resistance was the result of effective challenges to the entrenched position of existing managers. In Slovakia, the government changed the rules to limit the role of Investment Privatization Funds (IPFs) on the grounds that this would ensure 'no one shareholder would dominate, and to increase the role of small shareholders'. In reality, it seemed it was a response to the alarm of existing managers that they might be overturned if IPFs were able to build up shareholding positions that would allow them to do so (*Financial Times*, 5 April 1995).

CONCLUSION: DISARMING THE STATE

The countries now said to be in transition were the most extreme and thoroughgoing in creating war-making states, embedded in the case of Eastern Europe and the Soviet Union in a giant international MIC. The system proved incapable of incremental self-reform as had proved possible in Western economies through the operation of the market. As a result, reform could come only through an extraordinary crisis, a political implosion and disintegration.

With the benefit of hindsight, we can see that the old structures were much more resistant to change than first prognoses suggested. Macro economic reform was relatively easily accomplished (even if with some violent social changes), and also allowing the extraordinary growth of new private sectors, legal and illegal. But on the reform of the old institutions, real privatization to secure the separation of the units of capital from the State and their subordination to market competition, progress made remained frustratingly modest (van Brabant 1994: 80).

The MIC was able to keep powerful hold on its entrenched positions – the social relations of the old order were not abolished by edict. The old war-making state was pulverized, part of it destroyed, part retained on sufferance and part converted to new commercial tasks, but the bulk of it has not been transformed.

The hopes for rapid fundamental change were often based on a utopian assessment of the power of markets. The experience of the transitional economies might provide a test-case for the Brenner thesis (Aston and Philips 1985) – put crudely, that social relations predetermine the impact of markets. The reformers and their Western supporters saw the triumph of the market as automatic and the transition period as brief. In much the same way, the IMF and the World Bank saw the role of structural adjustment lending in Africa as essentially short term – 'sound' policies to accommodate markets would swiftly allow the resumption of growth. The combined wisdom of the IMF, the World Bank, the OECD and the EBRD found in the Soviet Union in 1990 that

A recovery from the reduced level of output should be able to get underway within two years or so . . . Further, strong growth of output and rising living standards could be expected for the remainder of the decade and beyond (World Bank *et al.* 1990:18–19).

At the heart of the rigidity of the structure was the MIC and the set of purposes which it embodied – the political will of the state to secure its survival regardless of the operations of markets. While that structure existed – and was sustained by the power of the state to tax, to borrow or to print money – it was legitimate to question, as Fan and Woo (1993: 27) do: 'whether any State where the predominant mode of ownership is public can have the political will to enforce tight budgetary constraints on SOEs'. The evidence from many different types of economy encouraged little confidence. But in market economies, privatization could be employed to secure this end. In transitional economies, it appeared not to be so – painting the signboard of the firm a different colour did not change the managers nor the social networks within the bureaucracy of which they remained a part.

Part of the over-confident optimism in the West derived from orthodox economics. The ethical vindication of this system of thought lay in the idea that the criterion for judging policy lay in the aim of optimizing popular welfare. But the central purpose of the state is quite different (although it might choose to express that purpose in terms of the nation's welfare) – it is to maximize its power to deter invaders and, if required, extend its power against its rivals. The criterion of its achievements is thus not the extension of welfare nor conformity to commercial criteria of efficiency, but success in pursuing its political purposes. The criterion of success of a war-making state is its capacity to wage war. In this context, both state planning and the role of the SOEs have a quite different significance than that envisaged in orthodox economics. And there is less disagreement between East and West – the European governments in the Second World War also employed central planning and a public sector that encompassed the entire civil economy. Thus, the 'mistake' that the old centrally planned economies were alleged to have made was the same one which in practice guided all the Great Powers in the planning of war.

The economic rationale of the state's endeavour is better expressed theoretically in mercantilism, in the corporatism of the 1930s and its later derivations, in the doctrines of radical economic nationalism (mystifyingly identified as something to do with Marx). The theory was a response to a world dominated by the competition of the Great Powers, not what came later, the domination of world markets (and with it, the restoration of neoclassical economics). Today, orthodox economics confuses the war-making with the rent-seeking state. Yet paradoxically, reform supposedly to reach a 'market-facilitating state' is exactly what is pushing the transitional economies into rent-seeking.

Left simply to the forces of domestic reform, it seems unlikely that the state and its public sector, even if privatized, will wither away. There will have to be a sharp destructive break – writing off a major part of the capital stock, breaking up the giant corporations, redistributing the labour force – to achieve this, to sever the relationships to government and end the purposes for which they were created. It is in slump that ordinary capitalist economies achieve these therapeutic transformations, renewing capital through its destruction. Presumably, therefore, if the newly privatized economies keep open their economic frontiers, the world at large will through slump achieve similar if painful effects. But that requires the state to keep open the borders, to be willing to sacrifice major units of capital to renew the economy. We return, not to the independently operating market, but to the political discretion of the state. There is little to encourage optimism there. It seems that, faced with the test of slump, the transitional economies will wish, and will be able, to retreat to shore up the old structures.

Western economies are now so closely integrated that it seems almost impossible for them to restore the old form of economic nationalism. We have seen, however, that in the defence sector and other elements of the modern economy, the instincts of governments remain centrally protectionist. The same is true on a much broader basis where national economies are not as integrated in the global system – India, for example, with 1000 or so SOEs (producing about a quarter of the non-farm GDP) resists privatization.

Thus, the 'revolution' may prove to be rather like China's Cultural Revolution. Despite all the damage and the destruction of particular people, when the dust subsided – and the Chairman was safely interred (or embalmed) – much of the old Establishment was found to be still in place, blinking perhaps with surprise in the unfamiliar sunlight. The communist parties of Eastern Europe and the Soviet Union may have disappeared, but the original nucleus of power – government, banks, heavy and military industry, the army and the police – still remain intact.

REFERENCES

Amsden, A. (1985), 'The state and Taiwan's economic development' in P.B. Evans, D. Rueschmeyer and T. Skocpol (eds), *Bringing the State Back In*. New York, Cambridge University Press: 78–106.

Aston, T.H. and C.H.E. Philips (eds) (1985), *The Brenner Debate: Agrarian Class Structure and Economic Development in Pre-industrial Europe*. Cambridge: Cambridge University Press.

Balcerowicz, L. and A. Gelb (1994), 'Macropolicies in transition to a market economy: a three year perspective'. Paper for World Bank Annual Conference on Development Economics, Washington, DC: World Bank, April.

Berliner, J.S. (1988), *Soviet Industry from Stalin to Gorbachev*. New York: Cornell University Press.

Blaho, A. (1994), *Russian Transition – Chinese Reforms: a Comparative View*. Helsinki: United Nations University-WIDER (Research for Action).

Block, F. (1980), 'Beyond relative autonomy: state managers as historical subjects' in R. Miliband and J. Saville (eds), *The Socialist Register 1980* London: Merlin Press: 227–42.

Brenner, R. (1986), 'The social basis of economic development' in J. Roemer (ed.), *Analytical Marxism*. New York, Cambridge University Press: 23–53.

Brown, A.N., B.W. Ickes and R. Ryterman (1992), 'The myth of monopoly: a new view of industrial structure in Russia'. *Working Paper*, 1331, Washington, DC: World Bank.

Burtin, Y. (1994), 'Nomenklaturnaya sobstvernost'vchera icegodnya'. *Moskovskie Novesti*, 35.28.8/4, September.

Castaneda, J.G. (1994), *Utopia Unarmed: the Latin American Left after the Cold War*. New York: Vintage Books.

Commander S., F. Coricelli and K. Staehr (1991), 'Wages and employment in the transition to a market economy'. *Working Paper*, 736, Washington, DC: World Bank Economic Development Institute.

Easterly, W. and S. Fischer (1994), 'The Soviet economic decline', *Policy Research Working Paper 1284*, Washington, DC: World Bank.

Dabrowski, M. (1994), 'Ukranian way to hyperinflation'. *DP*, 94/12, Warsaw: Centre for Social and Economic Research.

Fan, G. (1994), 'Incremental changes and dual-track transition: understanding the case of China'. *Economic Policy: A European Forum*, 19 (Supplement).

Fan, G. and W.T. Woo (1993), 'Decentralization, socialism and macro-economic stability: Lessons from China'. *Working Paper*, 112, Helsinki: United Nations University-WIDER.

Gilbert F. (ed.) (1975), *The Historical Essays of Otto Hintze*. New York: Oxford University Press.

Goldman, M.M. (1994), *The Lost Opportunity: Why Economic Reforms in Russia Have Not Worked*. New York: Norton.

Gonchov, K. (1991), 'The economics of disarmament: a difficult matter'. *Problems of Communism*, 23(9).

Harris, N. (1992), *National Liberation*. London: Penguin.

Harris, N. (1994), 'Nationalism and development' in R. Prendergast and F. Stewart (eds), *Market Forces and World Development*, New York: St Martin's Press: 1–14.

Havrylyshyn, O. and D. Tarr (1991), 'Trade liberalization and the transition to a market economy'. *Working Paper*, 700, Washington, DC: World Bank.

Havrylyshyn, O. and D. Tarr (1994), 'Reviving trade among the newly independent states'. *Economic Policy*, 19 (supplement): 171–90.

Hewett, E. (1988), *Reforming the Soviet Economy*. Washington, DC: Brookings Institution.

Hintze, O. (1906/1975), 'Military organisation and the organisation of the state', in F. Gilbert (ed.), *The Historical Essays of Otto Hintze*. New York: Oxford University Press: 180–215.

Jessop, B. (1977), 'Recent theories of the capitalist state'. *Cambridge Journal of Economics*, 1.

Jones, C.T. (1987), *International Business in the Nineteenth Century: the Rise and Fall of a Cosmopolitan Bourgeoisie*. Brighton: Wheatsheaf.

Kargalitsky, B. (1990), *The Dialectics of Change*, London: Verso.

Kaufmann, D. (1994), 'Diminishing returns to administrative controls and the emergence of the unofficial economy: a framework of analysis and application to the Ukraine'. *Economic Policy: A European Forum*, 19 (Supplement): 52–70.

Lange, O. (1957), *The Political Economy of Socialism.* Warsaw.

Lieberman, I.W., and J. Nellis (eds) (1994), *Russia: Creating Private Enterprises and Efficient Markets*. Washington, DC: Private Sector Development Department, World Bank.

Lieberman, I.W., J. Nellis and S. Rahuja (1994), 'An overview of privatization in Russia', in I.W. Lieberman and J. Nellis (eds), *Russia: Creating Private Enterprises and Efficient Markets.* Washington, DC: Private Sector Development Department, World Bank: 7–33.

Lin, J.Y., F. Cai and Z. Li (1994), 'China's economic reforms : pointers for other economies in transition'. *Policy Research Working Papers*, 1310, Washington, DC: World Bank.

Little, I.M.D., R. Cooper, W.M. Corden and S. Rajapatirama (1993), *Boom, Crisis and Adjustment: the Macro Economic Experience of Developing Countries.* New York: World Bank/Oxford University Press.

Lopatin, V. (1990), 'Est'-li vykhod iz krizisal'. *Voprosy ekonomiki*, 4.

Ludin, I. (1989), 'Ekonomicheskie aspekty sokrashchenila vooruzhehhykh sil i konversi voennogo proizvodstia'. *Voprosy ekonomiki*, 6.

Ma, J. (1995), 'Macroeconomic management and intergovernmental relations in China'. *Policy Research Working Paper*, 1408, Washington, DC: World Bank.

McMillan, J. and B. Naughton (1992), 'How to reform a planned economy: lessons from China'. *Oxford Review of Economic Policy*, 8(1): 130–43.

McCarthy, D., C. Pant, K. Zheng and G. Zanalda (1994), 'External shocks and performance responses in the transition: the case of the Ukraine'. *Policy Research Working Paper*, 1361, Washington, DC: World Bank.

Nove. A. (1961), *The Soviet Economy: An Introduction.* London: Allen and Unwin.

Olsen, M. (1982), *The Rise and Decline of Nations.* New Haven: Yale University Press.

Sachs, J. and W.T. Woo (1994), 'Structural factors in the economic reforms of China, Eastern Europe and the former Soviet Union. *Economic Policy: A European Forum*, 18: 101–31.

Schleifer, A. and M. Boycko (1994), 'Next steps in privatization: six major challenges' in Lieberman, I.W. and J. Nellis (eds) (1994), *Russia: Creating Private Enterprises and Efficient Markets.* Washington, DC: Private Sector Development Department, World Bank: 75–86.

Shatalov, S. (1991), 'Privatization in the Soviet Union: the beginnings of a transition'. *Working Paper* 805, Washington, DC: World Bank.

Skocpol, T. (1979), *States and Social Revolutions.* New York: Cambridge University Press.

Solimano, A. (1992), 'After socialism and dirigisme: which way?'. *Policy Research Working Paper*, 981, Washington, DC: World Bank.

Sutela, P. (1994), 'Insider privatization in Russia: speculations on systemic change'. *Europe–Asia Studies*, XIV(3).

UNCTAD (1994), *Privatization in the Transition Process: Recent Experiences in Eastern Europe.* Geneva: Kopint-Datorg.

Vacroux, A. (1994), 'Privatization in the regions: Primorsky Krai' in I.M. Lieberman and J. Nellis (eds), *Creating Private Enterprises and Efficient Markets.* Washington, DC: Private Sector Development Department, World Bank: 35–44.

van Brabant, J.M. (1994), 'The hobbled transition: mined privatization paths in the East' in UNCTAD, *Privatization in the Transition Process: Recent Experiences in Eastern Europe.* Geneva: Kopint-Datorg: 61–83.

Vasiliev, S.A. (1994), 'Market forces and structural change in the Russian economy', *Economic Policy*, 19.

White, G. (1993), *Riding the Tiger: the Politics of Economic Reform in Post-Mao China.* London: Macmillan.

Winiecki, T.A. (1992), *The Structural Legacy of the Soviet-type Economy*. London: Centre for Research into Communist Economies.

Wong, C. (1993), 'Between plan and market: the role of the local sector in post-Mao China' in B. Reynolds (ed.), *China's Economic Reform*. Boston: Academic Press.

World Bank (1993), *Vietnam: Transition to the Market*. Washington, DC: Country Operations Division (East Asia and Pacific Region), World Bank.

World Bank (1994a), *Albania: Building a New Economy*. Washington, DC: World Bank.

World Bank (1994b), *China: Internal Market Development and Regulation* Washington, DC: Country Operations Division (East Asia and Pacific Region), World Bank.

World Bank, IMF, OECD, EBRD (1990), *The Economy of the USSR*. Washington, DC: World Bank.

5 The Starting Point of Liberalization: China and the Former USSR on the Eve of Reform[1]

Peter Nolan

The contrast in performance of China and the former USSR under reform policies has been dramatic. In China there was explosive growth, a large reduction in poverty and a major improvement in most 'physical quality of life indicators' (Banister 1992, World Bank 1992a). The economy of the former USSR collapsed, alongside massive psychological disorientation and a large deterioration in physical quality of life indicators, including a huge rise in death rates (Ellman 1994). The contrast in reform paths is well known. China's approach to economic reform was experimental and evolutionary, under an authoritarian political system. The USSR followed the 'transition orthodoxy' of revolutionary political change under Gorbachev, followed by shock therapy and rapid privatization in the Russian Federation under Yeltsin.

Systematic comparison of the two countries' experience under reform is still limited (but see, for instance, Aslund 1989, Sachs and Woo 1994, Goldman 1994: chapter 9, Nolan 1994, 1995). Much the most influential proposition in this literature is the argument that the difference in results is explained not by the difference in reform policies but, rather, by the different starting-points:

> It was neither gradualism nor experimentation, but rather China's economic structure, that proved so felicitous to reform. China began reform as a peasant agricultural society, EEFSU [Eastern Europe and the former Soviet Union] as urban and overindustrialised. . . . In Gerschenkron's famous phrase [China] had the 'advantage of backwardness'(Sachs and Woo 1994: 102–4).

This proposition has been absorbed rapidly into the mainstream of popular perception of the reasons for the difference in outcome from post-Stalinist reform in China and the former USSR.

100

This chapter examines the two systems of political economy on the eve of their respective system reforms in order to evaluate their respective possibilities for accelerated growth. It concludes that there were indeed large system differences. However, many of these were to China's disadvantage. It argues that despite the differences, the systems each possessed large possibilities for accelerated growth with the introduction of market forces in an incremental fashion, in a stable political environment with an effective state apparatus. These possibilities stemmed to a considerable degree from common features of the communist system. The chapter concludes that on the eve of reform China did not on balance possess greater possibilities for improved system performance than did the USSR. It argues that the main explanation for the differences in outcome must, therefore, be sought in the policies chosen, not in system differences. We begin by comparing both societies on the basis of economic factors crucial to the possibility of accelerated growth.

ECONOMIC FACTORS

Advantages of the Latecomer

There are three main 'advantages of the latecomer'. Firstly, it may be advantageous to have a large share of the population in agriculture, since a rural labour surplus provides the potentiality for rapid 'Lewis-type' growth in labour-intensive industries. Secondly, latecomers can draw upon a much greater pool of international savings than was available to the early starters. Thirdly, a latecomer can employ more advanced technology than was available to the early industrializers. However, there are many problems with these arguments as applied to the Sino-Soviet comparison.

Economic Structure

Industry   In the early 1980s a reported 62 per cent of Soviet GDP came from the industrial sector, which is a higher share than even for the advanced industrial economies (Table 5.1). However, China also was hugely 'over-industrialized'. In China in the early 1980s, industry reportedly produced 47 per cent of GDP, ahead of even the advanced capitalist countries (Table 5.1). There were serious inefficiencies in both Chinese and Soviet industry, but 'over-industrialization' may have been an even greater burden for China than for the USSR, since in China's case the 'over-industrialization' was in a vastly poorer country, with a much lower income level from which to generate savings to finance investment.

In the USSR in the early 1980s the proportion reportedly employed in industry (around 45 per cent: Table 5.1) was higher than in the advanced economies. However, the difference was not large, and it stood at a similar figure in several of the advanced capitalist economies. Moreover, to some degree the relatively high proportion employed in industry reflected the high levels of over-manning in industry in all the communist countries.[2] This was a form of 'disguised unemployment'(Arnot 1988). Suitable institutional reform could have raised labour productivity and encouraged state enterprise managers to release labour to be employed in other sectors.

Table 5.1   Economic Structure of Pre-reform China, the USSR, Compared to the Non-communist Countries, 1980 (%)

	GDP					Employment				
	USSR	China	LIEs	MIEs	IMEs	USSR	China	LIEs	MIEs	IMEs
Agriculture	16	31	45	15	4	14	71	73	44	6
Industry	62	47	17	40	37	45	17	11	22	38
Services	22	22	38	45	62	41	12	19	34	56

Notes
LIEs = Low Income Economies (excluding China and India)
MIEs = Middle Income Economies
IMEs = Industrial Market Economies
Source   World Bank, World Development Report 1982

Agriculture   China's employment structure was close to that of a typical low-income country, with around three-quarters of the population still employed in agriculture. Although the USSR had a much lower proportion of the workforce employed in the farm sector, the share was still large compared to the advanced capitalist countries (Table 5.1) and was probably much higher than the usually reported figure (see Table 5.13 for a much higher estimate). There were large possibilities in Soviet agriculture as in Soviet state industry for releasing surplus labour to undertake useful work in other sectors.

Having a large proportion of national output and employment generated in agriculture is not necessarily an advantage for a reforming communist country. An important reason for the succcess of the East Asian Four Little Dragons was that each had a relatively small farm sector at the start of their phase of accelerated growth (Little 1979: 450). In a densely populated economy such as China's the capital needs for expanding agriculture are large. If a sufficient condition of rapid growth was having a large share of output and employment in the farm sector, impoverished countries would long ago have 'caught up'.

Services   Both China and the USSR had a low proportion of employment in the service sector (Table 5.1). They each had large possibilities for improvements in welfare and for attracting surplus labour from industry, agriculture and from the state bureaucracy, simply by allowing people to set up service sector businesses. Under China's reforms the service sector's share of employment rose from 14 per cent in 1978 to 23 per cent in 1991 (derived from SSB, ZGTJNJ 1992: Section 4). In the USSR in the late 1980s, the Law on Individual Labour Activity (1986) and the Law on Cooperatives (1988) were followed by a rapid growth of small-scale service-sector activity.

State Sector   Most Soviet workers were employed in the state sector, which included industry, state services, notably government administration, as well as state farms. These workers had secure jobs, incomes and housing, and welfare provision. In China, only a small proportion of the workforce was in these sectors. Most of the growth in employment in the non-state sector during reform came from rural dwellers, and only a small part from the state sector. Obviously in this respect successful reform in the USSR would have taken a different path from that in China.

The Soviet state sector was far from homogeneous. Although the 'Pareto tails' of extreme inequality in income distribution were missing, there were wide differences in income and standard of living between different occupations and sectors (Yanowitch 1977: chapter 2). Moreover, there were quite wide differences in average income and large differences in labour force growth rates between regions (Feshbach 1983). Generally speaking, income levels were lower and population growth rates much higher in central Asia than in the European republics. As new employment opportunities emerged outside the state sector during a successful economic reform programme, then, it is not difficult to imagine how workers might have begun to migrate between sectors, occupations and regions. This could have happened in many ways, including the following:

- Direct bidding of full-time permanent labour out of the state sector through higher wages.
- 'Part-time' work in the non-state sector by state-sector workers.
- State-sector workers might retain their right to work in the state-sector enterprise but cease to be paid wages from that enterprise, and being allowed to more or less permanently work full-time in the non-state sector.

- Workers in the state sector could be allowed to retain their rights to work in the state enterprise and their social security benefits from it in return for some form of fee paid to their original enterprise.
- State enterprises could themselves invest in new enterprises (either directly or as joint ventures with capital from other sectors) in the production of goods and services, the areas for which demand was growing rapidly, allowing the redeployment of surplus labour from the original enterprise.

Some form of all these arrangements occurred in China during its reforms, but the rapid growth in the new entrants to the workforce and the huge rural labour surplus in farm employment tended to reduce the extent of migration from the state to the non-state sector.

Capital Markets

The accelerated globalization of capital after the 1970s provided a large potential 'catch-up' opportunity for reforming communist countries. Post-1978 China attracted substantial direct foreign investment because it provided political stability, cheap labour costs with a low probability of strike action, reliable investment guarantees and rapid growth behind high protectionist barriers which made it attractive as a potentially huge market. China did enjoy an advantage of having a large amount of capital in the hands of the Chinese diaspora. Some other reforming countries also have large diaspora. For example, the Indian diaspora's financial resources probably exceed those of overseas Chinese. However, only a small proportion of this has been invested in India despite India's economic liberalization. Clearly, a large diaspora is insufficient. The reforming country needs to implement policies which encourage its overseas citizens to invest in their native land.

At the start of its reform, the USSR had high potential to attract direct foreign investment. The core of the Russian economy to the West of the Urals was essentially a part of Europe, which was to become the largest single market in the world in 1992. It had vast natural resources and a much more educated and skilled labour force than China's (see below). They were prepared to work hard for much lower incomes than comparably skilled people in the advanced capitalist countries. Moreover, its infrastructure was vastly more developed than that of China. A successful reform strategy would have generated huge needs for foreign capital. The fact that it failed miserably to attract foreign direct investment (rated as the second riskiest country for investments in 1993: *The Economist,* 21 August 1993) is attributable to massive instability caused by policy choices in politics and economics.

Technological Catch-up

Both China and the USSR achieved low returns in terms of civilian technical progress from their investment in science. Scientific research workers were isolated in institutions and universities. Enterprise managers had a strong interest in resisting technical progress, let alone themselves attempting to pursue it (Nove 1983: 76). By introducing the profit motive to industry (alongside other necessary reforms), large increases in output could in principle have been achieved from existing scientific personnel. The potential for the USSR to gain from this was considerably greater than was the case for China.

In both cases a large share of scientific expertise was allocated to the military sector. This reflected the USSR's frontline position in the Cold War and China's post-1960 'war on two fronts' against both the US and the Soviet Union. In the early 1980s Soviet defence expenditure amounted to around 15 per cent of GNP (USCJEC 1983: 306), and the defence sector claimed a large share of the best resources (USCJEC 1982: 340). China's defence sector was much less technically advanced than that of the USSR in the 1970s. However, the share of industrial resources pre-empted by the military sector was at least as great as in the USSR, accounting for around 21 per cent of industrial output value in 1980 (USCJEC 1975: 477). In both cases there existed a large 'peace dividend' from the end of the Cold War which could have released scientific and material resources for civilian use. This dividend could have been especially large if the end of the Cold War coincided with well-devised policies to introduce competition to industry leading to the intensive use (in order to make profits) of scientific skills and capital stock formerly tied up in the military sector. The USSR's scientific expertise would have been hugely attractive to foreign investors if the correct institutional environment, such as peace and a suitable, enforceable legal framework, could have been constructed and steady growth of demand ensured. Tragically, under the conditions of collapsed domestic demand and shattered political institutions, foreign countries often preferred to import scientists rather than organize production within Russia.

Despite the 'turn to the West' in the 1970s resulting in increases in the USSR's technology imports, equipment imports still accounted for only around 2 per cent of total domestic equipment investment (Hanson 1978: 31). In the 1950s most of China's technology imports had come from the USSR. In the 1960s 'self reliance' had become the watchword and imports of equipment and technology were reduced to the selective acquisition of the most advanced technology: '[China's] stock of Soviet equipment was rapidly becoming obsolete and domestically produced equipment was primitive'(USCJEC 1978: 311). Both China and the USSR possessed a large opportunity for technical catch-up, provided the foreign exchange could be generated to pay for technology-enhancing imports. China was in a much less favourable position than the Soviet Union to select and absorb foreign technology, since its scientific capabilities had been badly damaged during the Cultural Revolution.

Size

The vast size of China and the USSR provided a considerable potential advantage compared to other reforming Stalinist economies. This provided them with the opportunity to restructure with a relatively small loss of efficiency behind protectionist barriers. Domestic industries could potentially move towards profitability at world market prices within a relatively closed economy with growing internal competition while simultaneously achieving economies of scale.

Social Capability

Poor economies mostly have failed to catch up with advanced ones. Catch-up tends to occur only above a certain income-level (Gomulka 1991). In order to 'catch up', countries need a certain level of 'social capability' to be able to exploit advanced technology: '[A] country's potential for rapid growth is strong not when it is backward without qualification but rather when it is technologically backward but socially advanced' (Abramowitz 1986, 388).

The Labour Force

General Educational Level   Socialist ideals of the communist countries were reflected in the relative equality of access to education. China's level of general education in the 1970s was advanced for a low-income country, at least in the urban areas (Table 5.2). However, a mere 17 percent of the labour force worked in industry (Table 5.1). In the mid-1970s the vast bulk of the Chinese population was a semi-literate peasantry, over one-third of whom lived in dire poverty (Nolan 1983, World Bank 1992a). Around 35 per cent of the adult population was estimated to have been illiterate, around the same figure as for Indonesia (Eberstadt 1986: 315). Moreover, the country's primary and secondary education was hugely disrupted by the Cultural Revolution, which led to schools being closed across much of the country for two to three years, and even when they reopened, ideological education took a high priority in the curriculum.

The USSR by the 1980s was a highly urbanized country. Its achievements in basic education compare favourably even with those of the advanced capitalist countries (Table 5.2). In the mid-1970s the USSR's per capita consumption of educational services was ahead of all Western countries except the USA (Schroeder 1983: 319).

Table 5.2   Educational Achievements in China and the former USSR, 1978

	No. enrolled in primary school as % of age group	No. enrolled in secondary school as % of age group	No. enrolled in higher education as % of population aged 20–4	Adult literacy rate %
Low-income countries*	74	20	2	43
Middle-income countries	95	41	11	72
Industrial market economies	100	89	37	99
China	93	51	1	66
India	79	28	8	36
USA	98	97	56	99
Austria	100	72	21	99
USSR	97	72	22	100

Note   * excluding India and China
Source   World Bank, World Development Report 1981

Higher Education   Maoist China concentrated its limited educational resources upon primary and (to a lesser extent) secondary schools. In 1978 only 1 per cent of the relevant age group were studying in higher educational institutions, compared to 2 per cent in lower-income countries as a whole, and 8 per cent in India (Table 5.2). Moreover, during the Cultural Revolution higher educational institutions had been closed for several years, resulting in an estimated loss of two million middle-level technicians and a million university graduates (World Bank 1981a: 106). In the late 1970s the ratio of scientific and technical personnel to total manpower was low. Moreover, even this fact conceals the:

poor quality and out-of-date character of much technical knowledge – the result of ten years of educational disruptions and isolation from the rest of the world. . . . In relation to China's desire and need to modernize, its supply of skilled manpower is inadequate (World Bank 1981a: 107).

The USSR had a vastly greater pool of scientific and technical personnel than did China. A consequence of its poor record in utilizing scientific skills to produce technical progress was that it allocated a large amount of resources in order to enable the supply of scientific and technical workers to grow rapidly. In the early 1950s the USSR possessed just 15 scientists and engineers per 1000 people compared to 26 per 1000 people in the USA. By the mid-1970s the USSR had overtaken the USA, with the respective figures standing at 66 and 62 per 1000 people (Bergson 1983: 56).[3]

In neither case was the stock of scientists and engineers used well. The absence of competition and profit-seeking greatly reduced the incentive of enterprises to undertake technical progress and even led enterprises to resist new technology. Pervasive shortages led to a widespread sellers' market so that in both capital goods and final consumption goods there was little incentive for enterpises to use available scientific skills to improve product quality. In the belief that technical progress was a public good, a large part of scientific capacities were located away from the enterprises.

A common consequence of the difficulties of the command economy was that both countries possessed a large stock of capital goods per unit of final product. In both cases, capital goods were unreliable, with a high propensity to break down. Compared to market economies, there was much less reliability in obtaining spare parts from specialist producers. These factors led to widespread engineering failures.

Motivation   A large array of factors combined to produce a workforce in both China and the USSR that was operating well inside its capacity.

The penalty of dismissal was virtually absent. Managers had a strong incentive to hoard labour as well as capital, since this made it easier to achieve the key planning targets, namely gross value or physical quantity of output. The absence of timely delivery of needed inputs prevented production running smoothly at full capacity. Consequently, the workpace was very uneven throughout each production period.

The slow workpace and low work effort which resulted from these factors were not fixed parameters. Rather, they represented a potential windfall gain if workers' motivation could have been harnessed through suitable policies. An important factor which was available to enable this force to be released was the widespread disappointment with the standard of living attained after long years with high rates of saving and investment. The introduction of suitable incentive systems could have released a greatly increased intensity of labour, and hugely raised output from existing resources.

Entrepreneurship

China possessed a powerful capitalist tradition. It had a highly developed entrepreneurial system for many centuries before the European industrial revolution. In the first three decades of the twentieth century in those areas in which there was some semblance of political order, rapid industrial growth did occur (Bergere 1981, Rawski 1989). Because the Chinese revolution had occurred relatively recently, in the 1970s the memory of capitalism was still alive. Over much of the Russian empire there had been severe natural barriers to commerce. By 1914, capitalist development had still 'as yet touched little more than the hem of Russia's economic system' (Dobb 1966: 35–6). Subsequently, the Soviet Union experienced almost 60 years under anti-capitalist policies.

However, the view that China possessed a much stronger base of entrepreneurship from which to launch its post-Stalinist reforms is erroneous. In Maoist China the private sector came under repeated attack as a 'snare both to poor peasants and to party cadres who still had bourgeois aspirations' (Walker 1965: 75). 'Capitalism' was likened to a 'dog in the water to be beaten and drowned'. During Soviet collectivization the Soviet rural private sector was crudely suppressed. However, the policies were quickly reversed. By the late 1930s the private sector was producing a large part of rural personal income. The USSR had no subsequent attack on the rural private sector to match the severity of that in China.

In European Russia before 1860 capitalism was much more advanced than was once supposed (Gatrell 1986: 144–50; Blackwell 1983). From the 1880s to 1914, Russian industry grew at around 4 to 5 per cent per annum (Gatrell 1986: 143). A powerful group of big businesses emerged, benefiting from foreign technology, often involving foreign capital, and centred particularly around St Petersburg (Blackwell 1983: 17). Alongside them went a continued growth of more primitive small-scale *kustar* industry involving as many as 15 million urban and rural craftsmen in the 1880s (Gatrell 1986: 154).

In both China and the USSR the Stalinist command economy produced simultaneous shortages and surpluses without the possibility legally to reconcile them through the market. As a result there was a powerful tendency towards illegal (black) market and quasi-legal (grey) market activity (Grossman 1979). In Berliner's view, much of the activity of the 'second economy' consisted of 'entrepreneurship of the classically Marshallian kind – redirecting resources towards an equilibrium state' (Berliner 1983: 196). Within the state sector of all of the Stalinist economies an army of people ('pushers') scoured the country to obtain desired inputs in exchange for unwanted surpluses. The second economy often provided personal services or produced consumer goods. In addition there was a large illegal output both from enterprises themselves as well as from private illegal factories using stolen materials and often employing many workers. In the USSR in the 1970s between 30 and 40 per cent of personal income came from the private sector (Aslund 1991: 155). Indeed, due to the pervasiveness of shortages, ordinary individuals in command economies needed to be far more entrepreneurial in the conduct of their daily lives than the bulk of wage earners in the West.

Industry

Heavy Industry Bias

The extreme inefficiency of the Stalinist economies meant that both China and Russia required a large amount of heavy industrial output to produce a unit of final product (Table 5.3). China was even more profligate in its use of inputs than was the USSR. The quality of much heavy industrial output, especially machinery, was below that required to compete on world markets. Both economies had large potential, through the introduction of competition, to greatly reduce the amount of inputs needed to produce a unit of output and to raise the quality of capital goods, with multiple efficiency gains for the users of these goods.

Table 5.3   Intermediate Inputs per Dollar of GNP (1979/1980)

	Steel (g)	Sulphuric acid (g)	Cement (g)	Energy consumption (kg of coal equivalent)
USSR	136	21	116	1.49
China	146	31	319	3.21
USA	42	17	27	1.16
West Germany	61	7	47	0.56
Japan	109	7	87	0.48

Source   World Bank 1981a, SSB, ZGTJNJ 1981

However, the share of heavy industry in industrial output in neither country was particularly large compared to the advanced capitalist economies (Table 5.4). Output per capita of key heavy industrial products was much higher in the USSR than in China, but was not especially large relative to the advanced capitalist countries (Table 5.4). A large part of heavy industrial output in most economies consists of intermediate inputs, such as basic chemicals, steel, cement and glass, in which the product is

Table 5.4 Output Per Capita of Selected Industrial Products
in the Late 1980s and Early 1990s

	electric power '000s kwh	coal '000s kg	steel '000s kg (a)	paper '000s kg (a)	cement '00s kg (a)	sulphuric acid '000s kg (b)	chemical fibre '000s kg (b)	TV sets no 1000 people (b)	motor vehicles no 1000 people (b)(c)	share of heavy industry in GVIO* (%)
USSR	5.6	2.3	557	22	471	94	5.1	36	7	74
China	0.4	0.8	45	8	137	10	1.6	23	0.4	64
USA	11.1	3.4	339	136	321	147	15.8	60	35	70
Japan	5.5	0.1	872	99	621	56	14.5	122	107	70

Notes
(a) 1985
(b) 1991
(c) including both commercial and passenger vehicles
* various years
n.a. not available
Sources (i) Liu 1988: 56–7 and 116; (ii) SSB, ZGTJNJ 1993, appendix; (iii) World Bank 1981: 16

relativly homogeneous and quality often is a less important element in competitiveness than in other industrial product markets. In both countries there was a huge pent-up demand for the products of sectors that directly used large quantities of intermediate inputs. These included housing, motor vehicles and the associated investment in road networks. In both countries levels of production and consumption of these items were relatively very low indeed. Moreover, a rapid growth in demand for other lower-value industrial consumer goods, such as textiles, toys, sports goods, and household electrical goods, all created demand for upstream inputs from heavy industries such as power, steel, chemical fibres, and plastics. Although the USSR's level of consumer durable and clothing consumption was much greater than that in China,[4] it is likely that there was a high income elasticity of demand for the replacement of old, unreliable and unstylish items purchased in the Soviet command economy period.

In sum, while it might be expected that succesful growth would have caused a faster growth rate of output in heavy industry in China than in the USSR, it is not self-evident that even in the USSR successful reform would have been accompanied by the absolute decline of the heavy industrial sector (Table 5.4). What both countries needed were policies that caused the quality of heavy industrial output to rise and increased the efficiency with which heavy industrial products were used.

Table 5.5   Role of Very Large Establishments (over 5000 employees)
in Chinese and Soviet Industry

	No. of establishments	Employment No. (m.)	(%)	Fixed assets (%)	GVIO (%)	Employees/ establishment ('000)
USSR (1983)	1316	14.4	38.1	46.7	35.9	10.9
China (1987)	885	11.9	16.8	33.9	18.9	13.4

Sources   Li 1988: 120, 145, 436 and SSB, ZGGYJJTJNJ 1989: 293

Industrial Organization: Similarities

Very Large Plants   In the early 1980s in both China and the USSR around one thousand very large plants (over 5000 employees) employed 12–14 million workers, accounted for around one-third to one-half of the total value of industrial fixed assets, and produced around one fifth to one-third of the total gross value of industrial output (Table 5.5).

Table 5.6 Industrial Concentration by Size of Establishment in China (1987) and the USSR (1983) (%)

Size of establishment (employees)	Establishments		Employees		Fixed assets		Gross value of industrial output	
	China	USSR	China	USSR	China	USSR	China	USSR
under 100	68.5	27.2	14.0	1.6	5.8	1.1	9.6	1.9
100–500	25.6	42.4	32.6	12.6	18.1	8.8	26.6	12.8
500–1000	3.6	13.1	14.7	11.2	12.2	9.0	15.5	10.8
1000–10 000	2.2	16.3	27.5	52.4	38.2	51.8	36.5	54.1
over 10 000	0.1	1.0	11.2	22.2	25.7	29.3	11.7	20.4
Aggregate	100	100	100	100	100	100	100	100

Source Liu 1988: 120, 145, 145 and SSB, ZGGYJJNTJNJ 1988: 7 293

Large Plants In both cases, large plants (over 1000 employees) massively dominated the total value of fixed assets, occupying 64 per cent in China's case and 81 per cent in that of the USSR (Table 5.6). In China, large plants produced 48 per cent of the total value of industrial output compared to 75 per cent in the Soviet case (Table 5.6).

Small and Medium-sized Enterprises (SMEs) In both China and the USSR, SMEs were under-represented in the size structure of industrial establishments (Table 5.7). In both cases, there were large possibilities for improved industrial efficiency, for meeting consumers' needs and for absorbing surplus labour from other sectors, simply by permitting entrepreneurial endeavour in the SME sector. There were many activities in the SME sector in both economies in which high profits could have been made as market forces began to take effect, especially in quick-gestating investments requiring small amounts of capital (for example, personal services, restaurants, leisure services, small-scale manufacturing as with toys, furniture, clothing, etc.). The potential for growth of SMEs was shown by the explosive growth of China's township and village enterprises (TVEs) in the reform period (see Chapter 7 in this volume). Such a possibility was not confined to China. If anything, these potential opportunities were greater in the USSR than in China due to the even greater degree of under-representation of SMEs in the industrial size structure in the USSR compared to China. In the USSR, less than two years after the passage of the Law on Cooperatives (1988), the number of small business cooperatives had reached 150 000, employing five million people (3.7 per cent of the total workforce), producing an estimated 7 per cent of national income, and already attracting substantial numbers of skilled staff from state factories and government ministries (Miller 1993: 103).

Table 5.7 Distribution of Employment in Manufacturing Industry by Size of Establishment %

Size of establishment	Capitalist countries				USA	India	China*	USSR
	Small type		Large type					
	1950	1970	1950	1970	1986	1987/88	1987	1983
10–100	40	35	23	20	31.0	27.6	14.0	1.6
101–500	30	33	30	30	32.0	23.8	32.6	12.6
501-1000	11	13	13	14	11.6	12.0	12.0	11.2
over 1000	19	19	34	36	25.4	36.7	38.7	74.6

Note *'Independent accounting enterprises' only. In 1978 independent accounting enterprises accounted for 96% of NVIO (SSB, ZGGYJJTJZL, 1949–84, 1985, 41–2. *Source* Erlich 1985, SSB, ZGGYJJTJNJ 1991, Acs and Audretsch 1993: 62, Liu 1988: 120, 145

The Nature of the Large Enterprise In both cases, there was a high degree of vertical integration at the plant level. The difficulties of constructing the 'plan' were reduced by maximizing plants' self-sufficiency. Plants could not rely on the supply of inputs through the command system. Almost all enterprises in the massive machine-building sector produced their own iron and steel rather than purchasing it from specialized suppliers (Granick 1967: 157). A large proportion of spare parts and machinery needs were produced within the large plants. There was a large stock of general-purpose machine tools with low utilization rates used to produce a wide variety of inputs in small batches.

Far from benefiting from large-scale specialized production, large Chinese and Soviet plants produced a large amount of small-batch output with below-optimal scale. Within each large 'plant' were many relatively small-scale 'shops' undertaking activities which in a capitalist economy would be undertaken mainly by specialist producers, often on a much larger scale.

Both countries had large possibilities for improving industrial efficiency. These were illustrated vividly by China's reforms after the 1970s. Increasingly managers were selected on the basis of ability. Profit retention contracts led to the rise of profits as the main goal of enterprise managers. By the mid-1990s domestic price control and the material balance system had been virtually eliminated. State industry had moved 'upstream' into mainly large scale, capital-intensive heavy industries, in which scientific and technical expertise is much more important to success than in the small-scale light industrial sector where entrepreneurship is much closer to that envisaged by the perfect competition model of economic behaviour. The small-scale state sector was allowed to shrink rapidly in relative terms, its place being taken over by a variety of non-state forms of enterprise. A group of large multi-plant state-owned firms began to emerge in each sector under a carefully orchestrated planning strategy intended to create a series of South Korean-style large corporations. Output in the large-scale state sector increased rapidly, growing at around 11 per cent per annum in real terms and even increasing its share of total industrial output (from 25 per cent by value in 1980 to 28 per cent in 1991 (Nolan 1995: ch. 6). Most studies show a rise in total factor productivity in state enterprises in the reform period (for example, Chen *et al.* 1992, Macmillan and Naughton 1992, Nolan 1995).

Industrial Organization: Differences

Spatial Distribution of Industry China's split with the USSR in 1960 and its isolation from the capitalist world left it deeply vulnerable in international affairs. A major economic consequence of this intense insecurity was the 'Third Front' policy, under which the share of total investment allocated to the inland provinces increased rapidly. Their share of total industrial capital stock rose from 28 per cent in 1952 to 56 per cent in the late 1970s (Table 5.8). The economic return to this investment was low (Table 5.8).

Table 5.8   Distribution of Industrial Capital, Employment, and Output Between Coastal and Inland Provinces of China, 1952 and 1978 (%)

	1952	*1978*
Workers:		
coastal	60.5	46.3 (1984)
inland	39.5	53.7 (1984)
Value of fixed assets:		
coastal	72.0	43.9
inland	28.0	56.1
Value of industrial output:		
coastal	69.4	60.9
inland	30.6	39.1
Capital-output ratio:		
coastal	0.45	0.54
inland	0.40	1.08

Source   SSB, ZGGYJJTJZL 1985: 137

Self-reliance   Maoist China encountered special problems that led to a distinctively 'self-reliant' pattern of industrial development. China is huge and the transport system was backward. Widespread political turmoil during the Great Leap Forward (1958–9) and the Cultural Revolution (1966–76), increased the desire of administrative units for self-sufficiency since they could not rely on normal trade networks. Local self-sufficiency made it easier for the central authorities to retain some semblance of political order. In a feudal fashion, lower-level leaders were made responsible for all activities social, political and economic within their boundaries, minimizing contacts of ordinary citizens with the outside and making a direct and easy chain of command in all respects from higher- to lower-level authorities. These factors produced a high degree of 'self-reliance' at every level of the economic system, far beyond that normally characteristic even of a command economy.

Small Plants   The policy of self-reliance tended to cause the number of small plants to rise rapidly. This tendency was given further impetus by rapid growth in the production of modern farm inputs in the countryside after the disaster of the Great Leap Forward (Table 5.9). Much of this growth came from small rural plants. A large fraction of China's farm machinery was supplied by these plants by the mid-1970s (Yu 1984, Perkins 1977).

Table 5.9 China's 'Green Revolution'

	1957	1978	1992
arable area:			
total (m. ha.)	112	99.5 (1979)	95.4
per capita (ha.) (index)	0.173(100)	0.103(58)	0.081(47)
irrigated area (m. ha)	27.4	45.0	48.6
% of arable area	(24.5)	(45.2)	(50.9)
of which.			
mechanically irrigated (m. ha)	1.2	24.9	26.3
% of arable area	(1.1)	(25.0)	(27.6)
mechanically ploughed area (m. ha)	2.6	40.7	51.5
% of arable area	(2.3)	(40.9)	(54.0)
farm machinery (m. kwh)	1.21	117.5	303.1
large/medium tractors ('000s)	14.7	557.4	758.9
walking tractors (m)	–	1.37	7.51
combine harvesters ('000s)	1.8	19.0	51.1
farm-use trucks ('000s)	4	74	642
chemical fertiliser use (m. tons)	0.4	8.8	29.3

Source SSB, ZGTJNJ 1993: 341,349 and World Bank 1981c: 61

In the mid-1980s within the factory sector ('independent accounting enterprises'), there were 286 000 small enterprises with less than one hundred workers per enterprise (the average was 35 per enterprise) which produced just 9.6 per cent of the gross value of industrial output from factories (SSB, ZGGYJJTJNJ 1988: 293). Data for 1979 show there were in addition 580 000 minuscule enterprises at the brigade or team level, employing an average of only 17 workers per plant, which produced under 4 per cent of total industrial output value (World Bank 1981b: 20–21).

Results These policies produced a relatively widespread technical capacity in China's rural areas. They reinforced the role of local governments as a key economic agent over a wide array of activities rather than simply an administrator of agriculture. However, China's industry failed to benefit from economies of scale and the advantages of specialization and exchange, even more than was normal in a command economy. A large proportion of the output produced under this strategy was of low quality, using large amounts of power and raw materials. Costs of production were widely acknowledged to be very high in a large portion of the small factories. They produced a large volume of capital goods which are normally characterized by strong economies of scale at the plant level. Like the USSR, China faced large tasks in restructuring the large-scale industrial sector. However, it faced a special problem in that it needed also to undertake a large-scale restructuring of its small-scale sector.

Agriculture: Differences

Population Pressure on Farm Resources   China occupies less than 7 per cent of the world's cultivated area but its population is around 22 per cent of the world's total. The USSR occupied around 17 per cent of the world's cultivated area but accounted for only 6 per cent of the world's population (SSB, ZGNCTJNJ 1989: 417–18). By the late 1970s, the amount of farmland per person in China was among the lowest in the world, much below that even of India, let alone the USSR (Table 5.10).

Table 5.10   Arable Area Per Capita in China and Other Selected
Countries, 1979 (hectares)

China	0.10	
within which:		
East	0.08	Shanghai, Jiangsu, Zhejiang, Anhui,
within which:		Fujian, Jiangxi and Shandong
'densely populated eastern provinces'*	0.05 (1992)	Jiangsu, Shanghai, Zhejiang, Fujian
Northeast	0.19	Liaoning, Jilin, Heilongjiang(4.1)
Northwest	0.18	Shaanxi, Gansu, Ningxia, Xinjiang
Southwest	0.07	Sichuan, Guizhou, Yunan, Tibet
Central-South	0.08	Henan, Hubei, Hunan, Guangxi, Guangdong
North	0.15	Beijing, Tianjin, Hebei, Shanxi, Inner Mongolia
Other countries:		
Japan	0.04	
USA	0.86	
India	0.26	
USSR	0.89	

Note   * Total population in 1993 was 156 million
Source   Ministry of Agriculture 1982: 12–13; SSB, ZGTJNJ 1993: 83, 332

Capital   The stock of large farm machinery in Maoist China was vastly below that in the USSR (Table 5.11). In the USSR, only a small fraction of farmland was irrigated (Li 1981, SLNYTJZLHB 1981: 6, 446). A major reason for China's ability to sustain its huge population on such a limited arable area was its highly developed irrigation works. China's high labour input per unit of farmland, high irrigation ratio, and rapid advance in farm modernization after the 1950s (Table 5.9), enabled China to attain high yields per unit of farmland. By 1987, China's annual grain yields per hectare of harvested land stood at 4.0 tons, compared to 2.4 tons in Bangladesh, 1.9 tons in the USSR, 1.8 tons in Mexico, and 1.5 tons in India (SSB, ZGNCTJNJ 1989: 419).

Table 5.11   Size of Collective and State Farms in China and the USSR
(average per farm)

	USSR(1985)*		China(1980)	
	Collective farms	State farms	Production teams	Production brigades
number of workers	488	529	56	449
sown area (hectares)	3485	4766	26	206
large animals	1930(cows)**	1850(cows)**	17	134
pigs	1109**	1163**	55	430
sheep/goats	1666**	2921**	33	263
large/medium tractors	20	57	0.1	1.1
walking tractors	–	–	0.3	2.6
combine harvesters	14	19	negl	negl
farm-use trucks	44	26	negl	0.2
agricultural water pumps	–	–	0.8	6.4
mechanical threshers	–	–	0.5	3.5
grain husking machines	–	–	0.5	4.3
fodder crushing machines	–	–	0.3	2.0
rubber-tired carts:				
animal-drawn	–	–	0.4	3.4
hand-drawn	–	–	6.4	49.6

Notes   * In 1985, state farms occupied 179 million hectares of sown area, and collective farms occupied 143 million hectares of sown area.
** publicly owned
Sources   Liu 1989: 287, 289, 303; SSB, ZGNCTJNJ 1985: 232–3, 244; SSB, SYC, section 3.

Demand for food   At the start of its reform process, China's level of food intake per capita was vastly below that of the USSR (Table 5.12). China's reforms resulted in large increases in per capita income which were reflected in increased demands for superior foodstuffs, taking China's food consumption towards that of Japan, the most relevant comparator country (Table 5.12).

Table 5.12 Nutrient Intake in China (1978), USSR, USA and Japan (1988/90)
(Per Capita Per Day)

	China	(China as % of Japan)	Japan	USSR	(USSR as % of USA)	USA
calories of which:	2311	(79)	2921	3379	(93)	3642
animal	142	(23)	616	949	(86)	1107
vegetable	2169	(94)	2305	2430	(96)	2535
protein of which:	71	(75)	95	107	(97)	110
animal	4	(8)	53	57	(81)	71
vegetable	67	(160)	42	50	(128)	39
fats of which:	30	(37)	81	106	(68)	155
animal	14	(37)	38	71	(89)	80
vegetable	16	(37)	43	35	(47)	75

Source SSB, SYC 1983: 509; SSB, ZGTJNJ 1993: 896

China's limited (and falling) arable area and the fact that yields were very high, placed severe technical constraints on raising farm output. Huge population growth and improvements in diet meant that China in the 1980s needed large agricultural investments in order to sustain the required large growth of farm output. The 'Green Revolution' continued throughout the reform period (Table 5.9), pre-empting investment funds from other uses. China's farm output growth from the late 1970s to the early 1990s was not achieved simply through making better use of existing resources, or 'taking up the slack'. Although the efficiency with which resources were used was much greater than in the Maoist period, a big effort of saving and investment by individual farmers, local communities and the state, was needed to sustain the growth of farm output.

At the start of its reform, the USSR's level of per capita consumption of farm products was vastly above China's and close to that of the USA (Table 5.12). The USSR's population was growing slowly. Even a large growth of per capita income in the USSR would not have led to a large growth in demand for farm produce. China's task in reforming the farm sector was both to improve efficiency and substantially increase farm output. The USSR's task was simply to increase efficiency.

Size of Collective Farms The basic level of ownership of the means of production, of work organization and income distribution in China was the production team. This averaged only around 50–60 workers and 26 hectares of sown area (Table 5.11). The Soviet collective farm averaged almost 500 workers and around 3500 hectares of sown area (Table 5.11).

Labour Force: Growth By the 1980s, the USSR's farm population was stagnant. China's rural workforce grew by more than 130 million (over 43 per cent)[5] over the same period. Despite a successful programme of rural industrialization and non-farm labour absorption, the agricultural labour force increased by 65 million (25 per cent) over the same period. The amount of farmland per person fell by around one quarter in these years (from 0.35 ha per worker to 0.27 ha per person). Both economies began their reform process with a large amount of surplus labour consequent upon the shortcomings of the Stalinist command economy. However, China faced vastly greater problems than the USSR in absorbing surplus labour due to the huge pressure of population growth which constantly added to the total numbers for whom employment needed to be found.

Labour Force: Skill Level A sharply rising share of the Soviet rural workforce was technically qualified. Alongside a fall in the total rural workforce from the 1950s through to the 1980s went a steady rise in the number of technically skilled personnel (Li R. 1981: 498–9). The proportion of illiterate workers was negligible. In China in the mid-1980s, a mere 0.05 per cent of the rural workforce had a high-level specialist education. Only 8.8 per cent had even been to upper middle school, while 21 per cent were reported to be illiterate (SSB, ZGNCTJNJ 1985: 232). The Cultural Revolution badly damaged China's rural research and extension service: 'The numbers of qualified staff, especially at the senior levels, are severely limited . . .'(World Bank 1981c: 46). The agricultural education system had still in the late 1970s not recovered from 'the long period of closure and anti-professional bias' and there were 'critical shortages of staff at all levels'(World Bank 1981c: 46).

Agriculture: Similarities

Institutional Setting The communist economies all based their agricultural policies on the erroneous assumption that agriculture contained wide possibilities for economies of scale in all aspects of the farm process. Although the Soviet collective and state farm was much larger than the Chinese production team, the latter was still a large institution compared to farms under capitalist systems. There are deep problems with the collective and state-farm method of farm organization due to the peculiar difficulty of labour supervision in agriculture (Nolan 1988). This caused large managerial diseconomies of scale in most aspects of the direct tasks of cultivation. However, there is large scope for benefit from cooperation in the ancillary aspects of the farm process, such as research, irrigation, crop spraying, processing, and marketing.

Memories of Private Farming   Soviet collective and state farms had, of course, been in operation much longer than those in China, so that there were no direct memories of private farming. However, even in China, by 1989 the epoch of private farming was at least 25 years away. Moreover, no one under the age of around of 45–50 (the vast majority of Chinese farmers) would have had direct experience of running a private farm.

Lumpy Inputs   Soviet reforms failed to devise institutions which would have allowed individual farmers continued access to large, lumpy inputs which dominated the capital stock of collective and state farms (Kiselev 1993). China's rural reform sustained individual farmers' access to lumpy inputs that were beyond the financial and organizational resources of individual farmers. In China the predominantly small-scale mechanical farm inputs (for instance, mechanical threshers, power-tillers, mechanical rice-transplanters) were more expensive relative to average Chinese peasant income in the late 1980s than was a truck or tractor was to the Soviet collective farmer. In the early stages of reform in China most important means of production remained in collective ownership. Only as incomes rose did the share of privately owned assets become more dominant. Most irrigation facilities were beyond the resources of individual farmers. Continued provision by the local and national state apparatus ensured that the irrigation ratio rose from 45 per cent of the arable area in 1978 to 51 per cent in 1992 (Table 5.9).

Quality and Variety of Farm Inputs   In both China and the USSR farm productivity suffered from poor quality and variety of farm inputs, as well as from decisions about farm inputs being taken in offices remote from farmers. A well-devised industrial reform had the potential to enable a large reduction in capital needs per unit of output for the farm sector through the supply of better and more appropriate inputs.

Sale of Farm Output   In both the USSR and China the vast bulk of farm marketings pre-reform was controlled by state compulsory purchases. Increased freedom of choice for farmers about what to produce could have increased efficiency through allowing greater specialization.

Role of the Private Sector   In neither China nor the USSR had rural dwellers lost touch with individual farming. Indeed, private sector activity was the main source of supply for many of their most important food products. In China the sector was subject to many more vicissitudes than in the USSR, being periodically subject to severe atttack. However, as in the USSR for much of the time there was substantial scope for private farming activity (Li 1981: 384; Nolan and White 1983: 252).

Waste of Resources Far from economizing on labour and capital, the communist approach to agricultural organization resulted in massive waste of resources. In 1980 in the USSR as much as 26 per cent of the workforce was in agriculture compared to under 4 per cent in the USA (Table 5.13). In China 71 per cent of the workforce was employed in agriculture, a similar proportion to that in the least developed countries in the world (Table 5.1). In both cases agriculture grew at a moderate pace only through absorbing a large share of investment. In the 1970s in the USSR the farm sector's share of total national investment was over 20 per cent, compared to around 5 per cent in the USA (Table 5.13). In China, agriculture's share of national investment in the late 1970s was around 20 per cent (World Bank 1981c: 49).

Table 5.13   Comparison of Soviet and US Agriculture, 1974/5

	USSR	USA
farm workers:		
total no. (m.) (1978)	27	4.1 (annual average)
share of total workforce (%)	26.3	3.7
share of total national investment (1971/5) (%)	26	<5
agriculture's share of GNP (%)	17.6	2.6
sown area (m. ha.)	217	137
fertiliser application (m. tons)	15.0	17.5
stocks of farm machinery:		
tractors: total no (m.)	2.3	4.4
farm	12	0.9
workers/tractor	1.3	2.9
farm trucks: total (m.)	20	1.4
farm	0.7	0.7
workers/truck	40	5.9
combine harvesters: total no (m.)		
farm workers/truck		
comparative yields:		
grain output per ha. (centners):		
foodgrain	13	21
feedgrain	16	38

Source   Li 1981: 67; USCJEC 1976: 578, 585

Implications

In both cases relatively simple institutional changes had the potential to produce large improvements in farm efficiency, and to release labour and investment for other sectors. Improvements in farm performance could have had beneficial effects on light industrial growth and exports through the supply of industrial inputs, as well as cementing support for system reform through improving an essential element in people's livelihood.

The most important and simplest institutional change was contracting farmland to individual households. This 'land reform' alone would have reversed the profound managerial diseconomies of scale and radically improved peasant incentives. Profit-seeking farm households would have become more demanding in their selection of inputs. The largest problem was lumpy farm inputs. In advanced capitalist countries a large part of lumpy inputs are owned either by non-farmers and hired out by specialist suppliers to individual farmers, or are cooperatively owned alongside individual farm operation. In principle, in China and the USSR the land contract process could have been combined with a maintenance of a large part of lumpy inputs in the hands of profit-oriented cooperatives or state machinery and irrigation companies. However, this required a state system committed to, and able to implement, such a policy.

In Russia right through to the present day, neither the basis on which farmland was to be operated by individual farmers nor the basis on which they might be able to have acces to necessary lumpy inputs had been placed in a clear, credible framework. Indeed, the World Bank (1994: 3) considered that the lack of secure access to machinery services and capital were more important factors in explaining farmers' reluctance to leave collective and state farms even than uncertainty over property rights in land.

Natural Resource Endowment

The former USSR was much the largest country in the world in terms of land area. Its territory accounted for 29 per cent of the world's total. It had massive reserves of timber (around one-quarter of the world total), coal (around one-half of the world's total), oil and natural gas. It also contained the world's largest gold reserves, a fifth of the world's diamond reserves, the world's second largest deposits of copper, iron ore, nickel, and zinc, as well as an abundance of other rare raw materials.

China also is a huge country. Like the former USSR it has massive coal reserves. However, it has not located large oil and natural gas reserves. China's continued need to depend heavily on coal as the main source of energy was a substantial burden during the reform period, since coal requires such large investments in transport per unit of power produced. Despite large foreign investment in oil exploration in the South China seas in the 1980s, significant reserves were not discovered. It is uncertain whether Chinese central Asia will reveal large oil and natural gas reserves. China's timber reserves are tiny for a country of its size, and its precious metals and minerals do not compare with those of Russia.

The willingness with which international oil companies were prepared to invest in exploration in China during its reforms demonstrates the ease with which the USSR also could have attracted a large amount of foreign investment to modernize natural resource production. The necessary conditions were political stability, secure property rights and a guaranteed share of the income from the investment. This would have provided a relatively easy path with which, through simple institutional reform, to raise export earnings. Unfortunately, despite the huge potential attractiveness to foreign investment the amounts invested have been negligible. This has been due to criminalization and corruption, strong links between the Russian government and the 'private' Russian oil companies, protection of the natural resource sector, and substantial popular hostility to foreign capital. The creation of political chaos by Gorbachev's political reforms destroyed the relatively easy avenue through which a Russian economy undertaking a serious economic reform programme might have enhanced its export earnings and helped modernize its economy through technology embodied in imports.

Population Pressure

In the absence of government measures to control fertility, China in the 1980s and 1990s would have faced the problems of high age-specific fertility rate common to most developing countries. In addition it confronted the special problem of a large age cohort entering the reproductive ages. China's system of basic needs guarantees under Mao left it peculiarly liable to explosively high rates of population growth in the absence of tough state action to control reproduction. In the 1960s death rates fell to low levels but birthrates were high during a period in which the government was too preoccupied with other matters to pay attention to policies to control reproduction. This exceptionally large cohort was moving through into the marriageable age groups in the 1980s and 1990s.

Under the people's communes China was successful in the 1970s in raising the average age of marriage. This, combined with greatly increased availability of contraception and strong sanctions helped to reduce sharply the overall birth rate in the late Maoist years which dropped from 36 to 23 per 1000 between 1968 and 1975 (SSB, ZGTJNJ 1990: 90). Although the age of marriage and the proportion of the population using birth control remained high throughout the 1980s, the bulge in the proportion of the population in the reproductive ages still presented large difficulties in controlling overall fertility.

If the Chinese reforming government had not been able to take tough measures to control population growth, then China's population might well have been around 200 million larger in the mid-1990s, presenting large problems for the rate and structure of investment, which in turn would have slowed down the rate of growth of income and output. The key to its ability to implement the 'One Child' policy was the continued effectiveness of the communist party.

Inflationary Potential

The rate of inflation in China under reform was higher than was reported in the Maoist years. However, compared to the rate of inflation in Russia under reform or, indeed, in most developing countries, China's inflation rate was modest.[6] Did China have an easier task in controlling inflation than did Russia?

It has been argued that Yeltsin's government inherited a legacy of substantial repressed inflation which was a special diffficulty for Russia's reforms. In common with the other communist economies, China inherited repressed inflation from the Stalinist period, not least through the excess demand for many goods and services in short supply under the administered economy. These problems were as severe in China in 1976 as in the USSR in 1985. In the USSR after 1985 the problems of repressed inflation rapidly intensified, but this was a direct result of Gorbachev's political reforms. These were in turn the fundamental element of the 'transition orthodoxy': political democratization was considered to be essential before economic reform could be implemented.

In China also there were large structural pressures associated with reforming the planned economy, such as bottlenecks in infrastructure, which tended to stimulate inflation. Moreover, the bottlenecks intensified with the successful achievement of a rapid rate of growth, with surges in demand for slow-gestating capital goods products.

In a country of China's size, there were peculiarly strong inflationary pressures in the reform period associated with the need to decentralize many economic functions of government. In the absence of a comprehensive reform of the financial system, there was, in a 'prisoner's dilemma' fashion, little incentive for local authorities or banks to control the supply of money in the interests of control over the national rate of inflation.

In sum, China's success in combining a reasonable rate of inflation with rapid growth cannot be interpreted as mainly a matter of good fortune in the inherited inflationary potential. It was a peculiarly difficult feat to accomplish simultaneous accelerated growth, large structural transformation and a reasonably controlled rate of inflation. The maintenance of an effective state apparatus was a necessary condition of sustaining the government's fiscal capacity and combining required financial decentralization with some degree of control over money supply growth.

SOCIAL AND POLITICAL FACTORS

Culture

The fact that many of the Asian Newly Industrializing Countries were Confucian revived theories linking culture and economic development, long neglected after Max Weber's attempt to explain the rise of capitalism in Western Europe by the Protestant ethic. Confucianism emphasises hard work, education, meritocracy, and hierarchy, which fits the popular conception of an efficient corporation. It is tempting to add China, the birthplace of Confucianism, to the list of countries whose growth can be explained by this value system. However, 'culture' is not a given factor. It is continually being reconstructed either consciously or unconsciously.[7] It is not clear that any type of Confucianism *per se* promotes economic development, as Morishima (1982) has argued. A long scholarly tradition argued that China's variety of Confucianism constituted a large handicap to economic development, due to long-ingrained habits of familism, nepotism and corruption (for example, Levy 1949). The values of the Chinese, family-oriented variant of Confucianism was long thought to be fundamentally opposed to those of the modern business corporation, due to its emphasis upon 'particularism and functional diffuseness' (Levy 1949: 12). Pessimism about China's economic prospects based on the deep-rooted problems of traditional cultural factors was a persistent theme of writing on China in the 1980s.

Administrative Capacity of the Bureaucracy

Both China and the USSR had a long tradition of centralized bureaucratic rule, though the tradition was of much greater antiquity in China. They each had a huge party apparatus, which was closely interwoven with the system of state administration. The Chinese communist party apparatus was no less corrupt or more professionally effective than that of the USSR in the late 1970s. Indeed, the Chinese Communist Party and administrative apparatus was seriously damaged during the Cultural Revolution. Even more than usual in a communist country promotions in China during this period had been based on ideological rather than professional criteria. Economics had been virtually killed in China during the decade of the Cultural Revolution. By contrast, Soviet economics was very much alive, despite the constraints on the boundaries of discussion. The Soviet central planning apparatus was vastly more technically sophisticated than its Chinese counterpart. Local authorities in the USSR while tightly constrained in the range of independence, were charged with vastly more complex administrative tasks than their Chinese counterparts, most of which were administering relatively self-sufficient units producing a narrow range of primitive products.

There is a long tradition of political analysis of China which argues that the main reason for China's failure to build on its great medieval technical breakthrough and experience an industrial revolution was precisely the inhibiting power of the bureaucracy (for instance, Needham 1969). A consensus of informed opinion both inside and outside China in the 1980s felt that the strength of this stifling bureaucratic tradition would prevent China advancing successfully towards a market economy (for instance, the former head of the Marxism Leninism Institute, Su Shauzhi; Su 1988).

The bureaucracy was regarded by almost all commentators as the major obstacle to the implementation of reform policies in communist countries. Most observers regarded it is as self-evident that the bureaucracy would be deeply opposed to economic reform, since reform would deprive them of power and status. Aslund (1991: 14) summarizes this, the most fundamental tenet of the 'transition orthodoxy', as follows:

A reform reduces the power of the bureaucracy by definition and most of the administration will inevitably oppose reform. Therefore, a successful reform must break the power of the anti-reform bureaucracy.... *To break the power of the party and state bureaucracy may be seen as the key problem of a reform.* (my emphasis)

However, the possession of an effective, competent state bureaucracy is a central element in explaining the rise of almost every successful industrializing country since Britain. There were two logical possibilities to the problems of the old state apparatus. One was to regard it as hopelessly unreformable, inherently opposed to any kind of reform measure and to destroy it. A second, reformist approach was to attempt to change its goals and methods of operation. This would involve a gradual process of professionalization, making the organization more youthful, introducing more rationality rather than quasi-religious principles into its ethical foundation, and giving the members of the apparatus a central role in the process of reconstructing the Stalinist economy. In the reformist approach the Party members are less threatened and although their tasks alter greatly over a given period of time, they retain their dignity, status and remain relatively well rewarded.

The Chinese leadership attempted to follow the second approach and was broadly successful in it. However, the Chinese bureaucratic apparatus had no greater capacity to be transformed successfully in this reformist way than did the Soviet one. Indeed, the reverse may well be the case. Consider Miller's (1993: 77) evaluation of the Soviet bureaucracy which Gorbachev inherited:

> The Party's quasi-military structure and traditions made it an effective and durable instrument in the hands of such a leader. It still produced officials who could serve a transformist cause with energy and selfless loyalty. It contained millions of others who would doggedly carry out orders even if they did not fully understand them – indeed who would accept surgery on the Party provided it was administered by one of their own.

The Soviet approach under Gorbachev was entirely different. In the face of great opposition at the top of the Party, Gorbachev, with the support of small group of advisers (especially those in the think-tanks set up by Andropov in the early 1980s, known collectively as the 'New Thinking'), put into practice the policies of *perestroika* and *glasnost* which led to the rapid disintegration of the entire communist edifice in the USSR and Eastern Europe:

> Gorbachev was unusual in that he saw and accepted the logic of human rights dissent, that it falsified the central assumptions of the regime he commanded. This 'New Thinking' of course ... was not his work alone. His contribution was to bring together the isolated and alienated intellectuals who orginated it, *to turn a dissident subculture into a policy and to work out a strategy for realising it* (Miller 1993: 206; my emphasis).

Mass Demands for Political Reform

Political outcomes are far from a matter of choice by governments. One line of argument is that the dramatic contrast in political outcomes in China and the USSR was not at all a matter of policy choice but was, rather, an uncontrollable consequence of the fundamental difference in political environment. The most important of such propositions relate to mass demands for democracy on the one hand and the propensity for the respective countries to split into separate political units (their 'fissiparous' tendencies).

Mass Demands for Democracy

The Soviet Union in the late 1970s was a much more highly urbanized society than was China. Its intellectuals had a much stronger interest in Western values. In the 1970s there was a more widespread hope in the USSR than in China that Western democratic institutions might be put into place.

However, the Soviet political system seemed stable. It had survived relatively intact since the 1920s without fundamental disruptions. Even in the post-Stalin and post-Khrushchev period it still was highly repressive. China's political system had only recently been through the huge upheaval of the Cultural Revolution, which had deeply damaged the communist party, unleashing a period of widespread anarchy. There is no counterpart in Soviet history.

In the Soviet Union, expectations of fundamental political change were low. It was the policy decisions of Gorbachev, namely *glasnost* and *perestroika*, that turned distant hopes into ardent expectations. In the sharpest contrast there was a near consensus among the Chinese leadership that political democratization was not a part of the political agenda in the near future in China. A series of campaigns against 'bourgeois' values ('spiritual pollution') attempted to reduce expectations of change among the politically active population.

Fissiparous Tendencies

In the 1970s both China and the USSR were huge multinational empires. However, the relative size of the 'national minority' population is a major difference between the two countries. The non-Russian population accounted for around one-half of the total Soviet population whereas the non-Han population in China accounted for well under 10 per cent of the total population. Once the minority nationalities began to pursue their demands for independence in a serious fashion in the USSR the situation was more difficult to control than would have been the case in China.

Successful market and income growth is the most powerful force leading to the disintegration of ethnic differences. Stalinism kept nationalism intact in a 'deep-freeze' beneath a veneer of new 'socialist man'. The national leadership of both countries perpetuated a public propaganda myth that the 'nationality' question belonged to the past. In both cases the 'national minorities' were disproportionately concentrated in more sparsely populated, remote, resource-rich regions. In both cases national liberation movements had been brutally suppressed. However, the severity of these struggles in recent times had been much greater in China than in the USSR. China fought major battles against the Uighur 'national minority' in Xinjiang province in central Asia over a long period, and conducted a protracted and violent guerrilla war against the Tibetan independence movement.

In the 1970s in neither country was the expectation of national minority groups high. However, the policies pursued by the national leadership were strikingly different. In the Soviet case the policy of political *perestroika* and *glasnost* greatly raised the expectation of national minority groups. In China national policy-makers repeatedly made it clear that attempts to break away from rule by Beijing would be brutally repressed.

Effective central rule in a country may not be undermined only by nationalism. China's long history has been dominated by regular cycles of national disintegration and reunification, even among the Han people. No theme is stronger in Chinese political history than the need to maintain national unity in the face of a high intrinsic propensity for the 'sheet of loose' sand to spin apart into 'great turmoil' (*da luan*). China is not an inherently unified state. National unity has only been maintained over substantial periods through effective government. Its modern history shows only too clearly the high propensity for central rule to fall apart.

CONCLUSION

This chapter has identified many important differences between the economic and political inheritance bequeathed to the leaders of the respective countries at the start of their reform programme. These included China's much lower level of farmland per capita, of per capita income, of urbanization, of industrialisation, and of scientific skills. In China small-scale industrial enterprises were much more important than in the USSR. China had a much more important role played by poorly located areas in its structure of industrial assets. China had a much higher rate of population growth, and a more ancient tradition of entrepreneurship. National minority populations occupied a much smaller share of total population in China than in the USSR. China possessed much larger concentrations of capital in the hands of overseas citizens. Some of these differences tended to work to the advantage of accelerated post-Stalinist growth in China, but many of them did not. It is not apparent that on balance the inherited system differences made it likely that well-chosen political and economic policies would lead to faster growth in China than in the USSR.

However, there were also important similarities. Both countries had a high potentiality for fissure into political anarchy and separate nation-states. Both countries had large reservoirs of entrepreneurial skill. They each possessed relatively well-educated populations for their level of income, and in both cases, there was massive underfulfilment of human productive capabilites. The basic 'planning' methods of the command economy were the same. The key features of both farm and the non-farm institutions were the same. Both systems had relatively large amounts of technical skill and capital stock locked up in the military sector. In each case the economic system was massively under-performing compared to the productive potential achievable with existing physical and human capital. In each case, relatively simple system changes were capable of generating an initial large improvement in system performance which could act as the springboard to further more fundamental change and improvement. In other words, despite important differences, both the former USSR and China possessed large catch-up possibilities, as did most of the former Stalinist countries.

If the analysis in this chapter is correct, then the main cause of the difference in outcome between China and Russia under system reform must be the differences in policy choice. The contrast in policies chosen was itself the result of complex historical factors leading to fundamentally different approaches towards the task of transforming the Stalinist system (for a more comprehensive discussion, see Nolan 1995). The contrast in policy choice applies both to narrowly economic policy and to the wider question of the relationship between political and economic reform.

The Soviet disaster stems primarily from the wholehearted embrace of the 'transition orthodoxy', policies of political reform (*perestroika* and *glasnost*) and subsequent economic change ('shock therapy') advocated by foreign advisers and commentators such as Kornai (1990), Sachs (for instance, Lipton and Sachs 1990), Prybyla (1991) and Aslund (1990, 1991) and their domestic counterparts in the USSR and the Russian Federation.[8] China's reform success stems primarily from its refusal to implement the 'transition orthodoxy' policies which in the 1980s were increasingly urged upon the leaders by both domestic and foreign 'reformers'. It released the growth potentialities embedded within the Stalinist system. It did so through maintaining an authoritarian political system which allowed the gradual unfolding of market forces, remained reasonably fiscally effective, provided a stable environment to encourage foreign direct investment and was able to intervene in a wide array of areas in which markets might be expected to 'fail' in such a turbulent period of system transformation (for further argument, see Nolan 1995).

This chapter contains two implicit counter-factual propositions. The selection of different policies in Russia could have produced rapid growth of output and a large improvement in popular living standards. The selection of a different set of policies in China could easily have produced a political and economic disaster, with a large decline in popular living standards.

NOTES

1. I am grateful to Trevor Buck of the University of Nottingham for discussions which led me to write this chapter. I am grateful also to Geoff Harcourt and Michael Ellman for their perceptive and lengthy comments on an earlier draft, and to Albert Schweinberger, Ajit Singh and Norman Stockman for inviting me to present seminars, based on the chapter, at the Universities of Konstanz, Cambridge and Aberdeen respectively.
2. Due to labour hoarding by managers and the slow workpace among workers.
3. In addition to its large pool of highly qualified scientists, the USSR possessed a large stock of moderately trained scientific workers – larger than the USA's, in fact (USCJEC 1979: 745).
4. In 1979 over 75 per cent of Soviet families had TV sets and refrigerators and 70 per cent had a washing machine (Schroeder 1983: 313).
5. The Chinese data in this paragraph are all from SSB, ZGTJNJ (1983: 81, 97–8, 115).
6. The rate of inflation from 1980 to 1989 was reported to be 5.8 per cent per annum (Word Bank, World Development Report 1991). Russia's inflation rate in the early 1990s accelerated to over 1000 per cent.
7. For example, the Japanese 'culture' of industrial harmony did not emerge spontaneously, but was deliberately invented (Hobsbawm and Ranger 1985).
8. Such as the authors of the '500 Day Plan' for the transformation of the Soviet economy, and subsequently, Chubais and Sobchak.

REFERENCES

Note: USCJEC = United States Congress, Joint Economic Committee SSB = [Chinese] State Statistical Bureau

Abramowitz, M. (1986), 'Catching up, forging ahead, falling behind'. *Journal of Economic History*, 46(2): 385–406.

Acs, Z., and D.B. Audretsch (1993),'Has the role of small firms changed in the US?' in Z. Acs and D. Audretsch (eds), *Small Firms and Entrepreneurship*. Cambridge: Cambridge University Press.

Arnot, B. (1981), 'Soviet labour productivity and the failure of the Shchekino experiment'. *Critique*, 15: 31–56.

Aslund, A. (1989), 'Soviet and Chinese reforms: why they must be different'. *World Today*, 45(11).

Aslund, A. (1991), *Gorbachev's Struggle for Economic Reform*. London: Pinter.

Aslund, A., 1990, 'Gorbachev, perestroika, and economic crisis'. *Problems of Communism*, January–April, 13–41.

Banister, J. (1987), *China's Changing Population*. Stanford: Stanford University Press

Banister, J. (1992), 'Demographic aspects of poverty in China'. *Working Paper*, The World Bank.

Bergere, M-C. (1981), *The Golden Age of the Chinese Bourgeoisie*. Cambridge: Cambridge University Press.

Berliner, J. (1983), 'Planning and management' in A. Bergson and D. Levine (eds), *The Soviet Economy: Towards the Year 2000*. London: Allen and Unwin.

Blackwell, W. (1983), 'The Russian entrepreneur in the Tsarist period: an overview' in G. Guroff and F.V. Kasterson (eds), *Entrepreneurship in Imperial Russia and the Soviet Union*. Princeton: Princeton University Press.

Brown, A. and M. Kaser (eds), *The Soviet Union since Khrushchev*. London: Macmillan.

Chen, K., G. Jefferson and I. Singh (1992), 'Lessons from China's reform'. *Journal of Comparative Economics*, 16: 201–25.

Dobb. M., (1966), *Studies in the Development of Capitalism*. London: Routledge and Kegan Paul.

Donnithorne, A. (1972), *China's Economic System*. London: George Allen and Unwin.

Eberstadt, N. (1986), 'Material poverty in the People's Republic of China in international perspective' in USCJEC, *China's Economy Looks Towards the Year 2000*, Vol. 1. Washington, DC: US Government Printing Office.

Ellman, M. (1994), 'The increase in death and disease under *katastroika*'. *Cambridge Journal of Economics*, 18(4).

Erlich, E. (1985),'The size and structure of manufacturing establishments and enterprises: an international comparison'. *Journal of Comparative Economics*, 9: 267–95.

Feshbach, M. (1983), 'Population and labour force' in A. Bergson and D. Levine (eds), *The Soviet Economy: Towards the Year 2000*. London: Allen and Unwin.

Gatrell, P. (1986), *The Tsarist Economy, 1850–1917*. London: Batsford.

Goldman, M. (1994), *Lost Opportunity: Why Economic Reforms in Russia Have Not Worked*. London: W.W. Norton.

Gomulka, S. (1991), *The Theory of Technological Change and Economic Growth*. London: Routledge.

Granick, D. (1967), *Soviet Metal-Fabricating*. Madison: University of Wisconsin Press.

Grossman, G. (1979), 'Notes on the illegal economy and corruption' in USCJEC, *Soviet Economy in a Time of Change*, 2 vols. Washington, DC: US Government Printing Office.

Hanson, P. (1978), 'The import of Western technology' in A. Brown and M. Kaser (eds), *The Soviet Union since Krushchev*. London: Macmillan.

Hobsbawm, E. and T. Ranger (eds) (1985), *The Invention of Tradition*. Cambridge: Cambridge University Press.

Kiselev, S. (1994), 'The state and the farmer'. *Problems of Economic Transition*, 36(10): 67–81.

Kornai, J. (1990), *The Road to a Free Economy*. New York: Norton.

Levy, M. and K.H. Shih (1949), *The Rise of the Modern Chinese Business Class*. New York: Institute of Pacific Relations.

Li, R. (1981), *Statistical Materials on Soviet Agriculture* (Sulian nongye tongji huibian). Beijing: Nongye Chubanshe.

Little, I. (1979), 'An economic reconnaissance' in W. Galenson (ed.), *Taiwan*. Ithaca: Cornell University Press.

Liu, N., Y. Chen and C. Zhang (1988), *Seventy Years of Soviet Economic Growth* (Sulian guomin jingji fazhan qishi nian). Beijing: Jijie Chubanshe.

Macmillan, J. and B. Naughton (1992), 'How to reform a planned economy'. *Oxford Review of Economic Policy*, 8(1): 130–43.

Macpherson, W.J. (1987), *The Economic Development of Japan, 1868–1941*. London: Macmillan.

Miller, J. (1993), *Mikhail Gorbachev and the End of Soviet Power*. London: Macmillan.

Ministry of Agriculture (1982), *Outline of China's Agriculture* (Zhongguo nongye jingji gaiyao). Beijing: Nongye Chubanshe.

Ministry of Agriculture (1988), *Statistical Abstract of China's Xiangzhen Enterprises* (Quanguo xiangzhen qiye tongji zhaiyao). Beijing: Xiangzhen Qiye Bu.

Morishima, M. (1982), *Why Has Japan Succeeded?* Cambridge: Cambridge University Press.

Needham, J. (1969), *The Grand Titration*. London: Allen and Unwin.

Nolan, P. (1983), *Growth Processes and Distributional Change in a South Chinese Province: The Case of Guangdong*. London: Contemporary China Institute.

Nolan, P. (1988), *The Political Economy of Collective Farms*. Cambridge: Polity Press.

Nolan, P. (1994), 'Democratisation, human rights and economic reform: the case of China and Russia'. *Democratisation*, 1(1).

Nolan, P. (1995), *China's Rise, Russia's Fall: Politics, Economics and Planning in the Transition from Stalinism*. London: Macmillan.

Nove, A. (1983), *The Economics of Feasible Socialism*. London: George Allen and Unwin.

Perkins, D.H. (ed.) (1977) *China: Rural Small Scale Industry in the People's Republic of China*. Berkeley and Los Angeles: University of California Press.

Prybyla, J. (1991), 'The road from socialism : why, where, what and how'. *Problems of Communism*, XL.

Rawski, T.G. (1989), *Economic Growth in Pre-war China*. Berkeley and Los Angeles: University of California Press.

Sachs, J. and W.T. Woo (1994), 'Structural factors in the economic reforms of China, Eastern Europe and the former Soviet Union. *Economic Policy*, 18

Schroeder, G. (1983), 'Consumption' in A. Bergson and D. Levine (eds), *The Soviet Economy: Towards the Year 2000*. London: Allen and Unwin.

Shmelyev, N. and V. Popov (1990), *The Turning Point: Revitalising the Soviet Economy*. London: I.B. Tauris.

Spechler, M.C. (1979), 'Regional developments in the USSR, 1958–1978', in USJEC, *Soviet Economy in a Time of Change,* 2 Vols. Washington, DC: US Government Printing Office.

State Statistical Bureau (SSB), *Statistical Yearbook of China (SYC)*. Hong Kong: Economic Information Agency.

State Statistical Bureau (SSB), ZGTJNJ (1984–93), *Chinese Economic Yearbook* (Zhongguo tongji nianjian). Beijing: Zhongguo Tongji Chubanshe.

State Statistical Bureau (SSB), ZGNCTJNJ (1985–93), *Chinese Rural Statistical Yearbook* (Zhongguo nongcun tongji nianjian). Beijing: Zhongguo Tongji Chubanshe.

State Statistical Bureau (SSB), ZGGYJJTJNJ (1986–93), *Economic Statistics on Chinese Industry* (Zhongguo gongye jingji tongji nianjian). Beijing: Tongji Chubanshe.

State Statistical Bureau (SSB), ZGGYJJTJZL (1985), *Statistical Materials on China's Industrial Economy* (Zhongguo gongye jingji tongji ziliao). Beijing: Zhongguo Tongji Chubanshe.

State Statistical Bureau (SSB), ZGGXHZSTJZY (1989), *Statistical Materials on China's Supply and Marketing Co-operatives,1949–1988* (Zhongguo gongxiao hezuoshe tongji ziliao). Beijing: Zhongguo Tongji Chubanshe.

State Statistical Bureau (SSB), ZGTJZY (1984–94), *Statistical Survey of China* (Zhongguo tongji zhaiyao). Beijing: Zhongguo Tongji Chubanshe.

State Statistical Bureau (SSB), ZGRKTJNJ (1989), *Statistical Yearbook of Chinese Population* (Zhongguo renkou tongji nianjian). Beijing: Kexue Jishu Wenxian Chubanshe.

Su, S. (1988), *Democratisation and Reform*. Nottingham: Spokesman Books.

United Nations Development Programme (UNDP) (1990), *Human Development Report*. New York: Oxford University Press.

USCJEC (1975), *China: A Reassessment of the Economy*. Washington, DC: US Government Printing Ofice.

USCJEC (1976), *Soviet Economy in a New Perspective*. Washington, DC: US Government Printing Office.

USCJEC (1979), *Soviet Economy in a Time of Change*, 2 vols. Washington, DC: US Government Printing Office.

USCJEC (1978), *Chinese Economy Post-Mao*. Washington, DC: US Government Printing Office.

USCJEC (1982), *Soviet Economy in the 1980s: Problems and Prospects*. Washington, DC: US Government Printing Office.

USCJEC (1986), *China's Economy Looks Towards the Year 2000*, Vol. 1. Washington, DC: US Government Printing Office.

Walker, K. (1965), *Planning in Chinese Agriculture*. London: Frank Cass.

World Bank (1981a), *China: Socialist Development*. Washington, DC: World Bank.

World Bank (1981b), *China: Socialist Development, Annex D, Challenges and Achievements in Industry*. Washington, DC: World Bank.

World Bank (1981c), *China: Socialist Development, Annex C, Agricultural Development*. Washington, DC: World Bank.

World Bank (1992a), *China: Strategies for Reducing Poverty in the 1990s*. Washington, DC: World Bank.

World Bank (1992b), *Russian Economic Reforms at the Threshold*. Washington, DC: World Bank.

World Bank (1979–94), *World Development Report*. New York: Oxford University Press.

World Bank (1994), *Land Reform and Farm Re-structuring in Russia*. Washington, DC: World Bank.

Xu, D. and C. Wu, (eds) (1985), *China's Capitalist Sprouts* (Zhongguo zibenzhuyi mengya). Beijing: Renmin Chubanshe.

Yanowitch, M. (1977), *Social and Economic Inequality in the Soviet Union*. London: Martin Robertson.

Yeh, K.C. (1984), 'Macroeconomic changes in the Chinese economy during the readjustment'. *China Quarterly*, 100.

Yu, G. (ed.) (1984), *China's Socialist Modernisation*. Beijing: Foreign Languages Press.

6 Institutional Change and Economic Development in East-Central Europe and China: Contrasts in the Light of the 'East Asian Model'

Dic Lo and Hugo Radice

The contrast in institutional transformation between Central and Eastern Europe (CEE) and the former Soviet Union (FSU) on the one hand, and China on the other, is often characterized as one of shock therapy versus gradualism, although recently Sachs and Woo (1994) have argued that 'structural' differences make comparisons between the two cases problematic. This is part of a more general debate among economists concerning the pace and irreversibility of change towards a 'market economy'. But at the same time, the predominant neoclassical approach of most economic analysts allows the divergent experience of the CEE/FSU and China to support a common standpoint on the desirability in particular of *ownership* change. In this view, the continuing poor macro-economic performance of the CEE/FSU is at least in part due to the failure to carry through the shock therapy logic fully, for example in allowing the continuation of soft budget constraints for large state-owned enterprises (SOEs) and ex-SOEs; while the good performance of the Chinese economy is partly because despite the continued existence of a soft-budgeted state sector, the private and local-state firms (township and village enterprises – TVEs) have been 'free' to respond to market forces.

The response of 'evolutionary' writers is to argue that the CEE/FSU experience demonstrates that such deep-rooted change is unavoidably gradual, so that 'muddling through' must continue with the further clarification of ownership rights and improvements in state policies for structural change; the Chinese experience, on the other hand, is seen as supporting the need for continuity in central direction while the balance between state and market gradually shifts.

Our view is that both schools of thought are wrongly fixated on the simple dichotomy of state (or plan) versus market. Without going in to the theoretical critique of the conventional schools, suffice it to say that the 'developmental state' or 'East Asian model', and the practical experience of the region's main exemplars, notably Japan, Taiwan and South Korea, offer a very different framework for analysing the political economy of firms, markets and states (we do not here go into the very real differences among these exemplars). In this chapter we are concerned in particular with the enterprise as such: its ownership, its control or 'governance', its relations with the market, and with the state. Our initial standpoint is that for developmental purposes, a capacity for technological development and structural change is essential; that at the level of the enterprise this requires institutional arrangements which encompass both conscious coordination and the 'invisible hand' of the market; and that the state has an irreplaceable role in the promotion of development and change. Furthermore, such arrangements do not emerge naturally from a sort of meta-market of competition between alternatives; rather, they are socially constructed.

In this chapter we try to undertake an initial phase of clarifying the recent experience of transformation in the SOE in the CEE/FSU and in China, 'in the light of' the East Asian model. The second and third sections deal with each case in turn, essentially in terms of existing debate, but looking towards the 'developmental' concerns indicated above; since the debates in the two cases have had rather different concerns, these sections are not presented 'in parallel'. The fourth section elaborates a bit more on some key aspects of the enterprise system in the East Asian model, while the final section links together the previous ones more explicitly and suggests an agenda for further work.

PRIVATIZATION, GOVERNANCE AND RESTRUCTURING IN EASTERN EUROPE

Whatever the apparent pace of transformation in the early years, all of the countries of CEE, including the FSU, find themselves enmeshed in a long-drawn-out process of institutional construction, when it comes to the privatization of the dominant large state enterprises. The discussion in this section will draw in particular on the experience of the Visegrad group (the Czech Republic, Hungary, Poland, Slovakia) but will be organized around issues which are more widely relevant in the region.

Principles of Ownership Transformation

Right from the start, mainstream Western economists foresaw a quite lengthy timetable for what they termed the 'transition to a market economy'. Fischer and Gelb's well-known diagram (1991: 102) proposed that the 'intense' phase of macrostabilization could be in the first two to three years; under the heading of liberalization, price and trade reform could be largely accomplished in 12 to 18 months, with labour and capital markets taking longer to prepare; however, while small-scale privatization might take three years, large SOEs would take ten years to privatize. We can see that the 'shock therapy vs gradualism' debate becomes much less stark once we focus on specific areas of institutional change. Instead, the shock therapy position is modified by specifying the sequencing of, and the interaction between, macro and institutional change. Strong adherents to the virtues of the free market argued that fiscal austerity and price and trade liberalization would establish a foundation on which SOEs could evaluate their activities (or be evaluated) accurately, while at the same time creating the space (in terms of 'freed' resources) for the 'new' private sector to expand. They criticized those 'gradualists' who were alarmed by the scale of output contraction for wanting to entrench the 'sectional' interests of workers and managers, which had operated through structures of vertical bargaining under central planning, even in the more reformed systems of Poland and Hungary. The risk of entrenchment meant, to the free marketeers, that the privatization of large SOEs should proceed as quickly as possible. But what sort of privatization, and with what consequences?

At first, the argument focused on the monetization of SOE assets, encompassing both the determination of meaningful asset prices, and the creation of money capital for their purchase. The pricing of SOEs was bound to be an intractable problem, given the gulf that was seen as existing between domestic and world-market price structures, and the demand and supply consequences of trade liberalization. Even a well-conducted auction or tender process could not overcome inadequate information and uncertainty; 'insiders' had an unavoidable advantage, and the state could dramatically affect valuation through tariffs, financial and fiscal preferences, or through pre-privatization restructuring. And once the population's savings 'overhang' had been absorbed by inflation and imported supplies, there was very little in the way of local funds available for purchasing SOE shares. For most Western advisers, however, none of these arguments were sufficient grounds for delaying the privatization of large SOEs. Hence, there appeared to be a stark choice between (a) voucher 'giveaways', (b) corrupt or at least unpopular *nomenklatura* privatization, and (c) foreign takeovers (which might easily be, or be perceived as, another sort of 'give-away').

A second argument concerned the correct sequencing between privatiz-ation and enterprise restructuring. One issue here was the concern with com-petition, carried over from debates on Western – notably UK – privatization (for example, Newbery and Kattuman 1992). If existing state monopolies were broken up with the aim of encouraging entrepreneurial behaviour, this would inevitably reduce the market value of the assets, at least initially. It might also hit exports through the disruption of production. A second issue was financial (van Wijnbergen 1993). With the emergence of a two-tier banking system, the main assets of the banks consisted of inherited loans to SOEs; restructuring would lay bare the precarious nature of these loans and risk a financial crisis, as the interests of owners must prevail over those of managers, workers and other stakeholders – including the state – who are perceived as 'rent-seekers': in the Anglo-Saxon tradition, it is only the in-centives of owners (in terms of both risks and rewards) which coincide with allocative efficiency. However, a solution must be found to the free-rider problem, which causes underinvestment by owners in the information which they require to avoid 'melt-down'. Additionally, matters were con-stantly being made worse by the rapid accumulation of inter-enterprise debts. What is more, newly-privatized SOEs would need access to new cred-its on manageable terms; and in the long run, the privatisation of the banks themselves was seen as wholly desirable.

The third argument, which was already present in some early contribu-tions (Corbett and Mayer 1991, Frydman and Rapaczynski 1994), re-arranges the first two approaches in terms of Western debates on corporate governance, including both the form of financial intermediation (Anglo-Saxon capital markets vs 'continental' universal banking) and the strategic direction of the firm (owners versus managers: see Radice 1995). The main concern here among the more free-market-oriented writers was that if post-privatization corporate restructuring was to be swift, then owners had to pre-vail over the managers as the principal agents of restructuring. The common solution to this problem was to move towards more concentrated ownership. This has led to widespread approval for the use of financial intermediaries such as the Czech/Slovak investment privatization funds, which have been interpreted as being similar to mutual funds in the US or pension funds in the UK. Such financial institutions have been traditionally seen as lacking in strategic perspective in the US and the UK, where they are passive share-holders, exercising 'exit' rather than 'voice'. More recently, some US funds such as CalPERS have become much more active, especially in mobilizing shareholders to unseat incumbent management; but in their single-minded pursuit of shareholder value-maximization, they do not necessarily take a long-term strategic view of the corporations they invest in. The alternative approach (for example Corbett and Mayer 1991) is to argue that circumstances require a much more committed and strategic interventionism: this may emerge by default if CEE/FSU stock markets remain in their present primitive and illiquid state, because larger investors will be locked in and unable to realize short-term capital gains by exiting. There still remains the question of whether funds (or for that matter banks as 'locked-in' creditors) are actually competent to provide strategic direction in restructuring firms.

The curious thing is that despite very wide apparent differences in the actual privatization processes in the region, the reality is much the same everywhere. Whatever their supposed legal status, in every country a powerful core of old SOEs continues to exist with very little real change. This group is based typically in heavy industry (steel, engineering, chemicals) but extends into mass consumer durable goods, retail, wholesale and foreign trade and even agriculture; above all, it embraces the all-important banking sector. These SOEs or ex-SOEs have been judged, in practice, to be crucial to the maintenance of acceptable levels of production, employment and exports. Although their ownership has usually been 'corporatized' even when the state remains the sole or the dominant owner, in one way or another they are protected from the full rigours of the market, and they are governed by a pragmatic if uneasy alliance between owners, bankers, managers and the state (and even sometimes workers). At the same time, the absence of effective securities markets means that firms rely heavily on bank and inter-enterprise credits (not to mention, in the FSU, the forced intra-enterprise credit of unpaid wages!), which also promotes 'managed' solutions.

Country Experiences

In the Czech Republic, the state, through the National Property Fund, remains an important owner, along with the investment funds (controlled mostly by banks), foreign capital (both direct and portfolio) and managers (Brom and Orenstein 1994). The banks, it turns out, are owned by the state and by each other (via the funds; or even by themselves). The position of the banks as controllers of the funds sits uneasily with their role as creditors – at least, uneasily from the standpoint of other stakeholders. The first question is: does this not have something to do with the fact that the Czech Republic has the lowest unemployment in the region? Or is this achievement the result of other favourable circumstances (low labour costs, undervalued exchange rate, proximity to Germany), which would yield even greater benefits to growth and employment if the SOEs were 'liberated' from the cosy nexus of state–bank–management control? A second issue is whether the investment funds will emerge as 'strategic' controllers of the ex-SOEs and act to 'discipline' management and enforce restructuring (as the independent, non-bank Harvard Group has always threatened), and if so, to what effect? And thirdly, what will foreign capital – including the increasingly useful (for the balance of payments) portfolio investors – think of this nexus of control, which places Czech securities and their markets a very long way from the 'transparency' of the dominant Anglo-Saxon tradition?

The abrupt entry of Stratton, set up in 1995 by the American financier Michael Dingman in alliance with the Harvard group of investment funds, has brought both these latter issues into sharp focus: one of Stratton's first targets was the paper company Sepap, which had already sold a minority stake (34 per cent) to the Swedish firm AssiDomän, and when Stratton acquired a controlling 51 per cent, AssiDomän was forced to negotiate a strategic partnership with it. By mid-1996, some Czech investment funds were being converted into holding companies to obtain greater freedom of manoeuvre in soliciting or supporting such strategic moves; meanwhile, the supposedly liberal Klaus government was still resisting any moves towards foreign ownership or control of major banks, and still failing to provide adequate regulation of securities and related markets.

Since then, the 'velvet divorce' progress has been much slower in Slovakia, at least during the two periods of government under Meciar's alliance of so-called left and right nationalists. No second round of voucher privatization has taken place such as happened in the Czech Republic, and the attempt to accelerate sell-offs (including to foreign investors) in the Moravcik interregnum in 1993–4 achieved little. Apart from political instability, the problem is made worse by the greater importance in Slovakia of large military and heavy industry producers which face the need for massive restructuring. In 1995, the government proposed cutting the maximum stake of an investment fund to 10 per cent, and its maximum vote to 5 per cent (*Financial Times,* 5 April 1995: 32), in order to strengthen the position of incumbent managers and the state; more recently, the government has been selling SOEs by heavily-subsidized management buy-outs (*Business Central Europe* 1996)

In Hungary meanwhile, the only 'mass' element of privatization – the system of restitution vouchers – was a failure as far as large SOEs are concerned. Attention has focused first on the intractable problem of the 'dirty dozen' – the old SOEs which seemingly cannot find a buyer, and many of which were in fact the object of special 'intervention' already twenty years ago because they could not, or would not, adapt to the relatively mild exigencies of the 1968 reforms. It is very difficult for the Hungarian government now to attempt to deal with these through a late 'mass' privatization, because everyone regards them as valueless: the inert mass of their Czech equivalents was leavened by the presence, in both 'rounds', of other SOEs which were patently profitable, whether by virtue of monopoly power or proven adaptability. Hungarian industry has already been 'cherry-picked' by early *nomenklatura* privatization, by foreign takeover, or by flotation; while the infrastructure monopolies are being privatized (partially) by tender to foreign capital in order to raise hard currency and to inject modern technology. The 1994 fiascos of HungarHotels and the Budapest Bank demonstrated the dangers of relying on foreign capital where the investment is more risky: a price acceptably low to the investor will be unacceptably low to the government in the context of domestic politics. However, the very successful 1995 sell-offs of utility companies, and the eventual sale of a strategic stake in Budapest Bank to GE Capital, have confirmed the dominance of foreign capital in Hungarian privatization and restructuring: foreign firms are now responsible for around 60 per cent of all Hungarian exports. There remains a small but growing number of management and/or worker buyouts within the framework of 'self-privatization', mostly of smaller firms, especially after the 1992 Employee Share Ownership law (Karsai and Wright 1994): in these cases, management appear to be dominant in terms of control, with the support of bank creditors.

Turning to Poland, by all accounts the progress of privatization has been even more erratic than in Hungary. While the 'new' small-scale private sector has flourished more than anywhere in the region (having started from a higher base, and also a private agriculture), the sale of large SOEs has been much weaker. Two features stand out: the much stronger voice of labour, expressed through the unions, the Workers' Councils and several political parties; and the continuing delays in launching a long-promised mass privatization programme. At the enterprise level, workers and managers played a central role in so-called 'liquidation privatizations'. However, overall workers have been steadily losing influence: their shareholdings have been falling away in already-privatized firms (Tittenbrun 1995), they have been divided as a result of the differentiation of enterprise performance and pay, and their bargaining power has been weakened by heavy unemployment (again, with big regional differences), inter-union rivalries and the ideological confusions of *Solidarnosc* since 1989. The result has been to tilt the balance of power in firms dominated by 'insider' shareholders heavily towards management. The delays in mass privatization, together with the failure of the sectoral approach, which was intended to combine privatization with demonopolization, underscores the continuing role of the state as owner and controller. It is now expected that the bulk of the remaining SOEs will eventually be transferred to the new National Investment Funds, which make heavy use of Western banks and consultants as fund managers. Lastly, as in Hungary, a significant minority of more profitable SOEs have acquired foreign owners or controlling part-owners.

A 'Nexus of Control': But For What Purpose?

We draw two main conclusions from the above. Firstly, the former large SOEs, and the freshly created banks, are subject to a nexus of control and regulation in which the state plays a major role. However, secondly, the reality of this situation does not seem to satisfy either the major domestic political constituencies – including the nascent capitalist class – or the powerful foreign interests – both investors and governments. The 'nexus' has to manage an unavoidably gradual process of real economic restructuring, maintaining employment and exports, but at the same time achieving 'modernization' both of the structure of production, and of production processes. In the political realm, there is an equally gradual emergence of the sort of uneasy marriage between local capital, the state and foreign capital which typifies post-colonial and neo-colonial countries (Radice 1993).

There is no question that, at least in the Visegrad countries (and Slovenia), a great deal of enterprise-level restructuring is taking place. While reliable quantitative evidence for this is hard to find – and financial performance data particularly unreliable – Carlin *et al.* (1994) review a substantial body of case-study evidence. Their conceptual framework is a conventional neoclassical one:

> The aim of transforming the enterprise sector in the transition economies is to create value-maximizing firms. This will typically require that owners have some control over managers who in turn have some control over employees (Carlin *et al.* 1994: 6)

They then assess restructuring along four dimensions: 'internal organization (for example, unbundling, shedding social assets), employment (for example, labour shedding, wage differentiation), output (for example, marketing, product mix) and investment (for example, in wholesale networks, capital equipment)'; and they are looking especially for actions 'contributing to the creation of a competitive market economy', although in addition 'managers exploiting monopolistic positions can be seen as responding actively to the opportunities for making profits' (Carlin *et al.* 1994: 6). The authors therefore look first for evidence of harder budget constraints (imposed by old or new owners) and the emergence of a managerial labour market: here they recognize the limitations arising from the continuing importance of 'idiosyncratic knowledge' and informal networks and contacts. With regard to the restructuring of output and employment, they are concerned about the very low levels of lay-off and job mobility, which is coupled with the continuing monopolization of markets.

Other writers have offered approaches to restructuring that are less abstract, and focus on the need for a *strategic* response, both at the level of the firm, and at the level of sectoral industrial policy. A Hungarian study by Brada *et al.* (1994) focused at the enterprise level on 'a strategic vision of what their competitive advantage was and how it ought to be exploited and nurtured'; in more detail, 'strategic thinking that would combine market analysis and an understanding of the firm's competitive advantages into an integrated vision for developing production had to do with explanations of actual or anticipated changes in products or technology' (Brada *et al.* 1994: 62). The companies under study were clearly finding it difficult to arrive at such a strategic vision, given the legacies of the past (structure of management, products, markets) and the short-term exigencies of ownership change and financial difficulties. Similarly, Laki (1994) finds that crisis management by Hungarian firms has concentrated on short-term adjustment, with little fundamental restructuring except in relation to organizational (including ownership) change and lay-offs. In their case-studies of Czech firms, Clark and Soulsby (1995) focus on organizational change and managerial values, and uncover parallel obstacles and ambiguities. Moving to the sectoral level, Hare and Hughes (1991) sought to find out in which sectors Poland, Hungary and Czechoslovakia might possess comparative advantage. In an almost complete antithesis to the East Asian 'developmental' approach, they assessed the viability of a sector in terms of their current profitability when all inputs and outputs are revalued at world market prices. Their aim was to identify desirable patterns of specialization based on the ratio of value added to world prices. Although the conceptual framework and methodology derive from the standard neoclassical model of a competitive market economy, the results were quite plausible, suggesting that Poland had an advantage in some light industries, Czechoslovakia in plastic products, pottery and glass, and metallurgy and transport equipment, and Hungary in a wider range including chemicals and electrical equipment as well as several light industrial sectors. They concluded with the hope that 'industrial policy in Eastern Europe could be based on a well-founded analysis of long term competitiveness', but doubted whether either the state or the financial institutions were equipped to undertake or act upon such an analysis (Hare and Hughes

1991: 42). Landesmann and Szekely (1991) looked at the structure of output, employment and trade of the same countries in the 1970s and 1980s, finding them to display much more rigidity than Western economies, implying a backlog of needed change, to which the shock of the collapse of intra-CMEA trade had to be added. They identified a risk that currency undervaluation might allow heavy industry, especially in Czechoslovakia, to postpone change.

The story so far points in the direction of the East Asian model primarily for two reasons. First, in the East Asian model negotiated, and where necessary institutionalized, consensus is generally seen as a central part of the formation of stable, long-term economic and political structures. On this score, the emerging nexus of interests controlling large CEE firms, whether pre- or post-privatization, has more to do with enforced mutual dependence than with negotiated and purposive consensus. This is not just a question of providing carrots and sticks with which to encourage the emergence of more 'market-oriented' structures and practices, as the 'evolutionist' approach would argue. A dynamic corporate structure and strategy *orchestrates* a diversity of interests within the firm, and *articulates* it as a collective organization with its economic environment. This is especially important in relation to technological change. While the environment remains so uncertain and ungoverned, there is little with which new and inexperienced owners and managers (or indeed other stakeholders) *can* articulate. 'Outside' owners – foreign firms or determined and independent investment funds – may have a clearer strategic vision of structural change, but they still cannot rely on other actors to respond in predictable, 'market-oriented' ways.

Secondly, in the East Asian experience, this corporate framework is linked to a development strategy which aims to guide resource allocation for structural change at the sectoral level. Up to now, it is very hard to see any such strategy even being on the agenda in CEE and the FSU. There is a great reluctance to engage openly in anything that resembles the forced redistribution typical of pre-1989 central planning (even in the more 'reformed' economies). However, despite their apparent commitment to *laissez-faire* principles, governments in the region have clearly been using their very considerable influence to block such developments in selected key sectors. But the failure even to discuss a systematic sectoral approach, along 'East Asian' lines, carries with it the risk that each national economy will become internally differentiated – with growing regional, sectoral and inter-enterprise inequalities in wages, profits and above all technological change – and externally fragmented – with key enterprises coming under the strategic direction of foreign capital.

BREAKTHROUGHS IN CHINESE ENTERPRISE REFORM

Turning to the Chinese case, economists have now recognized that the widely publicized myth of the 'ailing Chinese state industry' does not live up to the reality, and in particular, the country's mostly state-owned large- and medium-scale enterprises (LMEs) have in fact performed well (Jefferson and Xu 1994, Naughton 1994). Between 1980 and 1993, amid Chinese industry as a whole growing at an average annual rate of 15 per cent, LMEs have maintained their output share in the total at the 42 per cent level. This runs counter to the belief that Chinese state-owned enterprises, just like their counterparts in Central and Eastern Europe and indeed SOEs everywhere, are inefficient and non-reformable (Sachs and Woo 1994; Woo 1994).

At the institutional level, the contradiction between China's reality and the prevailing views on the transformation of the Soviet-type economic system is especially stark. There is now a growing consensus in the literature that even collectively owned enterprises (COEs, of which most are township and village enterprises – TVEs), which big-bang advocates have often contrasted to SOEs to show the superiority of private ownership, are not reducible to the canonical capitalist firm. They are better conceptualized as public, community firms (Bowles and Dong 1994, Weitzman and Xu 1994).

The most enigmatic reality, of course, concerns LMEs: they are at the heart of China's traditional Soviet-type economy, their operations have been the least marketized, and their institutional arrangements conform the least to private ownership. The fact that LMEs have performed well thus especially calls for an interpretation of Chinese enterprise reform that transcends the exclusive focus on marketization and privatization. Following the conventional concerns in the literature on reform and transformation, and in line with the discussion on the East Asian experiences of economic development, we focus on three issues: namely, soft budget constraint, government intervention, and labour market rigidity. We conclude the section by considering the implications for economic development.

Soft Budget Constraint

Kornai (1990) contends that the soft budget constraint is not simply a characterization of firm behaviour under the traditional Soviet-type economic system but rather, more generally, that it refers to the institutional arrangements where the inside members (managers and workers) of firms are not fully responsible for their own receipts and expenses. In property rights terms, soft-budgeted behaviour is an expression of 'shirking' or 'perquisites' which are at the expense of the 'residual claimant'. In China, soft-budgeted behaviour takes the form of investment and bonus expansion. The explanation is that, because the residual claimant is the population at large which must rely on the state in monitoring enterprises, there is inevitably the problem of 'two-tier collusion': collusion between local or sectoral state agencies and enterprises, and that between managers and workers, striving for their own welfare at the expense of the accumulation of state assets (Lee 1991).

From a development perspective, the emphasis of property rights theory on strict control of owners (the residual claimant) over the firm, while in line with the logic of allocative efficiency, can be criticized for being detrimental to productive efficiency. At one level, the calculative atmosphere and strict power hierarchy that underpin owners' control are harmful to the long-term commitment and hence the collective learning of employees. At another level, there is the problem of short-termism on the part of owners, focusing on the maximization of dividends, which can hinder the realization of productive efficiency arising from endeavours of a long-term nature. It seems that what is more feasible-cum-desirable is to institute an appropriate degree of softness of the budget constraint, not eliminating softness altogether. As for constraining the down-side effects of soft-budgeted behaviour, Hua *et al.* (1986) argue that an essential condition is the clarification of the boundaries of the interests of enterprises. Zhang (1987) further makes the point that so long as the soft external financing does not blur the enterprise's cost–revenue structure, it would not leave much room for soft-budget behaviour.

China's enterprise reform thus can be seen in a more favourable light. The granting of autonomy and incentive, together with the increase in competition, tends to institutionalize enterprises' distinctive interests. Not only do enterprises need to become profit-oriented, but also they have to strive for good performance in market competition in order to increase the income of inside members. This arises mainly from two developments: the increase in inside members' commitment, and the hardening of the budget constraint from without.

The contractual management system which has been adopted since 1987 appears to be in line with the kind of institutional set-up whereby enterprises are accountable to their major stakeholders. This is particularly related to the composition of contract-issuing committees which have involved the participation of – and indeed the mutual checks and balances among – local authorities, related business entities, the banks, and the workers. In respect of external financing, the lending-for-appropriation financial reform after 1983 also appears to have brought about the hardening of the budget constraint. By replacing state allocation with bank lending, the reform largely reduces the shortcoming of the previous system which blurred the cost–revenue structure of enterprises. By requiring payment for the cost of external financing, the reform also forces enterprises to economize on its uses. It goes without saying that the lending-for-appropriation reform is not necessarily sufficient to constrain soft-budgeted behaviour. Indeed, the pre-1989 reform experience in some CEE countries seems to be different: enterprises continue to exhibit soft-budgeted behaviour after the substitution of bank lending for state appropriation as the main source of external financing. The difference may lie in the wider context of *de facto* corporate control: while in China a genuine 'nexus of control' has emerged, bringing together distinct and divergent interests, in pre-1989 reformed Hungary and Poland the supposedly-distinct interests of managers, workers, bankers and bureaucrats were all still subordinated to the central party-state apparatus.[1]

In terms of actual performance, it is observable that Chinese enterprises have become sensitive to the cost and utilization of external financing. In particular, it is reported that, during the austerity period of 1989–91, to sustain production many enterprises replenished working capital by drawing on retained profits and even by reducing payments to employees (Wang and Li 1991). It is also evident that, in contrast to the widely-held perception, many Chinese enterprises have become far less prone to expand bonuses at the expense of state asset accumulation (Tang 1992). This is especially true for LMEs which, compared with small-scale enterprises, have a far stronger inclination to emphasize long-term development instead of short-term employees' welfare (Ma 1992, Zhang 1987). There are reports that, rather than indulging in 'plundering', enterprises significantly increased their productive investments following increases in their autonomy (McMillan and Naughton 1992). In view of the good performance of LMEs, it can be further inferred that the significance of the reformed Chinese enterprise system is not simply the improvement in allocative efficiency as a result of budget hardening, but also the improvement of productive efficiency.

Government Intervention

That local and sectoral authority intervention seriously hampers the autonomy of enterprises (especially but not exclusively SOEs) is a fact frequently reported by the Chinese press. That this is related to the ownership system of enterprises is also widely agreed among economists (Du and Guo 1993, SCESR 1992).

But does ownership *per se* explain government intervention? It seems straightforward for Chen *et al.* (1992: 221) to claim that 'a key to limiting the *ad hoc* interventions of Chinese bureaucracy in enterprise operations is private ownership and a code of property rights'. This is indeed the target model pursued by many Chinese intellectuals. The problem is that the connection between ownership and government intervention is not simply a legal matter but one of political economy, which implies that the power structures in the economy and polity must be brought into the analysis. At an intuitive level, in view of historical experiences in both China and elsewhere, it is doubtful that private ownership as such is antithetical to bureaucratic intervention. Indeed, the phenomenon of *de facto* 'renationalization' in some countries after mass privatization appears to turn this proposition on its head (Roland 1995).

And must government intervention be *ad hoc*? For neo-liberal writers, intervention is always associated with distortions, protected inefficiency, rent-seeking, corruption, and so on. But it is arguable that there are also economically conducive effects of government intervention. There is a well-founded case from the late industrialization literature that supports government promotion of structural change in transcendence of the given comparative advantage (Amsden 1989, Wade 1990). Zhang (1987) further points out that, in the context of a dualistic economy or one characterized by an extreme unevenness in the development capacity of firms, it is necessary for government intervention to reach individual firms. Finally, as we shall discuss in the next section, government intervention – as well as other forms of non-market regulation, for example the bank's cushioning of firms from bankruptcy or take-over bids in the Japanese system – can foster the long-term commitment of inside members of the firm.

The discussion above implies that what is more feasible-cum-desirable than simply cutting the government-enterprise ties is to institute an appropriate degree and form of intervention. Viewed this way, China's experience of government intervention in enterprise operations cannot be judged as nothing but detrimental. The contractual management system implies the institutionalization of a bargaining regime, whereby local and sectoral authorities are involved in enterprise decision-making, while abandoning the pursuit of an arm's-length regime of state-enterprise relationship. It is precisely because of this continued existence of bargaining that the call for ownership reform runs high. Nevertheless, there is a crucial difference between the new bargaining regime and the old: namely, that the bargaining centres largely around financial performance, rather than around input allocation and output delivery as under the traditional physical planning system. This change, as discussed, means curtailing the room for soft-budgeted behaviour on the part of enterprises. It also implies that government intervention is more formal, or less *ad hoc*, because it is largely carried out through the unified contract-issuing committees rather than the industrial bureaus and other offices which are not mutually coordinated.

The formation of industrial concerns since the late 1980s has seemed capable of restructuring the state–enterprise relationship in a way that reduces some crucial deficiencies of government intervention. This is related to its dealing with the immobility of productive assets across localities or ministerial affiliations. Especially in fast-growing industries like automobile, electronics and steel, there are cases whereby nation-wide industrial concerns by means of shareholding take over the control of some enterprises from local or sectoral authorities. The latter thus become shareholders, and their intervention with enterprise operations becomes less *ad hoc*. Famous cases in point include the take-over by the First Auto Works (in its capacity as the core member of the Jiefang Auto Group) of several enterprises in Jilin province to form its light commercial manufacturing arm, and Shenzhen SEG Electronics Group's take-over of a number of enterprises in Heilongjiang province.

In a related development, the wave of mergers and take-overs which took place in the early 1990s, largely under the auspices of local and sectoral authorities, has proved to be conducive in rationalizing the industrial system. The same applies to cases of inter-enterprise joint R&D activity initiated by the authorities in recent years. To the extent that these would not have taken place purely by the initiatives of enterprises, or by the regulation of the existing market mechanism – where the underdevelopment of Schumpeterian entrepreneurship and the capital market makes it impossible for enterprises to undertake activities of long-term development at the expense of short-term profitability – the government intervention can be regarded as entrepreneurial.[2]

Labour Immobility and Enterprise Rigidity

One prominent feature of the Chinese enterprise system is the rigidity of labour employment, characterized not only by low labour mobility but also the rigidity of wage adjustment. The factors accounting for this feature are well known. In the context of a rural–urban dualistic economy, there is the phenomenon of 'unlimited supply of labour' under the existing wage rate for industrial workers. This rate is determined against an institutional background in which not only is the right of employment guaranteed by the state, but also the workers, through a collective bargaining regime, can considerably influence the distribution of the enterprise surplus. What are the economic implications of this systemic feature, in terms not only of labour cost and distribution but also of productivity?

For neoclassical economists, a bargaining regime which implies some degree of endogeneity of wage determination by economic agents must impede the working of the labour market. The rigidity of the wage in downward adjustment also implies unduly high labour costs for firms. In the context of the Soviet-type economic system, the state guarantee of job security further implies the rigidity of enterprises, especially expressed in the difficulty for inefficient enterprises to go bankrupt, and hence the structural adjustment of the economy. Nevertheless, in the theoretical literature there are alternative perspectives through which rigidity in the labour employment system can be seen as both inevitable and desirable in certain circumstances. Transaction cost theory says that, because of uncertainty of future market demand, firms would normally enter into long-term contracts with incumbent workers – the rigidity of employment fosters the flexibility of production and supply. Also, because of the firm-specific skills acquired by incumbent workers, the notion of idiosyncratic exchange underpins the desirability of a long-term employment relationship (Williamson *et al.* 1975). Thus, rigidity and flexibility should not be viewed in a dichotomous way. Both are necessary for the functioning of an economy, and their relative desirability depends on the specific growth pattern of the economy. From this perspective, the reform of China's labour employment system appears to be more complex than the orthodox diagnosis and prescription.

The effects of the employment system reform are often inferred with reference to a comparison between SOEs and COEs (especially TVEs). According to Zheng (1993), in the recession period of 1989–91, whilst almost one-third of TVEs stopped operations or went bankrupt, the same phenomenon was rare on the part of SOEs. This in some ways explains the divergence of financial performance between the two during this period: by 1992, SOEs were outperformed by COEs in terms of profit rate (9.7 per cent versus 10.1 per cent), loss–profit ratio (19.0 per cent versus 10.7 per cent) and particularly the proportion of loss-making enterprises (23.4 per cent versus 13.7 per cent) (ZGJTN 1993: 90, 116, 130, 142). Two reasons stand out. First, without the exit option, SOEs have to keep on running even in times of recession whereby market demand for their products is week. Second, because of the rigidity of wage adjustment, the unit cost of production goes up during the contraction of the production scale.

Nevertheless, to be balanced, the above depiction should be seen in connection with the good performance of SOEs in the boom period of 1985–8, when they outperformed COEs in terms of all the three financial indicators. Thus, the experiences seem to confirm our proposition that labour employment rigidity is bad for the capability of enterprises in responding to severe market fluctuations, but good for improving productivity in the context of expanding market demand. Institutionally, the reform of the labour employment system has fallen far short of official targets. Measures like dismissal of workers and widening wage differentials among workers, albeit being given top priority in official reform targets, have seldom been practised by enterprises. The most radical measure which has been adopted is, after all, a mild one: 'unemployment inside the enterprise'. This is to promote competition for formal jobs, with outcompeted workers becoming 'unemployed' but continuing to stay in the enterprise. These workers thus receive only the basic wage, rather than wage plus bonus, and have to face the embarrassing status of working at informal jobs. The competition also puts pressure on workers who retain their jobs (Liu 1993). Given the mildness of the reform, with workers still being cushioned by the enterprise (and ultimately the state) from the regulation of the market, the employment system is far from the orthodox ideal. Nevertheless, by strengthening the link between reward and performance, it is helpful in enhancing work incentives. The strengthening of the link between the income of the inside members as a group and that of the enterprise under broader reforms is also helpful in bringing about peer-group pressure on individual workers for good performance.

Implications for Economic Development

In order to conceptualize the character of firm organization in China, Japan and South Korea, Lee (1991) uses three labels: 'collusive', 'cooperative' and 'confrontational', respectively. A question thus arises as to whether the reforms have transformed China's enterprise system from a collusion-dominated one, which in a sense is an appropriate characterization of the early reform reality as well as the traditional Soviet-type enterprise in general, to a cooperative one. The answer seems to be affirmative. This can be seen in relation to the organizational restructuring of the production system of LMEs, which has proceeded along two lines: namely, rationalization and flexibility.

Rationalization refers to the promotion of economies of scale and specialized division of labour. At the intra-firm level, the multidivisional (M-form) model – whereby the enterprise is organized in a three-tier way consisting of the headquarters responsible for strategic decision-making, product- or geographically-differentiated divisions as profit centres, and workshops as cost centres – has been widely applied to large-scale manufacturing industries. This model, in a sense, mimics the capital market (and hence is dubbed the 'internal capital market' in transaction cost economics). At the inter-firm level, the formation of industrial concerns and with it the restructuring of the productive capacity of member enterprises appear to be in line with the pursuit of rationalization.

As for flexibility, or the capability of quick response to the demand for continuously improving product quality and output-mix, the adoption of Japanese just-in-time practices, mainly in intra-firm work organization but also in the coordination between assembling firms and parts suppliers, is a case in point. By lifting the buffer of input stocks, the practice implies rigorous demand for on-site quality control and problem-solving, as well as intensive cooperation along the production chain. In this respect, organizational set-ups like quality circles and management suggestions by participants of the production system have been instituted to foster cooperation.[3]

Flexibility-oriented practices like just-in-time cannot be instituted with-out the active participation of major agents of the production system, espe-cially the workers. This, in turn, requires their long-term commitment which has been underpinned by the rigidity of the employment relationship, the soft financing of banks and the protection of local governments; the latter two cushion enterprises from the threat of severe short-term fluctuations in the market environment. On the other hand, however, the formation of in-dustrial concerns cannot have taken place without the mobility of product-ive inputs. This requires overcoming the fragmentation of the industrial system associated with the domination of local and sectoral authorities, that is, instituting a relatively detached government–enterprise relationship, whereby the granting of government protection is conditional upon the good performance of the enterprise. The relatively successful organizational re-structuring so far indicates that an appropriate balance (however fragile) between the two principles, which in a sense can be mutually contradictory, has been reached under reform.

But what is so significant about being cooperative? After all, what neo-classical economics regard as of paramount importance is competition, the ideal of which can only be achieved by arm's-length exchanges based on parametric prices. The crucial question, then, is whether the possible gain of productive efficiency from collective learning can fully (and more than fully) compensate for the loss of allocative efficiency due to rigidity.

Here, we touch upon the East Asian model of economic development once again. But it is also possible to derive from China's experience some tentative answers to the question. To begin with, it is noted that an essential feature of the growth pattern of China's economy over the past 15 years is the explosive expansion of 'new (consumer durables) industries', the impact of which has been felt by the entire population. Because most new industries are ones with a high income elasticity of demand, their expansion has been especially capable of generating economies of scale and learning effects. Because the industries were established mainly through technology imports, the effect of their expansion was just like continuous technical change. Finally, because the rise of these industries has been induced by consumption demonstration effects from the advanced capitalist world, there has been continuous changing or upgrading of the product-mix (Lo forthcoming: ch. 3).

Given this market environment, particularly the rapid shifts of demand towards new products which imply good rewards for early entrants, successful adoption and improvement upon imported technology has been a major competitive advantage for enterprises. In this regard, the widely observed behaviour of Chinese LMEs to enhance their innovation capacity can be seen as entrepreneurial. One indication is their R&D activity. Between 1985 and 1993, the number of LMEs with in-house R&D centres increased from 1913 to 9503, or 29 per cent and 51 per cent respectively of the total. By 1993, the number of government-contracted R&D projects accounted for 32 per cent of the total, with the remainder being initiated by enterprises in response to market demand (ZTN 1994: 602, Ma 1993). In the context of rapidly expanding market demand, continuous and incremental technical change from collective learning has perhaps been an even more significant source of competitive advantage. Thus, the organizational restructuring in the pursuit of rationalization and flexibility mentioned above is likely to have been crucial for LMEs' good performance.

THE EAST ASIAN MODEL OF LATE INDUSTRIALIZATION

Technological development lies at the heart of East Asian industrialization, and the institutional environment within which technological development takes place has become a growing concern in development economics. In this section, we first briefly discuss the significance of technological development, and then turn to the institutional aspect. For the latter issue, we focus on corporate governance, while also devoting some space to the broader aspects of sectoral structure and state industrial policy.

In neoclassical economics, technology is treated as exogenous. The assumption of the existence of global production functions gives rise to the notorious proposition that the per capita income of countries tends to converge over time. This has now been seen as unsatisfactory even by leading neoclassical growth theorists (Solow 1994), but, ironically, it is still the basis of advice to the CEE countries (for example, Lipton and Sachs 1990).

The now fashionable theory of endogenous growth centres precisely around the recognition that technological development deliberately promoted by economic agents explains much of the observed experiences of development and underdevelopment (Romer 1994).

What causes technological development? The residual approach that is typically used in growth accounting analyses has been criticized as obscuring rather than illuminating. As for endogenous growth theory, despite all its efforts to develop an alternative to perfect competition and Pareto optimality, '(it) relies on externalities and R&D at precisely the time that a sense is emerging that one of the important factors determining intermediate and perhaps long-term productivity growth is organizational' (Pack 1994: 60). At one level, the significance of this remark can be grasped in connection with Alfred Chandler's thesis of the strategic firm that invests in governing the market (Teece 1993), as well as the notion of the entrepreneurial firm which portrays the firm as a collectively learning entity (Best 1990). At a broader level, the emphasis on organizational innovation can be incorporated into the discussion on techno-economic paradigms that is now the focus of various dissident strands of economics: structuralism, neo-Schumpeterian theory, flexible specialization, regulation, and so on. A common theme of these strands is on the connection between the nature of technical change and demand-side conditions, the latter being in turn regulated by social institutions. Succinctly, an appropriate match between the two sides (for example, mass production and mass consumption) can greatly promote productivity growth, while a mis-match would often result in crisis. But late-developing countries are far more prone to mis-match, because of their position as technology followers or receivers. The possibility of being trapped in a vicious circle of specializing in low skill/technology industries coupled with a low income level must, therefore, be taken seriously with respect to both China and the CEE countries.

The discussion thus points to the need for the state in late-developing countries to act strategically in mediating technology transfer and the inward investment of transnational corporations. It also pushes to the forefront the need for a sectoral approach to economic development: the promotion of dynamic industries in transcendence of the given international comparative advantage. Indeed, the endogeneity of technical change renders trivial or irrelevant the orthodox emphasis on 'getting the relative prices right': as Amsden (1989) has pointed out, in their early stage of industrialization, South Korea and Taiwan still could not compete with Japan in labour-intensive sectors on the basis of market-determined production costs. Ultimately, therefore, the crux of successful late industrialization rests with organizational innovations at the micro-level, in terms of governing-the-market investments, as well as collective learning which fosters the achievement of international competitiveness by domestic industries.

Amsden explains East Asia's experiences of successful late industrialization by the 'learning paradigm' (Amsden 1989: ch. 1). If they are to achieve industrialization in the context of an increasingly integrated global economy, latecomer nations must import foreign technology in order to avoid falling behind the rapid technical change taking place on the world scale. The crux of success is that learning – collectively for major participants of the production system – is the key to adopting, adapting and improving upon imported technology. It is by means of collective learning, together with the strategic mediation of the state, that South Korea and Taiwan have subsequently become competitive not only in labour-intensive sectors but also in a range of high-tech industries that did not accord with their initial international comparative advantage.

Focusing on corporate governance, and in a comparison between the Japanese and American firms, Aoki (1990: 9) proposes: '(in the situation) where external environments are continually changing but not too drastically, the J-mode is superior. In this case, the information value created by learning and horizontal coordination at the operational level may more than compensate for the loss of efficiency due to the sacrifice of operational specialization'. The 'J-mode' centres on three main features: horizontal coordination, long-term commitment and accountability to stakeholders. This links to the emphasis on the appropriate match between the organization of the production system and the pattern of economic growth. The competitive strength of Japanese firms rests on their capability of promoting horizontal coordination, and this mode of coordination covers major aspects of the production system: between workers, between workshops and divisions of the same firm (for example just-in-time practices), between separate firms in the same production chain which often takes the form of subcontracting, and between the firm and the externally financing entity as is expressed in the bank-oriented financial system.

What underpins such a capability? Conceivably, for participants of the production system to be willing to share with each other the tacit information/knowledge learnt from their work, it requires in the first place their long-term commitment to the system. The life-time employment system, the insulation of the management by the bank from takeover raids through the open market, the cross-shareholding among enterprises (*keiretsu*), and so on, therefore come into play. Ultimately, all these imply that an institutional arrangement whereby firms are accountable to major 'stakeholders', including both the external financing entities and the employees, rather than to shareholders alone, can be more conducive to productive efficiency, even if at the expense of allocative efficiency (Radice 1996).

This explanation of the East Asian experiences thus necessarily implies an erosion of the principles of market regulation and private property rights. The relative merits of the two contrasting approaches in promoting economic development, or avoiding underdevelopment, rest on the conceptualization of technological development which is ultimately an empirical question. A growing body of writing in the literature of both pure growth (and trade) theory and empirical studies of East Asia, and now China, tends to support the approach that we have outlined.

CONCLUSIONS

In this chapter we have sought to lay the groundwork for a more productive comparative study of the transformation process in CEE/FSU and in China – and indeed, hopefully, the wider study of the shift from central planning to forms of market economy. While disagreeing with much of their specific argument, we agree with Sachs and Woo (1994) that the comparison is difficult, because there are important differences not only in the starting-points of change, but also in ongoing circumstances that are in some sense exogenous to both economic management and institutional innovation.

The focus in section two on privatization and governance reflected the fact that, in the Visegrad countries at least, the early distinction between macroeconomic shock therapy (Poland) and gradualism (Hungary) is past history. The issue now is whether these economies can shift from short-term adjustment to renewed economic growth, and whether this growth will be 'developmental', or merely based on the exploitation of low labour costs and protected domestic markets: we argued that the conventional focus on establishing 'strong owners in a free market', with a minimal role for the state, will not be helpful. On the other hand, the focus in the third section was on explaining the actually rather good performance of Chinese SOEs, in terms of some incipient similarities with the East Asian model. The relative budget 'softness' has not prevented improvements in productive efficiency; state intervention has transcended the structural rigidities usually associated with central planning; and the cushioning of workers from the full rigours of the labour market provides a loyal resource for the management of change. In the fourth section, we then drew out those aspects of the East Asian model that seem most relevant for effective long-run development in the transforming economies. We highlighted in particular the development of technological capabilities through an enterprise system conducive to learning, and a coordinated and managed market system in which the state undertakes a strategic role.

Overall, then, our conclusion is that, making due allowance for very different circumstances, the differences in relative economic performance between CEE and China may be more to do with the degree of *de facto* emulation of the East Asian model, rather than the spread of market forces in the neoclassical conception. We are reminded of Chalmers Johnson's quote from a Chinese economist – this in about 1984: 'we write many articles about the Hungarian economy, but as you read them, you should understand that Hungary is a euphemism for the Republic of Korea' (Johnson 1986: 383–4). But are Hungarians studying the Republic of Korea in 1997?

NOTES

1. Since 1989, of course, this has changed. See the second section above.
2. For an analysis of the mergers, agglomerations and joint venture activities in the electronics industry, see Lo forthcoming: ch. 6.
3. On the organizational restructuring in the Chinese automobile industry, see Lo forthcoming: ch. 7.

REFERENCES

Amsden, A. (1989), *Asia's Next Giant: South Korea and Late Industrialization.* New York: Oxford University Press.
Aoki, M. (1990), 'Toward an economic model of the Japanese firm'. *Journal of Economic Literature*, 28: 1–27.
Best, M. (1990), *The New Competition: Institutions of Industrial Restructuring.* Cambridge: Polity Press.
Borensztein, E. and M. Kumar (1991), 'Proposals for privatization in Eastern Europe'. *IMF Staff Papers*, 38(2): 300–26.
Bowles, P. and X.Y. Dong (1994), 'Current successes and future challenges in China's economic reforms'. *New Left Review*, 208: 49–76.
Brada, J., I. Singh and A. Török (1994), *Firms Afloat and Firms Adrift: Hungarian Industry and the Economic Transition.* Armonk, NY: M.E. Sharpe.
Brom, K. and M. Orenstein (1994), 'The privatized sector in the Czech Republic: government and bank control in a transitional economy'. *Europe–Asia Studies*, 46(6): 893–928.
Business Central Europe (1996), 'Monopoly capitalism', June: 27–9.
Carlin, W., J. Van Reesen and T. Wolfe (1994), 'Enterprise restructuring in the transition: an analytical survey of the case study evidence from Central and Eastern Europe'. *EBRD Working Papers*, 14.
Chen, K., G. Jefferson and I. Singh (1992), 'Lessons from China's economic reform'. *Journal of Comparative Economics*, 16: 201–25.

Clarke, E. and A. Soulsby (1995), 'Transforming former state enterprises in the Czech Republic'. *Organization Studies*, 16(2): 215–42.

Corbett, J. and C. Mayer (1991), 'Financial reform in Eastern Europe: progress with the wrong model'. *Oxford Review of Economic Policy*, 7(4): 57–75.

Du, H.Y. and J.G. Guo (1993), 'Zhongguo guoyou qiye gaige: shidu, xingwei yu xiaolu' (China's state-owned enterprises reform: institutions, behaviours and efficiency). *Dongyu Luncong* (East Mountain Forum), 1: 35–48.

Fischer, S. and A. Gelb (1991), 'The process of socialist economic transformation'. *Journal of Economic Perspectives*, 5(4): 91–105.

Frydman, R. and A. Rapaczynski (1994), 'Privatization and corporate governance: can a market economy be designed?' in R. Frydman and A. Rapaczynski (eds), *Privatization in Eastern Europe: Is the State Withering Away?* London: Central European University Press.

Hare, P. and G. Hughes (1991), 'Competitiveness and industrial restructuring in Czechoslovakia, Hungary and Poland'. *Centre for Economic Policy Research Discussion Paper Series*, 543.

Hua, S., J.C. He, X.J. Zhang, X.P. Luo and Y.Z. Bian (1986), 'Weiguan jingji jichu de chongxin gouzao' (Reconstruction of the microeconomic foundation). *Jingji Yanjiu* (Economic Research), 3: 21–8.

Jefferson, G. and W.Y. Xu (1994), 'Assessing gains in efficient production among China's industrial enterprises'. *Economic Development and Cultural Change*, 42(3): 597–615.

Johnson, C. (1986), 'The non-socialist NICs: East Asia'. in E. Comisso and L. Tyson (eds), *Power, Purpose and Collective Choice: Economic Strategy in Socialist States*. Ithaca, NY: Cornell University Press.

Karsai, J. and M. Wright (1994), 'Accountability, governance and finance in Hungarian buyouts'. *Europe–Asia Studies* 46(6): 997–1016.

Kornai, J. (1990), *The Road to a Free Economy. Shifting from a Socialist System: the Example of Hungary*. New York: W.W. Norton.

Laki, M. (1994), 'Firm behaviour during a long transitional recession'. *Acta Oeconomica* 46(3–4): 347–70.

Landesmann, M. and I. Székely (1991), 'Industrial restructuring and the reorientation of trade in Czechoslovakia, Hungary and Poland'. *Centre for Economic Policy Research Discussion Paper Series*, 546.

Lee, K. (1991), *Chinese Firms and the State in Transition: Property Rights and Agency Problems in the Reform Era*. Armonk, NY: M.E. Sharpe.

Lipton, D. and J. Sachs (1990), 'Creating a market economy in Eastern Europe: the case of Poland'. *Brookings Papers on Economic Activity*, 1: 75–147.

Liu, S.J. (1993), 'Guangyu guoyou qiye laodong tizhi gaige de jige wenti' (Several issues concerning the reform of the labour employment system of SOEs).*Jingji Lilun yu Jingji Guangli* (Economic Theory and Economic Management), 5: 30–3.

Lo, D. (forthcoming), *Market and Institutional Regulation in Chinese Industrialization, 1978–1994*. London: Macmillan Press.

Ma, J.T. (1992), 'Woguo guoyuo qiye xingwei mupiao de shizheng fengxi' (An empirical study of the behavioural objectives of our country's state-owned enterprises), *Jingji Yanjiu* (Economic Research), 7: 20–6.

Ma, X.L. (1993), 'Quanguo dazhongxing gongye qiye jishu kaifa he jishu maoyi zhuangkuang de tongji fengxi' (A statistical analysis of the situation of R&D activity and technology transactions by large-and-medium industrial enterprises),

Kexue yu Kexue Jishu Guangli (Sciences and Scientific and Technical Management), 2: 32–7.

McMillan, J. and B. Naughton (1992), 'How to reform a planned economy: lessons from China'. *Oxford Review of Economic Policy* 8(1): 130–43.

Naughton, B. (1994), 'What is distinctive about China's economic transition? State enterprise reform and overall system transformation'. *Journal of Comparative Economics*, 18: 470–90.

Newbery, D. and P. Kattuman (1992), 'Market concentration and competition in Eastern Europe'. *The World Economy*, 15(3): 315–33.

Pack, H. (1994), 'Endogenous growth theory: intellectual appeal and empirical shortcomings'. *Journal of Economic Perspectives*, 8(1): 55–72.

Radice, H. (1993), 'Global integration, national disintegration? Foreign capital in the reconstitution of capitalism in Central and Eastern Europe'. *University of Leeds School of Business and Economic Studies Discussion Papers*, E93/09.

Radice, H. (1995), 'Organising markets in Central and Eastern Europe: competition, governance and the role of foreign capital' in E. Dittrich, G. Schmidt and R. Whitley (eds), *Industrial Transformation in Europe*. London: Sage Publications: 109–33.

Radice, H. (1996), 'Stakeholder capitalism'. *University of Leeds Centre for Industrial Policy and Performance Bulletin*.

Roland, G. (1995), 'Political economy issues of ownership transformation in Eastern Europe', in M. Aoki and H.K. Kim (eds), *Corporate Governance in Transitional Economies: Insider Control and the Role of the Banks*. Washington, DC: The World Bank.

Romer, P. (1994), 'The origins of endogeneous growth'. *Journal of Economic Perspectives*, 8(1): 3–22.

Sachs, J. and W.T. Woo (1994a), 'Reform in China and Russia'. *Economic Policy*, 18: 101–45.

Solow, R. (1994), 'Perspectives on Growth Theory'. *Journal of Economic Perspectives*, 8(1): 45–54.

State Commission for Economic System Reform (SCESR) (1992) 'Jiushiniandai: zhouxiang chengshuo de zhongguo jingji' (China's economy in the 1990s: towards maturity), *Guangli Shijie* (Management World), 5: 11–20.

Tang, Z.K. (1992) 'Guoyuo qiye lirun zhuangyi he qiye zaishenchan nenli' (Drain and redistribution of profits and reproduction capacity of state-owned enterprises), *Jingji Yanjiu* (Economic Research), 7: 9–19.

Teece, D. (1993), 'The dynamics of industrial capitalism: perspectives on Alfred Chandler's *Scale and Scope*'. *Journal of Economic Literature*, 31: 199–225.

Tittenbrun, J. (1995), 'The managerial revolution revisited: the case of privatization in Poland'. *Capital & Class*, 55: 21–32.

Wade, R. (1990), *Governing the Market: Economic Theory and the Role of Government in East Asian Industrialization*. Princeton, NJ: Princeton University Press.

Wang, H.J. and B.X. Li (1991), *Zhongguo Zhongchangqi Changye Zhence* (China's medium and long term industrial policy). Beijing: Zhongguo Caizhen Jingji Chubanshe.

Weitzman, M. and C.G. Xu (1994), 'Chinese township–village enterprises as vaguely defined cooperatives'. *Journal of Comparative Economics*, 18: 121–45.

van Wijnbergen, S. (1993), 'Enterprise reform in Eastern Europe'. *Economics of Transition*, 1(1): 21–38.

Williamson, O. *et al.* (1975), 'Understanding the employment relation: the analysis of idiosyncratic exchange'. *Bell Journal of Economics*, 6: 250–78.

Woo, W.T. (1994), 'The art of reforming centrally planned economies: comparing China, Poland, and Russia'. *Journal of Comparative Economics*, 18(3): 276–308.

Zhang, S.J. (1987), *Jingji Yunxing yu Jingji Tiaojie* (Economic operation and economic regulation). Hanzhou: Zhejiang Renmin Chubanshe.

Zheng, H.L. (1993), 'Xiangzhen qiye zhidu gouzhao tedian ji qidui guoyou qiye gaige de qishi' (Characteristics of the institutional set-ups of TVEs and revelations for the reform of SOEs), *Jingji Lilun yu Jingji Guangli* (Economic Theory and Economic Management), 1: 46–51.

Zhongguo Gongye Jingji Tongji Nianjian (ZGJTN) (China Industrial Economics Statistical Yearbook) (1993). Beijing: Zhongguo Tongji Chubanshe.

Zhongguo Tongji Nianjian (ZTN) (China Statistical Yearbook), various years. Beijing: Zhongguo Tongji Chubanshe.

Part III
National Specificities

7 Institutional Foundations of Robust Economic Performance: Public-Sector Industrial Growth in China[1]

Victor Nee and Sijin Su

China's economic reform was launched by fiscal decentralization, the gradual delegation of decision-making from the central state to local authorities and enterprises. The reform resulted in prodigious economic growth. From 1978 to 1991, the deflated growth rate of China's national income was more than 10 per cent per year. By 1991, its national income was nearly three times as large as that of 1978, transforming China into the third largest economy in the world after the United States and Japan. This sustained economic growth is difficult to explain. China lacks many of the conditions that economists look for in accounting for sustained economic growth. No plan for the privatization of public property was implemented as in Eastern Europe and Russia. Private property rights remain insecure and poorly enforced. The state does not serve as a neutral third party enforcer of contracts. The monitoring and enforcement of laws and regulations are often arbitrary and inconsistent. Economic markets are intertwined with political markets in which officials secure rents in exchange for administrative favours. Such features of the institutional environment in China ought not to promote sustained economic growth according to orthodox economic reasoning (North and Thomas 1973, Eggertsson 1990). Why then has the Chinese industrial economy maintained such a spectacular rate of sustained growth?

This chapter examines the cumulative changes in institutional arrangements governing the Chinese industrial economy. A number of competing hypotheses contend to explain China's remarkable economic performance in recent decades. A provocative state-centred explanation of China's recent economic performance is provided by Oi (1989, 1992) and Walder (1995). They argue that privatization is not required as long as there are secure property rights for some organized unit and sufficient incentives for that unit to pursue growth. According to this view, China's fiscal reform has provided local governments rights over income generated by collective-owned firms, creating strong incentives for local officials to foster economic growth. Local governments have taken on characteristics of a multi-divisional firm, with state officials acting as the equivalent of a board of directors. In this capacity, officials plan and co-ordinate economic activities in their territorial jurisdiction much like the board of directors of a company. They make all investment decisions and take risks like capitalists in market economies. It is the local government that is responsible for shaping the outcome of reform; hence, according to this state-centred account, political actors are the real entrepreneurs, not economic actors in the fledgling private sector nor even managers in public-owned firms.

The state-centred analysis treats markets as a background factor, rather than as an explanatory variable. The success and survival of firms is still determined by the socialist state, albeit its local agent. Firms readily conform to a script written for them by local state officials as their autonomy has been strictly circumscribed by those same officials who are said to appoint managers, make investment decisions, and decide on business strategy for the network of local firms owned by government. Rather than the shift to markets improving economic performance, the state-centred approach attributes the success of Chinese reforms to improved incentives for political actors. Above all, the state-centred approach posits that change in the structure of property rights is not needed to produce dramatic improvements in economic performance in rural enterprises under local government control. Individual agents need not have rights over the firm's profits for economic growth to occur, because there is no inherent reason why secure property rights will be an incentive only if they are assigned to private interests.

Economists influenced by the work of Janos Kornai are sceptical about the claims of the state-centred account outlined above. Just the sort of monitoring and enforcement activity by government that Walder (1995) contends has been a key ingredient of China's success in rural industrial growth, would in Kornai's (1990) view, be the cause of what he has identified as the dilemma of partial reform. Such state interventions, according to Kornai, perpetuate the institutional dynamics of the shortage economy in which persistent micro-interventions in the firms' investment decisions and management operate to confound the effort to introduce market discipline. In the Kornai-inspired account, local state control results in the same outcome as state ownership at higher levels of government (Wong 1987, 1990, 1992). Fiscal reform transferring bureaucratic control of public property to local governments gives rise to incentives for a single-minded pursuit of industrial growth as a means to offset the decline in budgetary revenues and to generate needed extra-budgetary revenues in order to finance growing local expenditures. As a result, political actors have an incentive to pursue extensive economic growth whether or not it results in profitable ventures. In the process, Wong (1992: 198) asserts they have created problems of persistent over-investment, duplication, regional blockages and continuing bureaucratic management of industry. This Kornai-inspired interpretation rejects the argument that public property rights poses no problem so long as the local state has secure rights over the revenues of industrial firms.

Despite their differences, however, both the Oi/Walder and Kornai/Wong interpretations emphasize an underlying continuity in the institutional structures governing the post-socialist industrial economy. In both accounts, government still behaves like the state did in the Maoist era, dictating and manipulating local economic life according to a state-imposed logic of extensive economic growth. Both interpretations undervalue the effect of expanding economic markets on the behaviour of public-sector firms and governments.[2] A reconciliation of the two seemingly conflicting accounts is seen in Walder's (1995) argument that the Kornai position accounts for the poor economic performance of enterprises owned by higher levels of government. However, at the lower levels of the industrial hierarchy, local government has clearer incentives and '*a greater ability to monitor firms and enforce their interests as owners*' (Walder 1995: 266, emphasis in the original). This, combined with harder budget constraints, in his view accounts for the remarkable economic performance of township and village firms.

The strength of the state-centred account of robust economic performance in the Chinese industrial economy is that it provides a consistent interpretation of weak and strong performance of state-owned firms at the higher and lower rungs of the industrial hierarchy. Its limitations, however, are: first, information even at the local level is costly. Methodical capital accounting is not commonly practised by rural enterprises. Although local government is in spatial proximity to the firm, the cost of monitoring and enforcement can be considerable, especially in industrial districts where firms are numerous and large. Local governments in fact experience growing costs of monitoring and enforcement relative to the pre-reform era because the shift to markets increases the scope and pay-off for malfeasance and opportunism, not only for economic actors, but also for agents of the state. Second, if local political agents are unrestrained in their capacity to intervene, as Walder argues, the local state is also free to redistribute economic surplus from the firm. Oi (1989) portrayed the state as a predatory agent with respect to its efforts to appropriate resources from rural communities. What institutional constraints keep the socialist state from persisting in its past predatory behaviour?[3] The state-centred account does not have an answer to this question because it must argue that local government has clear and undisputed property rights over the firm: control of the firm, its income and use of its assets (Walder 1995). Third, although local governments have limited financial capacity to subsidize loss-making firms, nonetheless, local agents of the state have a political incentive to maintain full employment, and hence like the central state, they redistribute resources to subsidize loss-making ventures. The board of directors analogy used to describe the role of local government stretches thin at this point: boards of directors of capitalist companies are not similarly committed to redistributive goals with respect to the local political economy.

By focusing only on changing incentives to political actors, state-centred analysis omits economic actors from an explanation of economic performance. Yet, an adequate explanation of sustained economic growth in China must focus on changing incentives for economic as well as for political actors. We argue that economic actors in firms, backed by corporatist governments, fuelled the remarkable growth of rural industry in China. The sinews of robust economic performance are institutional arrangements that bring economic and political actors into a compact in which devotion to market-oriented economic growth provides a basis for conjoint action. Geographical proximity and shared interests combine to buttress network ties that sustain flexible adaptation to the changing institutional environment. Our explanation of sustained improvements in economic performance in China emphasizes the interplay between institutions, networks and shared interests joining economic and political actors in local corporatist governance structures (Nee and Su 1996). This story is of the same genre as the studies of robust economic performance in industrial districts such as Silicon Valley and the Third Italy (Saxenian 1994, Piore and Sabel 1984). Rather than an emphasis on how interfirm networks provide the basis for rapid technological innovations and cooperation between firms, our account highlights the importance of flexible adaptation and shared interests between economic and political actors within Chinese local corporatist governance structures (see also Che and Qian 1996). The political economy of local corporatism is similar to other East Asian developmental states, except that more takes place at the local level in China (Amsden 1989, Wade 1990, Evans 1995). Local corporatism combined with central state interventions in maintaining macroeconomic policies favourable to market-oriented growth constitutes the essential core of the Chinese strategy of economic development (McMillan and Naughton 1996).

To be sure, fiscal decentralization provided sufficient incentives for local government to pursue growth-oriented measures (Oi 1992). But at the firm level, responsibility contracts specifying profit-sharing arrangements between local government and firms restructured the relationship between government and firm, providing the institutional foundations for sustained improvement in economic performance. Through profit-sharing, property rights in government-owned firms were in effect partitioned by means of *ex ante* agreements that specified the share of profits retained by the firm. Although formally the structure of property rights remained under state ownership, local government's rights over public-sector firms was attenuated through profit-sharing arrangements. Property rights are defined as rights over the use of assets, rights to earn income and the right to transfer ownership to another party. Alchian described the partitioning of property rights:

> By this I refer to the fact that at the same time several people may each possess some portion of the rights to use the land. A may possess the right to grow wheat on it. B may possess the right to walk across it. C may possess the right to dump ashes and smoke on it. D may possess the right to fly an airplane over it. E may have the right to subject it to vibrations consequent to the use of some neighbouring equipment. And each of these rights may be transferable. In sum, private property rights to various partitioned uses of land are owned by different persons (Alchian 1977: 132–3, quoted in Eggertsson 1990).

Profit-sharing arrangements diffused quickly in the Chinese industrial economy. By 1987, 80 per cent of state-owned enterprises and 95 per cent of collective-owned enterprises had negotiated some form of profit-sharing with government. Contracts backing profit-sharing arrangements furnished the institutional foundation for local corporatist governance structures. We define local corporatism as a social institution linking local government and a network of firms in a loosely coupled coalition aimed at promoting market-oriented growth. A characteristic feature of the Chinese corporatist governance structure is the use of dense network ties to promote flexibility and responsiveness in the relationship between government and firm. Local officials in local corporatist governance structures selectively interpret and enforce rules and regulations in dealing with economic actors in local firms. In local corporatist arrangements, local governments expend less effort in monitoring firms and enforcing their interests. This is because economic actors in the firm have a strong incentive to improve economic performance under profit-sharing arrangements. The better the incentives for gains in productivity for economic actors in firms, the less effort is required by local government to monitor firms.

The institutional arrangement of profit-sharing is in essence not a redistributive mechanism because it requires that government make a credible commitment to limit *ex ante* its appropriation of economic surplus. In unreformed state socialism, the state has the right to claim the entire surplus.

Profit-sharing subtly changes the structure of property rights in publicly owned firms by attenuating the rights of the state over revenues generated by the firm. Although the formal structure of ownership remains state-owned, the contractual agreement between local government and firm allows for a partitioning of property rights favourable to economic actors. Political actors likewise have an interest in the success of the firm, hence in working within the rules of the game specified by the hybrid governance structure. Profit-sharing contractual arrangements are highly variable in China, with some resembling long-term lease agreements between local government and private entrepreneurs. Such lease agreements amount to privatization of community property in so far as leases can be passed on to heirs and sold in secondary markets. Others involve rights to use state-owned property to generate income as in the Yugoslav model. In the latter type, managers in firms distribute profits to workers through salary increases and bonuses contingent on improved economic performance.

The emergence of profit-sharing contractual arrangements in China distinguishes the decentralization process in the era of reform from past experiments in non-market economic development. China's trial-and-error approach to economic reform experimented with institutional innovations aimed at improving incentives in order to stimulate gains in productivity. A variety of experiments were pursued in the Chinese effort to remake the economic institutions of state socialism. The responsibility contract, first used successfully in agriculture after decollectivization, became a model for enterprise reform. In the organizational setting of the industrial firm, the responsibility system quickly evolved into profit-sharing contracts negotiated between the firm and local government. As an institutional innovation, profit-sharing responded to broad parameter shifts in China's transition economy. These involved the weakening of the socialist redistributive economy through fiscal decentralization and the emergence of markets. The effect of these shifts in parameters was to increase substantially the cost of monitoring and enforcement by government at the same time as local governments acquired strong incentives to promote economic growth.

DECLINE OF SOCIALIST REDISTRIBUTION

In the 1980s, the Chinese economy shifted decisively away from non-market mechanisms for coordinating economic activity, to increasing reliance on markets and quasi-markets. This decline in socialist redistribution is evident in the trends reported in Table 7.1 which shows a broad-based dissolution of the redistributive mechanism controlled by the central government during the first decade of reform. First, a dramatic decline took place in the proportion of factor resources that were subject to allocation by central planning. This declined from 70 per cent in 1980 to under 14 per cent in 1991. With respect to the distribution of manufactured goods, the categories of products subject to mandatory distribution through non-market channels decreased from 120 in 1980 to 50 in 1988 to make up only 16.2 per cent of the total value of industrial output. By 1991, the number dropped to only 21 categories. Parallel to this, the number of commodities distributed by the state supply bureaucracy declined from 256 in 1980 to only 19 by 1989. These massive shifts away from central planning led to significant declines in the redistributive role of the central government.

The shift to reliance on market coordination is seen in Table 7.2 (page 175). At the outset of reform, market regulation of prices was restricted to a small number of agricultural and light industrial products sold in local marketplaces. The prices for all heavy industrial products, and most agricultural and light industrial products were set by the state. Although the state continued to set the prices for key agricultural and industrial products, the greater reliance on market clearing prices is clearly revealed in the far right column of Table 7.2. By the early 1990s, the state was no longer the dominant force in determining the prices of goods and services in the Chinese economy.

Prior to economic reform, the single largest item in the state investment budget was funds allocated for capital construction projects in state-owned enterprises. One aspect of the state's allocation of investment capital was that resources from profitable firms and manufacturing centres like Shanghai were redistributed to less developed inland regions. Table 7.3 (page 175) shows a rapid decline in this redistributive role of government. Prior to reform, state funds accounted for over 78 per cent of the cost of capital construction in state-owned firms. This had declined to 16.5 per cent by 1991.

The diminished investment capital provided by the central state for all firms is reported in Table 7.4 (page 176). This dropped from just over 62 per cent in 1978 to under 7 per cent in 1991. The category of self-raised investment funds refers to capital accumulated by local governments and firms. This increased from less than 32 per cent in 1978 (listed in the 'other' category) to over 52 per cent in 1991. At the same time loans from state-owned banks (23.5 per cent) and foreign-sources of capital (5.7 per cent) became significant sources of investment capital for industrial firms. Combined, Tables 7.3 and 7.4 show that by the end of the 1980s, state-owned firms no longer could rely on the central state as a source of investment capital. Instead, the

Table 7.1   Change in Degree of Economic Activities Subject to
Central Mandatory Plan

Areas/Year	1980	1987	1988	1989	1991
Production:					
Percent industrial materials subject to state mandatory plan[1]	70%		20%		13.8%
Distribution:					
number of industrial products subject to central state mandatory plan (kinds)	120	60	50[2]		21
number of commodities distributed by the Department of Commerce (kinds)	256	27		19	
number of industrial products allocated by state redistribution (kinds)	188	22			
Budgetary Investment by the Central Government:	63.3%		24.6%		
Project-Approving Authority:					
For production for single project (million yuan)	10		30		
For energy, raw materials & transportation	10	50			
For Guangdong, Fujian, Hainan and Shenzhen	10		200[3]		
Export Planning:					
number of export products subject to state unified export plan	800			27	
Import Planning:					
number of imports subject to state unified import plan (kinds)				13[4]	
number of imports subject to quota management (kinds)				470	
Foreign Currency Income:					
foreign currency income subject to state foreign currency control plan				50%[5]	

Notes to Table 7.1
[1] Out of the total demand of firms and localities for these materials.
[2] That is 16.2 per cent out of the total industrial output value. The figure was 40 per cent in 1978.
[3] For investment used for the purpose of production, innovation or investment in line with the state's industrial policy.
[4] Sharing 40 per cent of the total import volume.
[5] Out of the total foreign currency income.

Sources Zhongguo Jingji Tizhi Gaige Shinian 1989: 798.
Liu, Z. (1991), 'The new trends of planning system after the reforms', *Jingji Gaige* (China Economic System Reform Yearbook) 1992.

Table 7.2 Decline in Price Control by State (Calculation Based on Output Value)

Type	1979		1991	
	State control	Market regulation	State control	Market regulation
Agricultural products	92	8	24	76
Light industrial products	95	5	30	70
Heavy industrial products	100	0	42	58

Source China Economic System Reform Yearbook 1992: 779

Table 7.3 Sources of Capital Construction in State-owned Enterprises (Unit: 100 million yuan)

Year	Capital construction	State budgetary investment	B/A%
1977	382.37	299.23	78.26
1978	500.99	389.21	77.69
1979	523.48	396.92	75.82
1980	558.89	300.11	53.70
1981	442.91	222.62	50.26
1982	555.53	232.48	41.85
1983	3594.13	295.97	49.82
1984	743.15	359.85	48.42
1985	1074.37	381.67	35.48
1986	1176.11	417.39	35.49
1987	1343.10	437.85	32.60
1988	1574.31	381.67	24.24
1989	1551.74	323.33	20.84
1990	1703.81	363.59	21.34
1991	2115.80	348.45	16.47

Source Almanac of China's Economy 1992: 860

Table 7.4   Change in Sources of Fixed Capital Investment of Society (per cent)

Sources	1957	1978	1980	1985	1988	1989	1990	1991
State budgetary investment	88.6	62.2	44.7	16.0	9.0	8.3	8.7	6.8
Domestic loans	–	1.7	11.7	20.1	20.6	17.3	19.5	23.5
Foreign capital	–	4.2	7.2	3.1	5.7	6.6	6.3	5.7
Self-raised funds	11.4	31.9	36.5	60.3	54.5	56.9	52.4	52.3
Other					10.3	10.9	13.1	11.7

Sources Zhongguo Tongji Nianjian 1990: China Statistic Press 1996: 27; *Zhongguo Qiyue Guanli Nianjian* 1992: China Enterprise Management Press: 537.

sources of capital became more varied, and based more on assessments of the firm's performance and potential for profitability than on the political priorities of the state. The overall trend was towards greater reliance on local sources of investment capital, consistent with the policy of fiscal decentralization. By 1988, as shown in Table 7.5, a key reversal took place in which local governments became the primary source of budgetary expenditures by the state.

Table 7.5   Budgetary Expenditures: Central versus Local

Year	1957	1978	1980	1985	1988
Total Expenditures (%)	100	100	100	100	100
Central (%)	71.8	46.9	53.7	45.3	39.2
Local (%)	28.2	53.1	46.3	54.7	60.8

Source   *China Statistics Yearbook* 1990: 27

During the 1980s, the transition away from economic development directed by the central state to greater reliance on market-oriented local development is reflected in the changing distribution of labour in the non-farm economy. Table 7.6 shows that non-farm employment in the state sector declined relative to the non-state sectors. In 1980, the state sector employed nearly 57 per cent of the non-farm labour force. This declined to only 41.4 per cent by 1991. The data also indicate that the central state did not simply transfer control over local industrial growth to local government. Non-farm employment in township and village enterprises grew from 24.4 per cent to 36.4 per cent. Though still a small part of the total non-farm labour force, the growth rate of the private sector was considerably faster. The private sector emerged to provide a new source of non-farm employment not controlled by government, growing from 1.5 per cent of the non-farm labour force in 1980 to 8.2 per cent by 1991.

Table 7.6   Change in Distribution of Labour Forces Across Ownership Forms in Non-farming Sectors (per cent)

Year	State	Urban collective	Township enterprises	Private	Total
1980	56.9	17.2	24.4	1.5	100
1991	41.4	14.0	36.4	8.2	100

Source   China Economic System Reform Yearbook 1992: 766.

In the course of a decade, the redistributive power of the central state had declined markedly as the Chinese economy shifted to greater reliance on market coordination. Although fiscal decentralization transferred control over public-sector firms down the administrative hierarchy, local governments faced an institutional environment shaped increasingly by competitive markets. They could no longer rely to the same extent on clientelist politics, based on resource dependence on the state, to enforce their interests. The underlying problem of weak economic incentives which characterized industrial enterprises in the pre-reform era was not addressed by relying principally on negative sanctions. Fiscal decentralization fostered an interest on the part of government to generate revenues through market-oriented economic growth. But sustained improvement in economic performance could not be realized through the pre-reform political approach to control and intervention. It is in the context of changing parameters and the declining redistributive power of the central state combined with the penetration of competitive markets (which we describe below), that profit-sharing arrangements diffused quickly through China to provide a hybrid governance structure redefining the property rights relationship between local government and the industrial firm.

EMERGENCE OF MARKETS

In the 1980s the shift away from state socialist redistribution in China was accompanied by the rapid growth and diversification of market institutions. Table 7.7 reports the increase in the number of free markets, which more than doubled from 1978 to 1991. The volume of transactions in these markets increased at a even more rapid rate than the openings of new market places. Although rural markets were far more numerous than urban markets, the volume of trade in urban markets by 1991 was only a third less than the total volume of transactions in rural market places. Table 7.8 shows that not only did product markets increase, but so did the diversity of market institutions. Prior to economic reform, markets were limited to government-regulated free markets in rural areas. By the 1990s, market institutions included a wide variety of market arrangements, including many types of commodity markets, labour markets, real estate markets, financial markets and lending institutions. Moreover, regional and provincial market centres that flourished prior to the revolution quickly re-emerged to serve their purposes as central marketing hubs for intermediate and local markets. This is seen, for example, in the south-eastern provinces of Guangdong and Fujian where dense multiplex regional marketing networks became linked to the economies of Hong Kong and Taiwan to create the social bases for a newly emergent market economy. Likewise, in the Sunan region, marketing networks linked industrializing towns with the metropolitan economy of Shanghai.

Table 7.7   Rural and Urban Free Markets: Number and Transaction Volume

	1978	1980	1985	1990	1991
Total #	33 302	40 809	61 337	72 579	74 675
urban	–	2 919	8 013	13 106	13 891
rural	33 302	37 890	53 324	59 473	60 784
Total volume					
(100 million)	125.0	235.0	705.0	2168.2	2622.2
urban	–	24.0	181.0	837.8	1079.3
rural	125.0	211.0	524.0	1330.4	1542.9

Source   *Yearbook of China Economic Systems Reform* 1992: 797. Beijing: China Economic Reform Press.

Labour markets have expanded rapidly in recent years in China, especially in the south-eastern maritime provinces from Guangdong to the Yangzi Delta region surrounding Shanghai. Labour market institutions include service companies, employment agencies, professional and technical personnel exchange centres, and general contracting companies that export labour overseas. By the end of 1991, there were 65 000 labour contract companies through which about 8 million workers were employed. Complementing these were more than 10 000 employment agencies and 2000 career training centres. Thirty-six million contract workers, including two million who worked for joint ventures involving foreign firms and 20 million workers in the private sector, found their jobs through labour markets of some kind. In 1995, a contract employment system was extended to all employees in the state-owned sector, eliminating the socialist system of permanent employment.

Table 7.8   Market Institutions in 1991

Types of market	Number
Rural and urban free markets	74675
Agricultural and by-product wholesale markets	1509
Industrial general merchandise wholesale markets	3400
Industrial consumer goods wholesale markets	1000
Capital goods wholesale markets (annual transaction at least totaling 50 billion yuan)	1000
Property right markets	8
Real estate development companies	3700
Real estate management companies	4700
Labor markets/market institutions	65000
Real estate exchange centers	1500
Financial markets:	
a. Trust and investment companies	377
b. Securities companies	66
c. Foreign wholly-owned banks/branches	38
d. Urban credit associations	3000
e. Rural credit associations	60000

Source   *Yearbook of China Economic Systems Reform* 1992: 800, 776. Beijing: China Economic Reform Press.

A small but rapidly growing real estate market handling transactions involving urban and township land-use rights, the purchase and sale of private housing, mortgages, and the leasing and rental of homes and offices has emerged in China. The growth of the real estate market indicates that land, which remains state-owned, can now be bought and sold through market-like transactions. The market for land can best be described as a quasi-market because price-setting by local officials to favour clients with personal connections is a common practice. Local governments sell use-rights in real estate markets in which *guanxi* ties are routinely critical to successful deal-making.

The expansion of markets involves the rapid penetration of international markets into China's domestic markets, especially in the maritime provinces. This is seen in the growth of foreign-funded firms (*sanzi qiye*). The maritime provinces are increasingly linked to the broader East Asian regional economy. By 1991, there were 37 215 foreign-funded firms in China with a registered capital stock of US$46 billion. The south-eastern maritime provinces are rapidly emerging as the site of major manufacturing centres integrated into the global market economy. Foreign investments has been increasingly steadily, with overseas Chinese, Taiwan, Japan and the United States providing the largest sources of foreign capital. The number of joint ventures and wholly foreign-owned firms in Guangdong and Fujian provinces is unsurpassed in China.

Markets for capital goods expanded rapidly in scale during the decade of the 1980s. In 1985, there were very few capital goods wholesale markets in China. The total volume of any single market was no more than 1 billion yuan. By 1991, the volume of transactions in the capital goods markets grew to 1000 billion yuan. The total volume of securities of various types issued in 1991 came to 236.2 billion yuan, with 60 billion yuan of equity shares changing hands that year (YBCESR 1992: 776). By 1991, there were over two million shareholders, with the number growing by about 50 000 a week. China's stock market already reports the highest volume of trade in Asia outside of Japan (*New York Times*, 9 May 1993: B1).

The retail market has expanded rapidly in China. Table 7.9 shows that in Guangdong province, the density of the product market has increased from one retail market per 503 persons in 1980 to one per 89 persons by 1991 (*Outlook Weekly*, 24 May 1993). The number of retail stores increased from 13 per 10 000 persons in 1978 to 108.8 in 1991. Parallel with this, the number of customers served by a retail store employee dropped from 214 person for every employee to 52 in 1991. There are now over 75 000 local retail markets in China. These are combining into a vast national marketing network. It is estimated that of the 8.71 million retail firms nationwide, 89 per cent of them are privately owned (*Outlook Weekly,* 31 May 1993: 14).

Table 7.9   Density of Commercial Retail Market Networks

	1978	*1980*	*1985*	*1990*	*1991*
No. Average of customers served per retail sale employee	214	154	58	55	52
No. of retail sale services per 10 000 persons	13	–	101	104	109

Source   China Economic Systems Reform Yearbook 1992: 798, 804. Beijing: China Economic Reform Press.

The growth and diversification of markets described above have implications for the behaviour of local government and firms. The number and variety of markets and the dramatic increase in the sheer volume of market transactions comprise a significant source of discontinuous change. Firms are no longer dependent on the state supply bureaucracy for inputs and for the distribution of their products. Instead they now can go directly to producers, wholesale markets and even international markets in competitive bids to gain price advantages and market share. Also, with the emergence of regional marketing networks, competition is no longer limited to firms in a local market, but is regional and even global in scope.

Parameter shifts in the institutional environment alters the relative costs of alternative governance structures (Nee 1992). A thicker market environment intensifies competition for resources and market share, and contributes to the legitimacy of rules backing market processes. The old rules of the game, by contrast, are undercut as the market environment thickens. This disadvantages state-owned firms, while it especially favours private firms. Firms operating within the local corporatist governance structure also benefit from the shift to markets, notably if they are able to exercise competitive exclusion by maintaining barriers to entry for private firms. Firms operating within the local corporatist governance structure maintain a comparative advantage in so far as local government backing provides access to key resources and strategic connections in an industrial economy in which state-owned firms still comprise the dominant organizational forms. However, when private firms gain a critical foothold in market niches, competition intensifies for resources and market share.

PROFIT SHARING AS AN INCENTIVE STRUCTURE

The incentives for the state to maintain profit-sharing arrangements with publicly-owned firms are clearly seen in the rapid increase in revenues to state-coffers. Table 7.10 (a and b) shows that budgetary and extra-budgetary revenues for both the central and local state increased dramatically in absolute and relative terms. In 1991, the budgetary revenues of the central and local government were respectively nearly eight and over twice as large as in 1979. The central state's share of total budgetary revenues increased from 14.3 per cent in 1979 to just over 35 per cent in 1991.

Extra-budgetary revenues refer to the income generated from non-budgetary sources. Not well understood is that both central and local government has experienced rapid growth of revenues from extra-budgetary sources. The extra-budgetary revenue of central and local government in 1990 were respectively four and three times as large as they were in 1982. The increase in extra-budgetary revenue came mainly from profit-sharing arrangements set up in joint ventures between central ministries and local

Table 7.10   Budgetary and Extra-budgetary Revenues: Central and Local State
A: Absolute term (unit: 100 million)

Year	Total budgetary revenues	Central	Local	Total extra-budgetary revenues	Central	Local
1978	1121.12			347.11		
1979	1067.96	152.72	915.24	452.85		
1980	1042.22	166.74	875.48	557.40		
1981	1016.38	151.67	864.71	601.07		
1982	1083.94	218.45	865.49	802.74		
1983	1211.16	334.22	876.94	967.68	270.70	532.04
1984	1467.05	489.66	977.39	1188.48	359.90	607.78
1985	1837.16	678.63	1158.53	1530.03	470.54	717.94
1986	2184.52	840.93	1343.59	1737.31	636.10	893.93
1987	2262.42	799.36	1463.06	2028.80	716.63	1020.68
1988	2489.41	906.93	1582.48	2360.77	828.03	1200.77
1989	2803.81	961.43	1842.38	2658.83	907.15	1453.62
1990	3134.34	1189.66	1944.68	2708.64	1072.28	1586.55
1991	3409.10	1195.90	2213.20	2850.00	1073.28	1635.36

B: Relative terms (%)

Year	Total budgetary investment Central	(A) Local	Total extra budgetary investment Central	(B) Local	B/A
1978					31.0
1979	14.3	85.7			42.4
1980	16.0	84.0			53.5
1981	14.9	85.1			59.5
1982	20.2	79.8	33.7	66.3	74.1
1983	27.6	72.4	37.2	62.8	79.9
1984	33.4	66.6	39.6	60.4	81.0
1985	36.9	63.1	41.6	58.4	83.3
1986	38.5	61.5	41.2	58.8	79.5
1987	35.3	64.7	40.8	59.2	89.7
1988	36.4	63.6	38.4	61.6	94.8
1989	34.3	65.7	40.3	59.7	94.8
1990	38.0	62.0	39.6	60.4	86.4
1991	35.1	64.9			83.6

Source   *China Economic Systems Reform Yearbook* 1992: 773. Beijing: China
Economic Reform Press.

governments and firms. In 1978 extra-budgetary revenues for both central
and local governments was 31 per cent of the budgetary revenues. These

jumped to nearly 84 per cent in 1991. The central government's interest in profit-sharing is reflected in the rapid increase in its share of the extra-budgetary revenues, which increased from 33.7 per cent in 1982 to 39.6 per cent in 1990. Table 7.11 shows that in addition, revenues from industrial and commercial taxes increased rapidly after 1978, from 46.2 to 196.7 billion yuan in 1990. Tax revenues grew as a proportion of central budgetary revenues from 41.2 per cent to 63.8 per cent in 1990, off-setting deficits from loss-making state-owned firms (Nee 1992: 21).

Two conclusions can be drawn from the evidence presented above. First, decentralization did not result in a weakening capacity of the central government's fiscal power. Instead its share of the total state revenue grew.

Second, both central and local governments have strong financial incentives to establish and maintain profit-sharing arrangements with industrial and commercial firms, as documented by the growth and relative size of the extra-budgetary revenues.

Table 7.11 Central profit-sharing in form of tax revenue income: 1978–90

Year	Industrial & commercial taxes (100 million yuan) (A)	Share of A in the central revenues (%) (B)
1978	462.13	41.1
1979	482.30	45.2
1980	510.43	49.0
1981	547.48	53.9
1982	623.17	57.5
1983	688.75	56.9
1984	807.44	55.2
1985	1197.70	65.2
1986	1277.72	58.5
1987	1376.76	60.9
1988	1579.60	63.5
1989	1881.56	67.1
1990	1967.00	63.8

Source Zhongguo Suiwu Baike Qiansu (China Taxation Dictionary) 1991, Economic Management Press 1991: 795.

We have argued that China's economic reforms stimulated economic growth because it benefited economic as well as political actors. As shown in Table 7.12, profit-sharing resulted in a rapid increase in retained profits by firms. Retained profits per capita (employee) grew from 31.2 yuan in 1978 to 847 yuan in 1988. This was passed on to employees through bonus programmes and income growth. The income of Chinese non-farm employees has increased dramatically as a result. Reflecting this, rural and urban household savings grew considerably (*China Economic System Reform Yearbook* 1991: 775, 840). The aggregate savings of urban residents was 155 million yuan in 1978 (22 yuan per capita) and by 1991 had grown to 6790 million yuan (786 yuan per capita). The aggregate savings of rural households grew from 55.7 million yuan in 1978 to 2316 million yuan by 1991(ZNJTN 1992).

Table 7.12   Profit-sharing of state-owned industrial enterprises that are within state budget: 1978–88

Year	Profit actually retained within enterprises (100 million)	% of actually retained profits in total taxes profits	Actual retained profit within enterprises per capita
1978	7.8	1.1	31.2
1979	40.6	5.1	155.6
1980	69.2	8.1	254.2
1981	84.9	10.0	300.0
1982	112.0	12.9	376.0
1983	138.9	14.8	456.6
1984	160.1	15.6	536.4
1985	204.4	17.3	665.0
1986	214.3	18.0	674.1
1987	233.7	18.2	716.6
1988	285.9	18.8	847.0

Source   *The First Decade of Enterprises Reform in China*. Beijing: The Reform Press. 1990: 646.

CONCLUSION

Economic growth has been sustained in China because institutional innovations have framed incentives in a manner that benefits both economic and political actors. Within local corporatist governance structures property rights over industrial firms have been partitioned through profit-sharing arrangements. Although formal ownership rights are retained by government units, rights over the use of assets and over a substantial share of the income generated by the firm have been transferred through responsibility contracts to economic actors through profit-sharing arrangements. This has resulted in the attenuation of state-ownership of industrial firms. Even the right to transfer use rights to private operators is permitted in certain responsibility contracts that resemble long-term ground leases. Although such arrangements are more common among smaller publicly owned firms, informal privatization nonetheless has spread throughout the Chinese economy as improving economic performance has increased the incentive to secure private rights over community property (Nee and Su 1996). Informal privatization hollows out state-ownership; it is socially sanctioned, unlike corruption which is based on illegitimate rent-seeking by political actors.

The emergence of corporatist governance structures stems from local government response to broad parameter shifts in the institutional environment. Declining socialist redistribution and the shift to reliance on markets increases the costs of monitoring and enforcement for government. Firms are less dependent on the state for resources, diminishing the state's power to control economic activity in the firm. Similarly markets increase the pay-off and scope for opportunism and malfeasance. Local governments have an interest therefore in negotiating and abiding by contracts specifying the terms of exchange between government and public-sector firms. Improving rewards for productivity in firms not only proved to be a reliable means to generate growth in revenues to local government, but profit-sharing also reduces the costs of monitoring and enforcement. Stock-option and bonus plans for employees in capitalist firms operate in a similar manner.

The solidarity and trust generated by local corporatist governance structures may be more important than the effectiveness of formal monitoring and enforcement activity by government. Long-standing network ties between political and economic actors allow for flexibility and co-operation in adjusting to rapid changes in the institutional environment. Local governments selectively interpret rules issued by the central state in a manner favourable to the interests of local firms. A loose coupling between government and industrial firm also enables economic actors to respond opportunistically to changing market conditions.[4] Within small communities, frequent interactions between economic and political actors allow both parties to be well-informed. Informal monitoring takes place as a by product of on-going relationships between political and economic actors. Enforcement of the government's interests is implicit in the power to withdraw recognition of property rights stemming from informal privatization. Yet this is counter-balanced by the understood threat of diminished economic performance. The institutional arrangement works to promote economic growth not only because both parties to the contract have an interest in profitability, but network ties linking economic and political actors embody the checks and balances needed to sustain strategic cooperation and flexibility. In local corporatist arrangements, institutions and networks combine to provide the social underpinnings of robust economic performance.

NOTES

1. The research reported in this chapter was funded by grants from the National Science Foundation (SES9309651 and SBR9022192). Additionally Victor Nee is grateful for the support provided when he was a Visiting Scholar at the Russell Sage Foundation (1994–5) and a Fellow of the Institute for Advanced Study in the Behavioural Sciences, Stanford (1996–7). An earlier version of this chapter was prepared for the World Bank.

2. The Kornai/Wong perspective maintains that under partial reform, markets are so constrained by persistent state controls that they are unable to have their expected beneficial effect. In contrast Oi/Walder's state-centred perspective excludes markets as a significant causal variable.

3. Walder (1996) and Oi (1989) emphasize path dependence in their analysis of the reform era, yet their current view of the developmental state does not square with their earlier depiction of the socialist state as a predatory agent.

4. By 'loosely coupled' we refer to the insight that there is a gap between the formal rules of the game specified by the central state and the practical activities of actors in economic organizations. Our approach emphasizes the comparative institutional analysis of alternative governance structures, and shifts analytical attention to the effect of emerging markets and changing incentives for economic and political actors (Nee 1992). Oi's (1992) related concept, 'local state corporatism', introduced independently the same year, reflects the assumption of state-centred analysis that an adequate explanation of sustained economic growth need only focus on changing incentives to political actors.

REFERENCES

Alchian, A. (1977), *Economic Forces at Work*. Indianapolis: Liberty Press.

Amsden, A. (1989), *Asia's Next Giant: South Korea and Late Industrialization*. New York: Oxford University Press.

Che, J. and Y. Qian. (1996), 'Understanding China's township-village enterprises'. Unpublished manuscript, Department of Economics, Stanford University.

Eggertsson, T. (1990), *Economic Behaviour and Institutions*. Cambridge: Cambridge University Press.

Evans, P. (1995), *Embedded Autonomy: States and Industrial Transformation*. Princeton: Princeton University Press.

Kornai, J. (1990), *On the Road to a Free Economy: Shifting from a Socialist System*. New York: Norton.

McMillan, J. and B. Naughton (1996), 'Reforming China's state-owned firms' in J. McMillan and B. Naughton (eds), *Reforming Asian Socialism: the Growth of Market Institutions*. Ann Arbor: University of Michigan Press: 167–74.

Nee, V. (1992), 'Organizational dynamics of market transition: hybrid forms, property rights, and the mixed economy in China'. *Administrative Science Quarterly*, 37: 1–27.

Nee, V. and S. Su. (1996), 'Institutions, social ties and commitment in China's corporatist transformation' in J. McMillan and B. Naughton (eds), *Reforming Asian*

Socialism: The Growth of Market Institutions. Ann Arbor: University of Michigan Press: 111–34.

North, D.C. and R.P. Thomas (1973), *The Rise of the Western World: A New Economic History.* Cambridge: Cambridge University Press.

Piore, M.J. and C.F. Sabel (1984), *The Second Industrial Divide: Possibilities for Prosperity.* New York: Basic Books.

Oi, J.C. (1989), *State and Peasant in Contemporary China.* Berkeley: University of California Press.

Oi, J.C. (1992), 'Fiscal reform and the economic foundations of local state corporatism in China'. *World Politics*, 45: 99–126.

Saxenian, A. (1994), *Regional Advantage: Culture and Competition in Silicon Valley and Route 128.* Cambridge, Mass: Harvard University Press.

Wade, R. (1990), *Governing the Market: Economic Theory and the Role of Government in East Asian Industrialization.* Princeton: Princeton University Press.

Walder, A. (1995), 'Local government as industrial firms: organizational analysis of China's transitional economy'. *American Journal of Sociology*, 101: 263–301.

Wong, C. (1987), 'Between plan and market: the role of the local sector in Post-Mao China'. *Journal of Comparative Economics*, 11: 385–98.

Wong, C. (1990), 'Central–local relations in an era of fiscal decline: the paradox of fiscal decentralization in Post-Mao China'. *The China Quarterly*, 128: 691–715.

Wong, C. (1992), 'Fiscal reform and local industrialization'. *Modern China*, 18: 197–227.

8 The Developmental Alliance for Industrialization in East Asia: State and Business in South Korea and Taiwan[1]

Eun Mee Kim

The East Asian NICs of South Korea, Taiwan, Hong Kong and Singapore have attained some of the most rapid rates of economic development in the world in the last three decades. South Korea recorded 7.1 per cent in average annual growth rate of GNP per capita between 1965 and 1980, making it the second fastest growing economy in the world – after Botswana – during that period (World Bank 1992). Between 1980 and 1992, South Korea was the fastest growing economy in the world with an impressive 8.5 per cent in average annual growth rate of GNP per capita.

A common strategy for industrialization in all four East Asian NICs was export-oriented industrialization (EOI) based on light manufacturing. This strategy allowed them to take advantage of the relatively low wages of their workers, and of the expanding and less protectionist world economy of the 1960s and 1970s. EOI also helped companies hire more workers, albeit at lower wages compared to many Latin American nations which had adopted import-substitution industrialization (ISI) strategies. As a result, income inequality in the East Asian NICs did not rise concomitant with their rapid rate of economic development. More and more workers work in the manufacturing sector and in services rather than in agriculture, and some of these nations have already experienced labour shortages in certain sectors of their economies.

Looking at the four NICs today, we tend to forget that they have overcome tremendous obstacles and challenges in the last three decades, as the Eastern and Central European nations face today. These challenges included scarce natural resources, in particular oil, relatively small domestic markets, low levels of domestic capital accumulation, lack of indigenous technology, political instability, and in the case of South Korea, a devastating civil war in 1950–53.

The key to their success lay in a combination of the establishment of key institutions responsible for economic development, the creation of institutional alliances between the state and business, and effective implementation of the EOI strategy for economic development. This chapter focuses on the first two issues since they form the basic foundation for economic development, from which the latter was possible. My contention is that EOI would not have been successful had there been no appropriate institutional foundation for its implementation. Furthermore, this chapter sidesteps the tired debate between the state-centred and market-centred studies (which focuses on the question of which set of institutions played the more crucial role for attaining economic development), and provides an alternative framework where both the state and business are treated as key institutions for economic growth, and where both their roles, and in particular, the relations between them are explored in the context of economic and political development. The chapter deals with three topics: the key institutions for economic development, namely, the 'developmental state' and business; the 'developmental alliance' between the state and business; and the implications of the developmental alliance for the long-term economic development and political democracy.

KEY INSTITUTIONS OF ECONOMIC DEVELOPMENT

For South Korea and Taiwan, an overwhelming amount of evidence suggests that their respective states played much more interventionist roles in their economies than suggested by the World Bank (1993) and other market-centred studies. In South Korea the key institutions were the developmental state and large private business groups (*chaebol*). A developmental state was established in 1961 following the military coup led by General Park Chung Hee. The tight developmental alliance formed between the state and the *chaebol* dominated the South Korean economy during the first two decades of rapid growth (1960s and 1970s). In Taiwan the developmental state was also established under the guidance of a military general, Chiang Kai-shek, who fled the People's Republic of China in 1949. President Chiang's party, the KMT (Kuo Min Tang), established a number of state-owned enterprises to initiate industrialization. The developmental alliance was formed between the developmental state and a few state enterprises. On the other hand, small and medium-sized enterprises played a significant role in the Taiwanese economy for they hired a large number of workers and produced a large share of the manufactured products for exports. However, they were not part of the developmental alliance, and their growth was not guided and financed by the state as in South Korea. In fact, their growth occurred outside of the state's close supervision.

The Developmental State

Before a concerted effort for economic development began, key institutions were founded and/or reformed in South Korea and Taiwan. The creation of a developmental state was crucial for both nations. A developmental state focuses on economic development as its primary policy objective, and it invests capital and human resources in pursuit of its policy goal (Johnson 1982). A developmental state does not merely augment and regulate markets, but it actually *creates* and *changes* (distorts) markets (Amsden 1989, Wade 1990). Developmental states in East Asia, such as Japan, South Korea and Taiwan, have led, and controlled tightly, their markets, and by-and-large have been very effective in their endeavours. The role that these states played in their economies, however, goes beyond the connotation of 'state-intervention'.

In South Korea, the Park Chung Hee (1961–79) regime created a developmental state in 1961 by founding the Economic Planning Board (EPB), and expanding and strengthening the Ministry of Finance (MOF) and the Ministry of Trade and Industry (MTI). These three economic ministries formed the nucleus of the developmental state and performed the following functions:

- Provision of long-term goals for the economy. The state provides comprehensive economic development plans, long-term goals, and projections for the entire economy (Johnson 1987, Lim 1987, Mason *et al.* 1980).
- Provision of capital and technology. The state provides capital for investment through domestic and foreign capital loans, capital assistance for research and development, and technology and technical assistance through national and regional research facilities (Jones and Sakong 1980, E.M. Kim 1993, Krueger 1979, Lim 1987, Mardon 1990, Mason *et al.* 1980).
- Provision of indirect assistance. The state acts as a mediator with multinational corporations for foreign direct investment and technology transfers, establishes trade offices for expertise on exports and imports, provides tax breaks and tariff exemptions, and eases regulations (Jones and Sakong; E.M. Kim 1993; Krueger 1979; Mardon 1990).

These services, and in particular the last two, are designed to support the private sector in its infancy, when it cannot provide the services itself due to lack of resources, information, and know-how. I designate such a developmental state as 'comprehensive', since its intervention in the economy is complete and omnipresent. This is opposed to a 'limited' developmental state, which performs the above three functions, but in limited degrees. In the market, there will be sectors which are liberalized, while others remain under the state's close supervision and control. For the state, goals other than economic development, such as foreign policy, welfare, and security, are identified as other priorities of the state.

The Comprehensive Developmental State of South Korea

The clearest example of the comprehensive developmental state at work is the South Korean government's promotion of heavy and chemical industrialization (HCI) in the early 1970s, which was fostered against market signals and advice from various foreign and local specialists. Even the domestic private sector was initially opposed to this plan. It required a second overhaul of the economy, this time toward HCI, after less than a decade of EOI based on light manufacturing. The cumulative experience of the private sector in manufacturing was rather shallow. Furthermore, not enough capital or technology had been accumulated by individual businesses to support a massive campaign for HCI. Nevertheless, the South Korean government, in particular the President and his staff in the Blue House[2] was determined to promote HCI. More than economics was involved in this decision. The changing geo-political conditions with the US troops beginning a partial withdrawal from South Korea after President Nixon's Guam Doctrine in 1969, and President Park's narrow victory in the 1971 presidential election provided important political justifications for the Park regime's pursuit of HCI. Thus, although domestic and international market conditions were not ripe, President Park pushed HCI with determination.

The Park government announced that the goal of the Third Five Year Economic Development Plan (1972–6) was a 'balanced economy': a balance was to be achieved between the light and heavy industries, and between the urban and rural areas (EPB 1972, FKI 1987). Soon after, President Park announced the 'Plans for the Development of the Heavy and Chemical Industry' during his State of the Nation Message on 13 January 1973, underscoring the importance of HCI[3].

On 17 August 1973 the 'Long-Term Plans for the Development of the Heavy and Chemical Industries' were announced, and various institutional reforms took place. Within a year of the President's initial announcement, numerous plans were announced by the economic ministries, including the following:

- March 1973:   Long-term human resources development plan was announced.
- May 1973:   Ministry of Trade and Industry announced basic principles for the development of the heavy and chemical industries.
- August 1973:   The law for public investment fund was promulgated.
- October 1973:   A new long-term plan for energy was announced.
- November 1973: A plan for effective business management for the heavy and chemical industries was announced.
- January 1974:   A new plan to reduce taxes for heavy and chemical industries was announced (Chông 1985: 51).

Economic ministries underwent institutional reforms to help assist the development of the heavy and chemical industries. Within the EPB, the Department for Foreign Capital Management and the Department for Promoting Investment were both formed in 1973 to assist with attracting foreign capital (public and commercial loans and foreign direct investment). Similar departments within the Ministry of Finance were also expanded. In the Ministry of Construction, the Department of Industrial Plants was created in 1973. The Ministry of Trade and Industry underwent the greatest changes. The Department for Industrial Development and the Department for Management of Industrial Plants were expanded and promoted to higher status within the ministry. Many defence-related departments and heavy and chemical industry-related departments were created, and old ones were expanded to give them more prominence within the ministry. A new Bureau of Science and Technology was established in 1973 to consolidate and expand the research and development efforts for the heavy and chemical industries. In January 1974, the Development Association for Marine Resources was expanded and renamed the Development Association for Industrial Parks. Its new responsibility was to oversee the establishment and development of industrial parks for heavy and chemical industries.

The state established new long-term targets for the economy, along with institutional reforms in various economic ministries. These targets were designed to complete the transition toward HCI by the beginning of the 1980s. The goals for industrial restructuring included the following: the primary sector was to decrease to 15.9 per cent from 25.5 per cent in 1972; the secondary sector was to increase to 42.9 per cent from 26.3 per cent in 1972; and the tertiary sector was to decrease to 41.2 per cent from 48.2 per cent in 1972. In terms of manufacturing alone, the share of heavy manufacturing within it was to increase from 35.2 per cent in 1972 to 51.0 per cent by 1981. The export structure would change toward exports of more heavy manufactured products. Other more general economic goals included increasing the GNP per capita by 1981 to $983, and increasing foreign capital holdings to $2.7 billion (Chông 1985).

The state's support for the public and private sectors in terms of promoting HCI involved the selection of a few target industries and providing them with generous government support. Six target industries were chosen based on the following factors:

• Forward and backward linkages.
• Contribution for the whole country's economic development.
• Possibility of foreign capital earnings through exports, and foreign capital savings through import substitution.
• Use of natural resources.
• Inducement effect of foreign capital.

The six target industries chosen were iron and steel, nonferrous metals, machinery, ship-building, electrical appliances and electronics, and petrochemicals.

Pursuant to these guidelines, several state-owned enterprises were established. The Pohang Iron and Steel Company (POSCO) was founded in 1968 and began production in 1973. It took several years for POSCO to begin production since it was difficult to secure the necessary foreign capital loans to build factories. It was only after the Pronouncement for the Development of the Heavy and Chemical Industry that the POSCO finally began production (Y.H. Kim 1976, Nam 1979). Another state-owned enterprise, the Korea Chemical Company, was founded in March 1973.

The state also promoted HCI in the private sector by providing preferential treatment to specific private businesses. The EPB and the Ministry of Trade and Industry specifically sought the support and cooperation of the large *chaebol* in order to promote HCI. These *chaebol* were capable of financing, at least partially, the capital- and technology-intensive industries, and they had a proven track record of growth during the 1960s. As a result, many private businesses received financial assistance through foreign capital loans, the newly created National Funds, domestic loans, tax cuts, technology, and infrastructure. An annual average of 14.5 per cent of total development finances was used for the development of the heavy and chemical industry between 1971 and 1981 (Chông 1985). The law for tax cuts for the heavy and chemical industry was passed in 1974, and 40.1 per cent of tax cuts were subsequently given to the heavy and chemical firms. Other protective measures included removal of tariff barriers and relaxing bans on imports for certain heavy and chemical products. In addition, heavy and chemical firms received preferential treatment for foreign direct investment (FDI). Before other manufacturing firms were allowed to receive 100 per cent FDI, many heavy and chemical firms were allowed by law to do so. By 1974, metal, machinery, and electronics firms were allowed to accept 100 per cent, and by 1978 all six target industries were allowed to acquire 100 per cent FDI.

The role of the developmental state is undeniable in the HCI drive in South Korea during the 1970s. Various economic ministries were reformed to effectively coordinate research and development for HCI, to disseminate the findings of research and development related to HCI, to provide direct capital subsidies through low-interest-rate loans, and to provide other indirect assistance such as tariff and tax breaks and easing of import regulations. The state also established long-term targets for the economy, so that the private sector would be informed about the government's intended direction for the economy, and be assured of the relative stability which comes with long-term projections.

The Limited Developmental State in Taiwan

The Taiwanese government had dual missions since Chiang Kai-shek fled mainland China, and established the KMT's home base in Taiwan in 1949. The Chiang regime proclaimed that it would regain the mainland (People's Republic of China), and that it would also attain economic development in preparation for the conquering of the mainland. The sub-ethnic division between some two million people who crossed the Taiwanese strait with Chiang and the indigenous population helps explain the political agenda behind the KMT's decision to curb the growth of the private sector. The mainlanders took control of the military and the government, while it prevented potential opposition from the Taiwanese by declaring martial law immediately after entering Taiwan in 1949. Martial law lasted until 1986.

It appears that Chiang and KMT were concerned about potential opposition from the Taiwanese, in particular through the growth of economic elites. In an effort to prevent such a challenge of power from the Taiwanese, the KMT established state-owned enterprises and discouraged the growth of private large enterprises. Unlike in South Korea where establishing significant numbers of state-owned enterprises carried potential political risks, founding state-owned enterprises to be headed by the mainlanders appeared to be a more desirable alternative than to allow the Taiwanese to head large businesses. The Chiang regime announced various long-term economic development plans, which were mostly Four Year Economic Development Plans. A few early Four Year Development Plans involved building up the infrastructure, which was to be carried out primarily by state-owned enterprises. Aside from supporting the growth of the state-owned enterprises and their work in building the infrastructure, the state was relatively *laissez-faire* with the private sector. As noted above, the only stipulation was to discourage the expansion of private large businesses, and this was done by controls over domestic loan capital. Financial institutions, which were nationalized, had strict regulations which made it difficult for small and medium-sized Taiwanese-owned businesses to expand by utilizing bank loans, as was the case with South Korean large businesses.

Some of the state's economic development plans also did not produce results, as was the case with the development of heavy industries in the early 1970s. Unlike in South Korea, where the government itself went through institutional reforms and provided generous subsidies to a select group of private businesses, the Taiwanese government was relatively lax in its implementation of such plans. As a result, heavy and chemical industrialization (HCI) in Taiwan was left to the private sector to accomplish; initially it failed. After this setback, the Taiwanese economy entered a phase of HCI during the mid- to late-1970s, but even so, HCI was more oriented towards the electrical and electronics industries. This industrial sector was largely concerned with final assembly work and the production of certain components which required low to mid-level technological sophistication. Thus, Taiwan's attempt to develop HCI did not produce dramatic and immediate results as in South Korea. HCI in Taiwan was driven more by the private sector than by the state.

Thus compared to the South Korean state, the Taiwanese government was less interventionist in the economy. However, it intervened in two important ways: it provided long-term goals for the economy; and it provided indirect assistance including tax and tariff breaks, and in the case of Export Processing Zones, a complete withholding of taxes and tariffs. On the other hand, the Taiwanese government did not provide capital and technology to private businesses (which were largely small and medium-size enterprises), although such services were provided to the state-owned enterprises. As a result, the Taiwanese state was unable to influence the private sector during the 1960s and 1970s to the extent of its South Korean counterpart; the latter was able to control the private sector by controlling low-interest domestic loans and by procuring and distributing foreign capital loans.

Companies: South Korean and Taiwanese Comparisons

South Korea's rapid economic development based on exports is often lumped together with Taiwan's as a new model for Third World growth. However, there are significant differences in the way the private sector is organized, and in the state–business relations in the two nations. First, in Taiwan, the state has allowed small and medium-size enterprises to grow, while it has discouraged the growth of privately owned large business groups (Cheng 1990, Ho 1982). In contrast, the South Korean economy was dominated by large family-owned and -managed business groups, or *chaebol*. There are several reasons for this difference. In Taiwan, the Kuo Min Tang (KMT) established many large-scale state-owned enterprises, supported the growth of a myriad of small and medium enterprises, and actively discouraged the growth of huge conglomerates through loan policies (Cheng 1990, Gereffi 1991, Hamilton and Biggart 1988). Restrictions on domestic loans imposed by the financial institutions made it difficult for the Taiwanese firms to grow based on debt as was the case in South Korea (Cheng 1990). The cultural tradition of China and Taiwan, in which inheritance is more equitably distributed among all sons also made it difficult for family-based large conglomerates to prosper as in South Korea. In the latter, there is a stronger tradition of primogeniture, which allowed the family business to remain intact through generational successions. In addition, it is important to recognize that *guanxi*-based trust, which is prevalent in Taiwan, also contributed to the proliferation of small and medium-sized enterprises (Whitley 1992). These smaller enterprises allowed the Taiwanese to do business primarily within their *guanxi* networks. Secondly, the Taiwanese state has also been more aggressive in investing in state-owned enterprises compared to South Korea. In 1987, four out of the largest six corporations in Taiwan were government-owned (Gereffi 1990: 94–5). Thus, there are few large privately owned Taiwanese businesses comparable to the South Korean *chaebol*. In more recent years, thanks to the continued success in exports for small and medium-sized enterprises, Taiwanese private enterprises have grown to quite significant sizes compared to the past, and have begun to enjoy more political leverage against the government (Hsiao 1995).

South Korea's *chaebol*, such as Hyundai, Samsung and Lucky-Goldstar (now LG) formed a tight alliance with the South Korean state and spearheaded the economy's rapid growth based on exports. During the 1970s, the state provided low-interest loans for heavy and chemical industrialization, from which the large *chaebol* benefited disproportionately. The combination of the state's subsidized low-interest loans and the *chaebol*'s shrewd management generated tremendous growth for the largest ten *chaebol*. On average, the largest ten grew at a rate of 27.7 per cent per year during the 1970s.[4] Hyundai, the largest *chaebol*, grew at an average rate of 38.0 per cent every year during the 1970s. Daewoo, the youngest of the ten, grew at an astonishing rate of 53.7 per cent per annum during the same period (E.M. Kim 1991). The growth rate of the ten largest *chaebol* was 3.5 times faster than the entire South Korean economy. This is remarkable, since the average annual growth rate of real GNP was 7.9 per cent, which was one of the highest rates in the world (EPB 1988). The *chaebol* have become the most powerful group of domestic capitalists in South Korea. They dominate South Korean society and markets in several ways. First, they employ a large share of the workers. For example, the largest ten *chaebol* employed nearly 12 per cent of all workers in manufacturing in 1987. Second, they dominate the manufacturing sector, especially key heavy and chemical industries. In 1987, the largest ten *chaebol* were responsible for 28.2 per cent of total shipments in manufacturing (I and I 1990: 28). The largest *chaebol* have near monopoly status in many capital and technology-intensive sectors. The largest five are responsible for over 40 per cent of all shipment in fabricated metal products, machinery and equipment (I and I 1990: 29). Third, the *chaebol* produce an exhaustive array of manufactured products and services. Finally, the *chaebol*'s organizational structure has become a model for South Korean businesses. Partly as a result of the *chaebol*'s economic success, their organizational features have been emulated by small and medium-size enterprises in South Korea. Similar to the *chaebol*, they attempted to expand their businesses by investing in often unrelated sectors, and utilize family members in their businesses, often to great effect.

The *chaebol* exhibit the following organizational features: family ownership and management, with a centralized and hierarchical system of control based on filial piety and loyalty; flexibility in mobilizing and in exchanging capital, technology, and personnel among member companies; and horizontal diversification in an unusually wide range of often unrelated business activities. Each of these attributes distinguish the *chaebol* from Western business conglomerates. Despite important similarities, the *chaebol* are also somewhat different from the pre-World War II *zaibatsu* of Japan. Unlike the *zaibatsu*, the *chaebol* do not own banks, or engage in the well-known Japanese business practice of lifetime employment. The criteria for promotion are also different. Promotion in the *chaebol* is based on a combination of factors, including ability, credentials – advanced academic degrees, licenses, or in-house promotion examination scores – and seniority (C.S. Kim 1992). Chronological age, an important criterion for promotion in Japan, does not operate in the promotion dynamics of large *chaebol* (C.S. Kim 1992, Lie 1990). The employees of the *chaebol* also experience more mobility than their Japanese counterparts, although the mobility of *chaebol* employees is still less than that of US workers (Lie 1990).

In contrast, the Taiwanese economy is dominated by a small number of large state-owned enterprises, and myriad small and medium-sized enterprises. In fact, over 90 per cent of Taiwanese businesses employ less than 30 workers. The large state-owned enterprises were established during the 1960s and 1970s, in particular in the areas of infrastructure and energy. The KMT recognized the strategic significance of these sectors, and for political as well as economic reasons, decided to found state-owned enterprises. The largest of these include: Chinese Petroleum, Taiwan Tobacco and Wine Monopoly Bureau, China Steel, and Formosa Plastics. Taiwan's state-owned enterprises are not only numerous, but they are diversified as well including petrochemicals, plastics, steel, shipbuilding, construction, fertilizer, food and beverages (Gereffi 1990: 94–5).

There are several reasons that can explain the abundance of small and medium-sized enterprises and lack of large private business groups in Taiwan. Culture-centred studies argue that the traditional Chinese custom of inheritance, in which the wealth is relatively equally divided among the sons, tends to make it easier for family businesses to splinter off after only one generation (DeVos and Sofue 1984). This is accentuated by another traditional custom, in which sons leave the father's household upon marriage, except for the eldest son (DeVos and Sofue 1984). This has made it more likely for the family fortune to be dispersed, and for a myriad of small and medium-size enterprises to thrive.

Politics-centred studies provide a different explanation for Taiwan's abundance of small and medium-size enterprises. These studies argue that the Kuo Min Tang (KMT) of Chiang Kai-shek, which was an exile government from mainland China, designed policies to discourage, if not prohibit, the Taiwanese from entering positions of power (government, parliament, the military etc.), and of wealth (large businesses), fearing that the Taiwanese might usurp power (Cheng 1990). The KMT allowed the Taiwanese to operate businesses, ownership of large businesses was discouraged, and small and medium-size enterprises were promoted. The latter were deemed a more effective way of preventing the private sector from becoming a major social force (Cheng 1990). Therefore, the Chiang regime restricted access to domestic loans for business expansion, and invested heavily in state-owned enterprises (Hamilton and Biggart 1988).

The situation in Taiwan has changed significantly since the early days of the Chiang regime. The government, parliament, and the military have become more open to Taiwanese. Several firms have become large business groups due to their success in the export markets since the 1960s. But this success has been achieved *despite* the state, unlike in South Korea where the *chaebol*'s success was in part due to state support.

In spite of the different composition of the private sector, Taiwanese and South Korean businesses appear to share a cultural trait, which is found in many Asian nations. They rely on personal ties to recruit employees and to conduct businesses. In Taiwan, this is called *guanxi*, which translates as relationships, connections, or networks (Hamilton and Biggart 1988, Hamilton 1991). *Guanxi* appears to be a more encompassing concept than the personal ties utilized in South Korea. It refers to members of a family or kinship group, school alum, people who are born in the same region, or acquaintances of the above categories of people. Through *guanxi* one can have immediate rapport and trust. The argument goes that people seek out others who are related by *guanxi* when looking for business partners, subcontractors, or employees (Hamilton 1991). This practice of hiring and doing business almost exclusively within the *guanxi* network was conducive to the growth of small and medium-size enterprises in Taiwan. In comparison, the *chaebol* in South Korea, due to their size, cannot rely on hiring and doing business only with acquaintances. The usage of *guanxi* in Taiwan has resulted in the relatively slow development of formal entrance exams for hiring, official contracts, and legal documents. In contrast, in South Korea due to the early expansion of business groups, formal entrance exams, contracts, and legal documents have been more widely used (Janelli and Yim 1993, C.S. Kim 1992).

THE DEVELOPMENTAL ALLIANCE

The present study helps correct the one-sided analysis of both the market and state-centred studies by incorporating both state and the capitalists as institutional actors into the analysis. The two institutions are examined since they formed an alliance to attain rapid economic development. However, this alliance was neither an egalitarian nor a static one. The power balance shifted from state dominance, to symbiosis, and later to competition. This argument departs from earlier studies, which tend to assume that the institution in control (whether it is the state or the capitalists) will retain its power over time.

South Korea's rapid economic development was attained initially by a tight alliance formed between a strong, developmental state and big business. First, this alliance repressed labour and excluded it from enjoying the fruits of economic growth. The coexistence of a strong state and big businesses goes against arguments made in state-centred studies. These studies assume that a strong state exists on the basis of a weak society, which includes business (Evans *et al.* 1985, Migdal 1988). In other words, state and society are depicted in a zero-sum relationship with one group's interests at odds with the other's. However, the South Korean case demonstrates that a strong state is not necessarily antithetical to big businesses. Second, the relations between the state and capitalists changed in the course of successful economic development. The relationship is a dynamic one. This argument opposes earlier studies, which assume that the relationship is constant over time. In South Korea, the power balance between the two institutions shifted from state dominance to symbiosis, and later to competition. Conflict and tension, which are embedded in the relationship between the two institutions, intensified over time. Third, the *chaebol* were not complacent rent-seekers in spite of generous state subsidies provided to them. The largest and most successful *chaebol* did not rely solely on state subsidies and protection. The successful business groups cultivated new markets abroad, acquired technology and investments from multinational corporations, and took advantage of the state's shifting economic priorities.

The alliance formed between the state and the *chaebol* help illuminate the repression of labour. Relatively low-paid female and male workers provided the competitive edge in terms of prices for South Korean-made products in the international market. Yet these workers did not enjoy the fruits of their labour in terms of wage increases, improvement in working conditions, or enhancement of labour rights.

In Taiwan, the developmental alliance was formed more narrowly between the state and state-owned enterprises, while the large number of small and medium-sized enterprises, which make up the bulk of the economy, were pretty much left alone. This rather lax control of the small and medium-sized enterprises had some unintended consequences. On the one hand, it prevented the private sector from challenging state power through economic prowess, as in South Korea. On the other hand, it helped foster a growing middle class, who came to challenge the state's authoritarian rule, by utilizing their considerable experience in mobilizing and organizing. The ability of the middle class to organize and mobilize against the state appears to have been higher in Taiwan than in South Korea, where the middle class is still relatively unorganized in spite of its participation in the democracy movements of the late 1980s.

Social and Political Implications of the Developmental Alliance

The social and political implications of the developmental alliance are illuminated as they help us understand the costs and problems of economic transformation in South Korea and Taiwan. In South Korea, the growth of super-wealthy family-owned businesses has hastened the weakening of the developmental state. In South Korea and Taiwan, the rapid growth of the middle and working classes has contributed to social unrest during the 1980s, which led to political opening and democratization. The question addressed in this section is the costs of pursuing economic transformation without political transformation, and the long-term problems associated with postponing political transformation in order to attain rapid industrialization.

The costs of economic reform without concomitant political reform has caused the labour movements and social movements for democracy to escalate to the extent that the ruling party in each case was forced to make major concessions. In both South Korea and Taiwan, widespread labour strikes and movements for democracy erupted in 1986 and 1987. The short-term economic consequences were negative and disruptive. In the longer term, however, both economies have performed strongly in spite of labour volatility. Nonetheless one lesson to be learned from the industrialization of South Korea and Taiwan, which relied heavily on labour-intensive processes, is that labour cannot be perpetually bought at a cheap price, and that violent labour disputes and demonstrations for democracy will come if the political will of the people to be governed in a democratic system is not honoured. Thus, short-term economic growth without political reform may work, but in the long run, suspension of democracy and delayed political reform may cost nations dearly in terms of social and economic disruption.

CONCLUDING REMARKS

Economic development in South Korea and Taiwan has been rapid and quite successful. In record-breaking time, these two economies shed the traditional traits of agrarian societies and have become two of the most robust economies in the world. Their economic growth was not accompanied by growing income inequalities as in many Latin American nations. Even so, Taiwan and South Korea have also experienced volatile labour movements and social movements for democracy. Exploitation of workers, political repression, and suspension of democracy are part of their legacies. Concerted efforts for rapid economic development in South Korea based on a politically conservative alliance formed between an authoritarian state and large business groups contributed, albeit indirectly, to the most volatile labour movement among the East Asian NICs. This conservative alliance continues to orchestrate state–business relations and colours the substantive discussions of democracy, which include negotiations for the provision of welfare services to its citizens, and the rights of workers. Although democratic transition began in 1987, the conservative nature of the alliance continues to impede progress towards workers' and other human rights.

In the case of Taiwan, the state's tacit acceptance of small and medium-sized enterprises, and its active role in deterring the growth of large private businesses, contributed to a more egalitarian society, albeit under the authoritarian control of the KMT government. Unlike in South Korea, this provided the context in which the middle class could begin its political ascendancy. Although democracy in Taiwan continues to be weak, it is arguably more firmly grounded than in South Korea and consequently may well affect more significantly the subsequent course of economic development there.

NOTES

1. This chapter is drawn partly from the author's forthcoming book, *Big Business, Strong State: Collusion and Conflict in South Korean Development, 1960–1990* (Albany: State University of New York Press).
2. The official residence and offices of the President of South Korea.
3. Most industrial policies were announced by the relevant ministries. That Park should have used his State of the Nation address for this purpose demonstrated his strong personal support for HCI.
4. The growth rate was based on total assets. The average annual growth rate was culated using 1980 constant prices in Won.

REFERENCES

Amsden, A. (1989), *Asia's Next Giant: South Korea and Late Industrialization*. New York: Oxford University Press.

Cheng, T.J. (1990), 'Political regimes and development strategies: South Korea and Taiwan.' in G. Gereffi and D. Wyman (eds), *Manufacturing Miracles: Paths of Industrialization in Latin America and East Asia*. Princeton: Princeton University Press: 139–178.

Chông, K.Y. (1985), 'Kwanryojôk Kwonwijûûi Taedu wa Chunghwahak Kongôp Chôngch'aek' (Emergence of the Bureaucratic Authoritarianism and Policies on the Heavy and Chemical Industry) in Sang Chin Han *et al.*, *Hanguk Sahoe Pyôndong kwa Kukka Yôkhwal e Kwanhan Yôngu* (Studies on the Changes in the Korean Society and the Role of the State). Seoul: Hyôndae Sahoe Yônguso.

DeVos, G. A., and T. Sofue (eds) (1984), *Religion and Family in East and Southeast Asia*. Berkeley: University of California Press.

EPB (Economic Planning Board) (1960–93), *Korea Statistical Yearbook*. Seoul: Economic Planning Board.

EPB (Economic Planning Board) (1962–84) *Five-Year Economic Development Plans: I, II, III, IV.* Seoul: Economic Planning Board.

EPB (Economic Planning Board) (1978–91), *Major Statistics of the Korean Economy.* Seoul: Economic Planning Board.

FKI (Federation of Korean Industries) (1987), *Korea's Economic Policies (1945–1985).* Seoul: Federation of Korean Industries.

Gereffi, G. (1990), 'Big business and the state' in G. Gereffi and D. Wyman (eds), *Manufacturing Miracles: Paths of Industrialization in Latin America and East Asia.* Princeton: Princeton University Press: 90–109.

Hamilton, G. (ed.) (1991), *Business Networks and Economic Development in East and Southeast Asia.* Hong Kong: University of Hong Kong Press.

Hamilton, G. and N. W. Biggart (1988), 'Market, culture, and authority: a comparative analysis of management and organization in the Far East'. *American Journal of Sociology* 94 (Supplement): 52–94.

Hsiao, H.H.M. (1995), 'The state and business relations in Taiwan'. *Journal of Far Eastern Business*, 1(3): 76–97.

I, K.Ô. and C.H. I (1990), *Kiôp Kyôlhap kwa Kyôngjeryôk Chipchung* (Business Groups and Economic Concentration). Seoul: Korea Development Institute.

Janelli, R.L. and D. Yim (1993), *Making Capitalism: the Social and Cultural Construction of a South Korean Conglomerate.* Stanford: Stanford University Press.

Johnson, C. (1982), *MITI and the Japanese Miracle.* Stanford: Stanford University Press.

Johnson, C. (1987), 'Political institutions and economic performance: the government–business relationship in Japan, South Korea, and Taiwan' in F.C. Deyo (ed.), *The Political Economy of the New Asian Industrialism.* Ithaca: Cornell University Press: 136–64.

Jones, L.P. and I. Sakong (1980), *Government, Business and Entrepreneurship in Economic Development.* Cambridge, Mass.: Harvard University Press.

Kim, C.S. (1992), *The Culture of Korean Industry: An Ethnography of Poongsan Corporation.* Tucson: The University of Arizona Press.

Kim, E.M. (1991), 'The industrial organization and growth of the Korean chaebol: integrating development and organizational theories' in G. Hamilton (ed.), *Business Networks and Economic Development in East and Southeast Asia.* Hong Kong: University of Hong Kong Press: 272–99.

Kim, E.M. (1993), 'Contradictions and limits of a developmental state: with illustrations from the South Korean case'. *Social Problems*, 40(2): 228–49.

Kim, Y.H. (1976) *Hanguk Ch'ôlgang Kongôp ûi Sôngjang* (Growth of Iron and Steel Industry in Korea). Seoul: Korea Development Institute.

Krueger, A.O. (1979), *The Developmental Role of the Foreign Sector and Aid.* Cambridge, Mass: Harvard University Press.

Lim, H.C. (1987), *Dependent Development in Korea, 1963–1979.* Seoul: Seoul National University Press.

Mardon, R. (1990), 'The state and the effective control of foreign capital: the case of South Korea'. *World Politics*, 43: 111–38.

Mason, E.S., M.J. Kim, D.H. Perkins, K.S. Kim, and D.C. Cole (eds) (1980), *The Economic and Social Modernization of the Republic of Korea.* Cambridge, Mass: Harvard University Press.

Migdal, J.S. (1988), *Strong States and Weak Societies: State–Society Relations and State Capabilities in the Third World*. Princeton: Princeton University Press.

Nam, C.H. (1979), *Ch'ôlgang Kongôp ûi T'ûksông kwa Sugûp Kujo* (Characteristics and Structure of Demand and Supply of The Iron and Steel Industry). Seoul: Korea Development Institute.

Wade, R. (1990), *Governing the Market: Economic Theory and the Role of Government in East Asian Industrialization*. Princeton: Princeton University Press.

Whitley, R. (1992), *Business Systems in East Asia*. London: Sage Publications.

World Bank (1981–1991) *World Development Report*. New York: Oxford University Press.

World Bank (1993), *The East Asian Miracle*. Washington, DC, The World Bank.

9 Enterprise Strategies and Labour Relations in Central and Eastern Europe[1]

Sarah Vickerstaff, John Thirkell and Richard Scase

The majority of contemporary discussions of transformation in Eastern Europe are focused around either political changes or macroeconomic developments; enterprise-level labour relations have received considerably less attention. The institutionalization of new patterns of labour relations is highly contingent upon the prevailing economic and political conditions and this may lead some to argue that it is too early to try to study labour relations at the enterprise level. The function of this chapter, however, is to argue that developments at this level are a constituent element in change processes. The discussion draws upon research on processes of change in labour relations in Bulgaria, Czech and Slovak Republics, Hungary, Poland and the Novosibirsk region of Russia. It has been a basic hypothesis of our research that privatization of large state enterprises, and the resulting weakening in centralized control of the economy, would radically alter the context for labour relations in Eastern Europe and in particular, would greatly enhance the opportunities for strategy formulation at enterprise level.

The significance of the enterprise level has been systematically underplayed in many discussions of the transformations in Eastern Europe, (but see Whitley and Henderson 1995, Whitley et al. 1996). In this chapter we take the enterprise as our unit of analysis. First, we set the discussion in the context of the operation of the earlier socialist enterprise and its internal and external relations. Second, we look at the significance of privatization and consider why the role of the enterprise has been under-theorized in the 'transition' literature. Third, we draw on enterprise case-studies to explore the contested nature of transformation. The cases which are discussed are drawn from the traditional engineering and manufacturing sectors. Cases from other sectors, and involving foreign takeovers which may involve the direct transference of foreign managerial strategies and approaches to labour relations, are not discussed here. We do not claim that the cases reported here are representative of all sectors but rather that they point to key issues associated with the process of enterprise change. The main purpose of this discussion is to illustrate the contested and contingent nature of ownership change and the emerging enterprise strategies, with particular reference to labour relations.

ENTERPRISE STRATEGY IN THE COMMAND ECONOMY

The significance of the enterprise in the command economy of Eastern Europe had two important dimensions.[2] First, that the focus of management 'was mainly related to the macro level' and changes within the enterprise 'reflected the external requirements of the administrative-cum-political system rather than the problems associated with the functioning of the enterprise itself' (Federowicz 1994: 95). Second, that of all the different organizations inside the one-party state, the enterprise had a special significance as 'the constitutive institution of the new socialist society' (Szczepanski, quoted in Federowicz 1994: 124). It provided not only earnings and employment but a whole range of social and other services, in addition to the party organization and its membership which were based on the enterprise as the place of work rather than the locality.

Under the system of central planning the relationships of enterprises with both customers and suppliers were mainly determined by Ministry officials. These were 'allocated' from above through the mechanism of 'state orders'. There was substantial central control over prices of products and raw materials and over wages. The 'tariff' wage system prescribed the rates for the different grades while the Wage Funds were closely controlled. 'In a socialist economy the analysis of wages has to start from central wage policy because the latter is actually enforced' (Kornai 1980: 377). There was significant central influence over the design of the internal structures of the enterprise; as, for example, in the brigade system of work, which was widespread in the Soviet Union, Bulgaria and Czechoslovakia (see Petkov and Thirkell 1991). Although there were repeated attempts to reform the Soviet model and develop new mechanisms of enterprise organization, the strategies for such reorganization came from above rather than from enterprise management (Petkov and Thirkell 1991:160–201). Significantly, in the 1980s it was wage reform in Hungary associated with the Enterprise Work Partnerships (VGMKs) and the Law on Cooperatives in the Soviet Union which provided unusual opportunities for enterprise autonomy in which management could alter internal organizational structures and labour relations. In the traditional 'soviet' environment the most important activity of enterprise directors in these undertakings was bargaining over plan targets and seeking additional resources from central branch authorities. (Burawoy and Lukacs 1992, Myant 1993). Thus, as Markoczy (1993: 286) comments 'these companies did not make strategic decisions in terms of economic rationality'. In general the *importance* of the enterprise was defined according to the number of employees and the reduction of the labour force to increase efficiency was politically neither acceptable nor encouraged by the mechanisms of central planning.

The constraints on enterprise autonomy in the command economy meant that the scope for enterprise strategy was very limited, that is, in the choice of markets, the design of enterprise structures and in labour relations. The development of a market economy in theory enlarges the scope for enterprise strategy. It also places considerable emphasis on the skills and abilities of managers. As Burawoy and Lukacs (1992: 96–100) demonstrated, in the command system the role of middle managers (for example, plant managers, functional heads) was squeezed, with real managerial power residing above and below them. Senior managers were responsible for bargaining with the state and first line managers had discretion over allocation of work and the distribution of bonuses in order to try and meet plan targets at operational level. As has often been noted, this pattern of internal organization led to considerable shop-floor autonomy and a considerable degree of worker control over the labour process, at least by Western standards (see for example, Burawoy and Krotov 1992: 25–8, Petkov and Thirkell 1991: 160–8, Burawoy and Lukacs 1992: 65–78). This flexibility at shop-floor level was necessary to cope with shortages in supplies and poorly maintained or inadequate machinery and technology.

This brief discussion of enterprise strategy in the command economy demonstrates the gulf between traditional patterns of labour relations in these countries and the patterns and mechanisms of management strategy and control seen as typical to capitalist enterprises in the West. It is our contention that the difficulties of changing enterprise labour relations will be a significant factor in the success or failure of attempts to rapidly transform these economies. The freeing up of interests at enterprise level conditions and may constrain the processes of reform initiated at national level.

THE SIGNIFICANCE OF PRIVATIZATION

In the early days of the post-communist regimes the desire to move rapidly to a market- rather than a state-led system gave an enormous ideological significance to ownership changes and the assumption that privatization was a chief mechanism for industrial, economic and political reform. As Przeworski (1993: 141–2) has commented about Poland, this was often presented as the need to return to a 'normal economy' (see also Aslund 1992, Dabrowski *et al.* 1991). The advice and commentary of many Western economists who counselled the need for a rapid transformation of the economy reinforced such views (Kiss 1992: 1015). This has led Murrell (1993: 45), among others, to worry that: 'too many hopes have been invested in privatization'.

In much of the literature advocating rapid privatization it is deduced that the prerequisite for changing the behaviour of enterprises and the managers and employees who work in them is ownership change (see Aslund 1992, for example, and the discussion in Major 1993: 51). The only way to overcome the deficiencies of central planning and its consequences at the level of the individual firm is to restructure property relations. It is then expected that the discipline of the market will restructure the actions of both managers and workers (see, for example, Nuti and Portes 1993). Thus, the pattern of managerial incentives will be changed by creating real owners who will exert pressure on managers to behave in a profit maximizing manner. In time this will give managers the incentive to restructure industry as 'owners' seek to move out of unprofitable and into profitable areas. In the field of labour relations this is likely to require managers to restrain wage demands, shed excess labour and generally seek ways of improving labour productivity. Hence, the assumption is that to achieve economic renewal the behaviour of management has to be restructured by providing incentives to manage in a 'capitalist way' and that the behaviour of workers has to be changed by providing a capitalist system of discipline over labour.

At an abstract level the justifications for privatization as a means of restructuring managerial incentives are clear enough, however, this line of reasoning suggests that the main effects on labour relations will only emerge after privatization: that privatization is a precondition of labour relations reform. As Kabalina *et al.* (1994: 1) have commented: 'in the West restructuring is a condition of privatization, while in Russia it is the anticipated result'. The basic assumption or hypothesis is that as privatization proceeds, the autonomy of the enterprise will increase and management will be free of 'political interference': free to act like a manager in a capitalist enterprise. In Aslund's (1992: 70) phrase, privatization 'helps create a boundary between economics and politics'.

Given the integration of the Party and the management of the enterprise in the former regimes it is easy to understand the rhetorical appeal of separating politics from the enterprise or for the creation of 'autonomous industrial relations' (Deppe and Tatur 1995: 4). The problem with such assertions, however, is the oversimplification of the processes of transformation which they imply. Much of the discussion of property rights assumes that we can clearly delineate between a private market sector and a public bureaucratic sector, and that privatization can simply shift the bulk of Eastern European economies from the latter to the former. However, in most of Eastern Europe there is little or no private sector for enterprises to be 'transferred' to; in practice privatization is part of a process to *create* a private sector (Gradev 1996). In reality the processes of ownership change have not presented clear choices between 'private' and 'public' control, but rather a whole series of intermediate forms of ownership. Nor is it a simple matter to identify 'owners' or infer what their strategies in relation to labour relations might be.

Our approach hypothesizes that the relationship between ownership change, enterprise behaviour and labour relations is much more complex in reality, because ownership change is only one and not always the most important aspect of the process of marketization. Ownership change itself cannot be treated as an undifferentiated category. In practice, the process of ownership transformation has proved to be complex and slow. As Clague (1992: 18) has suggested, the use of the term privatization serves to obscure many important differences between recent sales of public enterprises in Western economies and the project facing eastern European governments. In our analysis of enterprise change we have found the concept of marketization more useful for unpacking the impact of ownership changes on labour relations (see Thirkell, Scase and Vickerstaff 1995: 11–14).

In considering the relationship between privatization and labour relations it is first necessary to draw a sharp distinction between the privatization of large industrial enterprises and that of small organizations. State enterprises, and those which form the majority of the cases studied in the project, were generally large. Exposure to marketization in these cases is frequently connected with internal restructuring of the enterprise, usually initiated by enterprise management but sometimes in collaboration with state agencies. Such restructuring, whether directly or indirectly linked to changes in ownership, is usually geared to linking different units of the enterprise with specific products. This process – often of divisionalization and decentralization – gives the opportunity to engage, usually for the first time, in the process of business strategy. That is, of deciding markets and products, and of formulating organizational strategy by developing appropriate organizational structures and mechanisms of change. Internal restructuring and divisionalization have implications for labour relations especially through the segmentation of internal labour markets. It also has consequences for the role of middle management.

Thus, prior to privatization or ownership change, senior management has to refocus its activities and develop new business strategies; this requires a spotlight on threats and opportunities in the external environment but also the need to develop new strategies for organizational and labour control. In the past, middle management played a largely regulatory role dependent upon first-line managers, mobilization of core workers to achieve production targets, which resulted in a tendency to hoard labour, tolerate low productivity, high absenteeism and poor quality, in which, as Thompson and Smith (1992: 19) comment:

> [a] dual control system of managers and party mobilize to meet production targets through a variety of mechanisms including an employment relationship based on a 'social contract' with the workforce; a technical division of labour frequently dependent on high degrees of flexibility and work group autonomy; piece work and normative reward systems. (See also Burawoy and Krotov 1992, Filtzer 1991, Clarke *et al.* 1994.)

The middle management group is in a particularly ambivalent position *vis-à-vis* ownership changes and the uncertainty they bring. However, this group is also crucial for the enterprise's success in terms of their ability to mobilize the workforce and translate corporate strategies into effective operational management. The key processes of organizational restructuring suggest a transformation of middle management roles in the process of divisionalization. It implies the need both for new skills and new accountabilities.

Relationships between ownership change, as a stage in marketization, and organizational restructuring and changes in labour relations are therefore complex. Attempts in Eastern Europe to transform the property structure have generally been much slower than was initially expected. For post-communist governments the central political issue has been to create structures and mechanisms for the creation of market economies while at the same time maintaining a minimum level of social and political integration. Specifically this has meant a debate about the pace and sequence of macroeconomic measures – either the shock treatment of rapid change (the liberal market) or, a more gradual approach (the social market). In such economic conditions trade unions often function as agencies of social integration through their negotiations with governments. The process of ownership change is also constrained at enterprise level by the market position of the organization, ambiguities in the implementation of new legislation, by the competences and abilities of managers and the potential for emerging interests to press for particular outcomes. The attempt to transform the property structure and the relations of production are constrained by the habits of management and workers at enterprise level developed over the long period of the command economy. The strength and persistence of these enterprise-based patterns and customs vary from country to country according to recent past policies of economic reform. Nevertheless, in all cases labour relations at enterprise level remain of crucial significance for the possible success of different reform strategies.

It is not surprising, but equally not defensible, that much of the economic literature on privatization in Eastern Europe and Russia has failed to focus on the complexities of ownership change and has ignored the enterprise level, changes in which have been seen as contingent upon ownership change (van Brabant 1990: 129–31). Thus, it is valuable to evaluate the extent to which the freeing up of interests at enterprise levels does or does not constrain reform processes. It is our contention that understanding the changing role of management, and in particular the emerging role of middle managers and the scope for other institutions, especially trade unions and other mechanisms of 'self-management', to mobilize to protect or promote their interests, is critical to an analysis of the changing role of the enterprise in post-communist societies and indeed, to understanding the wider processes of transformation in these countries (see also Henderson *et al.* 1995). Many of these points may be illustrated by reference to case-studies of enterprise change which, in collaboration with local-based research teams, were undertaken between 1992 and 1995.

PROTOTYPE RESTRUCTURING

In this section we discuss a prototypical case in which enterprise restructuring was identified as a strategic issue before the main political changes and while the main normative regulations from the socialist regime were still in force. It could be hypothesized that in such cases enterprise strategies would be more developed because of the longer time-span. At the Slovak enterprise, SPRINGS, a large engineering firm which in 1990 had a workforce of 2000 employees, organizational restructuring began in 1989 before the political changes later that year. SPRINGS is an example of the process that has been characterized as 'centralized decentralization' in that the process of structural divisionalization in certain enterprises was promoted or facilitated by the central authorities. The particular interest is in the impact of restructuring and ownership change on the different groups within the enterprise.

The election of a new director in August 1989 was an event which led to major organizational restructuring in advance of political change and economic reform. The conception was to produce an enterprise with a structure more similar to that of Western enterprises than that of most Czechoslovak enterprises. In essence, this was defined as involving the divisionalization of the different sections of the enterprise and increasing the autonomy of the divisions. It was developed by a group of consultants in conjunction with the candidate (from outside the enterprise) who won the election as director. The Enterprise Act of 1988, which required the election of directors organized by the Employee Council, provided the opportunity for mobilizing the change (Cziria 1995). There was opposition to the proposal from the regional party committee on the ground that it was a new and Western concept of management structure, involving decentralization, rather than a Soviet one that was being introduced. However, the internal enterprise coalition, including the enterprise party committee, was successful and the political changes in November removed all political obstacles. The programme for divisionalization was put by the external candidate and he secured 97 per cent of the votes.

Although consent to the principle had been secured from the workforce it was recognized that implementation of the programme would require further internal mobilization for a period of six months, in order to prepare and explain it fully to the employees. The central aim of the restructuring was to decentralize operational control to divisions which were given more financial independence. The size of the headquarters would be reduced and it would function primarily for strategy formulation. There was opposition from some headquarters staff so that cooperation was lost and the units of the chief engineer and the legal adviser were closed down. However, there was no opposition from the workforce.

It is significant that the concept of the restructuring was essentially managerial. It was designed to give some authority to operational managers but also to provide accounting information by which the costs of operations in relation to products could be assessed and inefficiencies could be identified. Although the consent of employees was needed there was no conception of new approaches to the motivation of the workforce. Increased efficiency was to come through changes in managerial structures and mechanisms.

The political changes of November 1989 coincided with the development of the divisional structure. The appointment of divisional heads was done by competition in order to avoid political influence on selection. Seven divisions were established in January 1990 and they came into operation in July with an internal market and internal prices which were fixed by the centre. Each division was a profit centre and had its own account at the enterprise bank which operates like a commercial bank charging interest on loans to divisions. However, although the top controlled 80 per cent of investments, 20 per cent remained with the divisions.

The process of restructuring (and political changes) led to a reorganization and separation of interests both vertically and horizontally. Thus, the trade union representatives ceased to be part of the management team and managers joined a separate association while there was a change in trade union office holders at the time of the political changes. Trade union sections were established for each division and the mechanisms of collective agreements were negotiated at both enterprise and divisional level. One aim of divisionalization was to relate bonuses to economic performance. It was noted that this fostered identification with the division. The members of less prosperous divisions particularly expressed dissatisfaction with the transfer of administrative and accounting staff from the top to the divisional level. First-line supervisors, on the other hand, were dissatisfied that divisions were not as fully independent as they had anticipated.

In the conditions of market crisis of 1991 the enterprise was successful in substituting its own distribution network for that of the established trade organization and in developing direct export links so that the values of exports in 1991 were almost four times as much as in 1989. The year 1991 saw a reduction of one third in the number of employees from 2100 to 1400. This however, was mainly the result of divestment of activities and employees to private firms and other companies rather than redundancy leading to loss of employment. This restructuring of activities through leasing of services and non-core activities was the first stage of privatization in 1991. Arising from the 1991 Privatization Act management prepared a project approved by the Ministry. By creating an external fund which they controlled and selling assets to a foreign joint venture they were able to achieve a controlling interest in the company's share for a group of 24 managers; in effect it became a management buy-out with the support of the divisions. The constitution of the joint stock company at the end of 1992 was an event that did not promote competing interests.

Decentralization in this context was set in the framework of business plans. The divisions had operational responsibility for implementing these plans but quality control, the wage system, the management of human resources and investment were centrally controlled. The formal institutions and mechanisms of labour relations have changed very little since 1991. There was an enterprise trade union committee composed of representatives from the divisions which met top management to negotiate the collective agreement within the framework of the branch agreement.

Between 1993 and 1995 there was a further process of internal restructuring and ownership change. Several divisions were merged and replaced by four joint-stock companies wholly owned by the holding company but who now became legally the employers of the workers – a process which initially provoked mistrust among the workers. However, the structure of trade union representation has not been altered by this change and the tariff scales remain the basis for grading. Actual earnings have, however, increased more than the general trend. The changes in the structures and mechanisms of the management have gradually resulted in increases in labour productivity and an intensification of the labour process.

Significance of the Case

This case is remarkable for the continuing, uninterrupted, succession of managerially led changes. The enterprise has been reshaped according to the criteria selected by managers, rather than externally driven. There were two main occasions when management had to cope with external constraints: the first event was in securing political acceptance of the restructuring in 1989; the second was when a top management group achieved a controlling share holding in 1991, when the national political strategy for privatization was designed to establish a preponderance of external governance. In SPRINGS, restructuring and ownership change has involved a series of stages: initial divisionalization, divestment of activities, formal ownership change and further internal restructuring changing divisions into companies. The initial restructuring required mobilization from the top to secure the consent of the workforce and the only opposition came from within groups of managers. The subsequent changes in internal structure evoked concern from sections of the workforce but management were able to reproduce consent through negotiations with their representatives.

Clarke *et al.* (1994) have argued in respect of Russian enterprises that restructuring is predominantly at the top of the enterprises and that the reorganization of the labour process itself remains unattempted, in part because management fears the conflicts that this might involve. In SPRINGS the reorganization of the labour process has been gradual and the most significant changes have occurred recently, resulting in improvements in labour productivity. What is striking about the case is the continuity of change from before 1989 and the enterprise-led nature of the ownership change processes.

BULGARIAN FLEXTOOLS AND POLISH POLTOOLS

This pair of cases come from the engineering sector and initially both had about 2000 employees. They both make tools, though Poltools is mainly for industrial uses while Flextools is primarily for the consumer market. Although there have been some changes in the ownership relationship, neither has been privatized. Consequently, the particular interest is how processes of restructuring have proceeded. This means assessing the influence of both external conditions and of internal agencies.

Poltools was a flagship company (part of a *Kombinat*) in the 1980s with good political connections through its director which enabled it to secure improved technologies at a time when such investment was rarely available to other enterprises. The new technology enabled some production to be made at world standards. The workforce is predominantly male. Its 'political' status led to it being selected for the introduction of the brigade organization of work in the period 1986–9. (Brigade organization of work was only adopted in a small number of enterprises in Poland.)[3] This restructuring, implemented through party activists, was designed to establish the brigades as cost centres with the brigade leaders negotiating with the departmental manager and eliminating the intervening level of management. One interpretation of this restructuring led by the director was that it would neutralize the influence of the Employee Council. In practice this top–down restructuring produced negative reactions among the workforce because its operation was seen as depending on an arbitrary system of payment and on personal connections. In 1988 the company was externally proposed for prototype transformation into a so-called 'nomenclature' company. This process was blocked by Solidarity, which had reestablished itself following the changed political climate in February 1989. Solidarity, which in this enterprise had been mainly an organization of blue-collar workers, became the leading agency in articulating worker interests in relation to the restructuring of the enterprise and the form of privatization. During the 1980s OPZZ had been dominated by middle management but after 1989 it became less active and stood aside from the interest issues around privatization.

The conflict in 1989 was centred on the form of privatization and specifically on the formation of internal companies, in which it seemed that the shares would go to persons inside and outside the company connected with the director. Solidarity organized a strike and the director resigned in 1990. His successor was appointed on the basis of a plan to restore the internal structures and end the internal companies. However, he failed to achieve the latter and the director of employee affairs concluded that the director was improperly involved in these companies. With the support of Solidarity and a proposal for privatization to include employee shareholding, the employee affairs director was able to organize a successful campaign against the director in 1991 and to succeed him as an 'administrative director'. The idea of employee shareholding was popular as a form of privatization with some teams of workers although the practicality of raising significant funds from them was doubtful.

In 1991 the Ministry of Property Transformation included Poltools in the list of four hundred enterprises scheduled for 'commercialization' followed by 'mass privatization'. Management used all its efforts in getting it withdrawn from this list, in which it was successful. The new director was appointed on the basis of a 'management contract' with the Ministry signed at the beginning of 1992. The intention was to strengthen the power of the director (the Employee Council was dissolved at this time), and to provide a financial incentive to produce a restructuring programme. Although the support of Solidarity had been a major factor in the Managing Director's appointment, he soon attempted to reduce its role. He aimed to build a strong management structure unhampered by 'social factors' and to exclude the trade unions from decisions on restructuring. However, this was a period of extreme financial difficulty for the enterprise. The Solidarity representatives demanded to see the programme for restructuring the enterprise but the director refused. The issue of the programme became the main source of conflict within the enterprise. Solidarity pressed for the establishment of the Management Board delayed by the director and later Solidarity complained to the Ministry of Industry. In June 1993 the Ministry ended the director's contract and announced a competition for the position. The grounds for the action were delays in setting up a supervisory board and developing the restructuring programme and the deterioration of financial results in 1992. (Solidarity immediately negotiated an increase in wages for employees with the interim director.) The commission for appointing his successor in 1993 consisted of five external representatives (three from the Ministry and two from banks) and four internal representatives (two from the Advisory Council and one each from Solidarity and OPZZ). There were ten candidates (four internal and six external) and they were asked to present programmes for the development of the enterprise based on study of enterprise documents. The candidate favoured by OPZZ, the former chief accountant, who was also supported by Solidarity, was successful. The researcher's judgement was that in the selection process the opinion of the employees' representatives was important but not decisive and that, within the commission, consensus was achieved on the appointment which was on the basis of a managerial contract. The enterprise remained a state company and privatization was deferred pending stabilization of the enterprise's financial and market situation. The outcome of the selection process was the establishment, for the first time for many years, of an internal consensus around the programme of restructuring.

Flextools was founded in the early 1960s but its main development dates from 1968 when it secured a licence from a foreign company to make electrical tools. This cooperation, which provided technical and managerial know-how, lasted until 1986 when Bulgarian failure to meet delivery targets led to the severance of the arrangement by the foreign partner. Production was oriented for exports – formerly the Soviet Union and more recently towards the West.

In common with other Bulgarian enterprises the principal change in labour relations in the 1980s was the introduction of the brigade organization of work and the increased powers given to the labour collective. Changes in trade union organization followed the political changes at the end of 1989 when about 100 employees were laid off: the formation of Podkrepa in the enterprise and the restructuring of the branch trade union affiliated to CITUB.[4] The basis of the Podkrepa membership was political: the initial common interest of its members, drawn from across the enterprise, was anti-communism. By 1993 its functions were primarily industrial but its 80 or so members continued as a separate organization.

The first major threat to the enterprise and its employees came with the market crisis of 1991–2. The management aimed to secure employment as far as possible and although 150 workers were laid off, the fall in production was proportionately much greater. However, the company was able to remain solvent because it could raise prices and secure credits. Recruitment was restricted and new workers were hired on short-term contracts.

In August 1992 the replacement of the General Director was a significant event in the development of the enterprise. In this year a large number of directors were replaced in the context of policies supported by the Union of Democratic Forces (UDF) government elected in October 1991. This event revealed the roles of internal and external agencies and the perceptions of interests of groups within the enterprise. The main driving force for change was the organization of Podkrepa inside the enterprise which floated the idea early in 1992 but it was soon linked with the national organization and with the ruling coalition of the UDF in the locality. The case against the director was nominally based on the need to secure the future of the enterprise – it was claimed that he had been responsible for earlier mistakes and the failure to move beyond a survival strategy. On the other hand, from the standpoint of employees, he had successfully reoriented the shift from the Russian to Western markets, maintained employment at relatively high level and a wage level which was high for the district. Consequently, the mobilization for the change was at the top of the enterprise and not positively endorsed by the base. At this time the Ministry initiated proposals for privatization which involved negotiations with potential foreign partners. Top management saw ownership change in this form as a potential threat rather than an opportunity to operate with more freedom. The fear was that a foreign owner might buy the plant and close it to remove competition.

Changes in labour relations were strongly influenced by developments in policy at the national level. The process of collective bargaining began in the summer of 1991 stimulated externally by the national tripartite initiative (Thirkell and Teseneva 1992). In the joint negotiations the unions were the leading agency and wages were the most contentious issue. There were similar annual negotiations in 1992 and 1993. In 1993 the negotiations were set in the context of the new labour code which extended the range of issues for negotiation. Commissions of management and union representatives were set up to agree issues of interpretation of the agreement and to assess the competence of those threatened with dismissal.

There were major events in 1994 and 1995. At the end of 1994 the enterprise was officially placed in the privatization procedure which made it open to offers, including those from foreign investors as well as Bulgarian business groups. However, by August 1995 the privatization agency had made no decision about ownership. In May 1995 the General Director was dismissed, as was the Production Director with whom he had been in conflict, while the former director dismissed in 1992 returned to the Board. These positional changes were the result of external events, including the sessional meeting of the regional Bulgarian Socialist Party in May which decided on the replacement of politically unacceptable directors. However, more significant in the context of prospective privatization were the internal links with competing external business groups. The General Director had connections with one of these groups but the Production Director did not support this. A second group sought support from the trade unions in Flextools and in other enterprises in the competition for control of enterprises through privatization. CITUB finally decided in favour of the Director's dismissal. Podkrepa, on the other hand, had at one stage threatened a strike if the Production Manager was dismissed.

There has been a significant shift in the attitude of management towards privatization. As explained above this was formerly seen as a threat which might lead to the takeover of its markets and the closure of the enterprise by a foreign buyer. Until recently their position was that the enterprise should remain state property but with provision for shares to be held by management, the workers and external holders. The shift in approach has been caused by recognition that substantial investment for modern technology is essential to meet growing competition from China and that prospective Bulgarian business groups may be a source of capital to ensure a prosperous company. For the workforce, apart from the issue of managerial appointments which was mainly one for the union leadership, the main issue in privatization was the acquisition of a 20 per cent block of shares allocated for employee purchase at half price, for which 80 per cent of the workforce has applied. However, the vouchers and workers' savings will not be sufficient to buy all the block and the trade unions will press potential buyers of the enterprise to cover the remaining part of the block as part of the deal.

THE CASES COMPARED

Both of these cases had a legacy as leading enterprises in terms of products and technology but Solidarity as a revived agency from the early 1980s was a more significant institutional inheritance and focused around the hostility to the imposed changes of the 1980s which were not an issue at Flextools. At Poltools restructuring and the position of successive managing directors became the salient issue over the whole period. The constellation of internal forces was sufficient to block restructuring until 1994 and the external agencies were unsuccessful in directing the enterprise towards a viable form of privatization. The trade unions in this case seem to have developed as institutions with the support of their members, whereas management were unsuccessful in developing institutional structures and mechanisms. At Flextools the replacement of managing directors was more closely related to developments in the party-political arena although the internal agencies had an active part, but the issues were not primarily about enterprise restructuring.

The presence of two trade unions in both enterprises and their development makes an interesting contrast especially in the shifting balance between political and industrial functions. Thus, both Solidarity and Podkrepa had political functions but these shifted to mainly industrial functions in post-socialist conditions. The reformed unions – CITUB and OPZZ – both limited their functions to those of interest representation within an employment rather than a political framework. In the Polish enterprise the range of issues which came within the field of management–union labour relations were wider than in Flextools mainly because of the salience of restructuring as an issue at Poltools. In the Bulgarian plant, external standards from the tripartite negotiations and the labour code were more apparent than at

Poltools and the periodic process of collective bargaining was more institutionalized, including the development of commissions. Both of the cases indicate the negotiated and contingent nature of privatization; in neither enterprise was it a simple exercise for external agencies to implement their reform agendas. Employees at Poltools were attracted to employee share ownership as an aspect of privatization. This was also apparent later in Flextools.

CONCLUSIONS

This chapter has set out to show examples of the enterprise level dynamics of restructuring and privatization. These cases, drawing on evidence gathered over a number of years, dispel any assumptions that the process of enterprise transformation in Eastern Europe is a relatively straightforward one, involving one or two stages carried out over a short period of time. The cases also suggest the importance of understanding both the general economic and political heritage and the enterprise-specific legacies from the past. In this sense there may be more continuity in strategy formulation in some enterprises than might have been expected.

An important general issue is the relationship between the external environment and the articulation of interests within the enterprise, and the effects of these on the dynamics of restructuring and privatization. Processes within the enterprise are generally related to the attempts by senior management to increase their autonomy and hence their room for manoeuvre. Specifically, this may involve the mobilization of internal interests and/or contacts outside the enterprise to foster the outcomes of internal restructuring and to promote or prevent ownership change. The replacement or appointment of enterprise directors has emerged as a key issue and stage in organizational change. Here we can see clearly the struggle between the competing interests of Ministries and state privatization agencies, the managers themselves, the trade unions, mechanisms of worker involvement, such as the Employee Councils in Poland, and local political interests.

In the case of the SPRINGS enterprise we see an example of a managerially driven change which succeeded in achieving a high degree of enterprise autonomy from external controls and a share structure with a high proportion of internal ownership. This was accomplished after initial political and internal opposition from some managerial groups had been overcome. The Poltools case shows five years of mainly internal conflicts in which a succession of managing directors failed to secure consent for their restructuring proposals from the workforce whose interests were articulated by Solidarity. The external privatization agency was continuously involved but was successfully resisted by the coalition of the managing director and the workforce, when it included the enterprise in the list for early privatization. In Flextools the restructuring of sales has been more important than the restructuring of the enterprise. Here the relationship to the external institutional environment has been influenced more directly by the changing fortunes of political parties which have been reflected in the changing managing directors. The role of the trade unions as agencies in these changes were significant, although their actions cannot be seen as autonomous but rather the result of interaction with outside organizations. As the privatization of Flextools approached in 1995, it was notable that potential owner groups from outside have sought trade-union as well as managerial support for their strategies.

This discussion has necessarily been limited to a few enterprises, and caution must be exercised in generalizing from these cases.[5] Nevertheless, the experience recounted here of three post-communist enterprises at least suggests that they are very much participants in transformation processes and not merely passive recipients of privatization projects devised elsewhere. They also indicate the enduring significance of the specific legacies in each country. Thus, a diversity of outcomes is likely from country to country and indeed within each country. This casts doubt on the likelihood, and possibly the feasibility of, a rapid 'transition' of Eastern European countries to a depoliticized labour relations system akin to those in Western Europe. Indeed, as other chapters in this book also suggest, our findings imply that models of labour relations (and of human resource management) developed within the market economies of Northern Europe and the United States may be inappropriate for projecting future trends in Eastern Europe. Instead, it could be that paradigms of management control of the kinds that have emerged in southern Europe or even Asia have greater applicability.

NOTES

1. This chapter draws on research funded by the Economic and Social Research Council under its East–West Initiative. We are grateful to the following consultants and researchers who prepared the case study reports on which this chapter is based: Bulgaria – consultant: Professor K. Petrov, researcher: G. Gradev; Poland – consultant, Professor W. Morawski, researcher: Dr M. Ferderowicz; Slovakia – consultant and researcher, Dr L. Cziria.

2. On the significance of the distinction between 'command' and 'planned' economies, see Nolan (1995).
3. In 1988 Gorbachov and Jaruzelski visited Poltools to consider the viability of the brigade model for *perestroika* reforms.
4. Podkrepa was the first new trade union in Bulgaria after the political changes of 1989. The older trade unions declared their independence from the Party and re-formed themselves as the Confederation of Independent Trade Unions (CITUB) in 1990 (see Petkov and Gradev 1995: 41–3)
5. A broader range of cases, including enterprises involving foreign ownership, is discussed in Thirkell *et al.* (1997).

REFERENCES

Aslund, A. (1992), *Post Communist Economic Revolutions: How Big a Bang?*. Washington: Centre for Strategic and International Studies.
Burawoy, M. and J. Lukacs, (1992), *The Radiant Past: Ideology and Reality in Hungary's Road to Capitalism*. Chicago: University of Chicago Press.
Burawoy, M. and P. Krotov (1992), 'The Soviet transition from socialism to capitalism: worker control and economic bargaining in the wood industry'. *American Sociological Review*, 57.
Clague, C. (1992), 'The journey to a market economy' in C. Clague and G.C. Rausser (eds), *The Emergence of Market Economies in Eastern Europe*. Oxford: Blackwell.
Clarke, S., P. Fairbrother, V. Borisov and P. Bizyukov (1994), 'The privatization of industrial enterprises in Russia: four case studies'. *Europe–Asia Studies*, 46(2).
Cziria, L. (1995), 'The Czech and Slovak republics' in J. Thirkell, R. Scase and S. Vickerstaff (eds), *Labour Relations and Political Change in Eastern Europe*. London: UCL Press.
Dabrowski, J.M., M. Federowicz and A. Levitas (1991), 'Polish state enterprises and the properties of performance: stabilization, marketization, privatization'. *Politics and Society*, 19(4).
Deppe, R. and M. Tatur (1995), 'Trade union configurations and transformation policy in Poland and Hungary'. Paper given to the ICCEES 5th World Congress. Warsaw, 6–11 August.
Federowicz, M. (1994), *Poland's Economic Order: Persistence and Transformation*. Warsaw: Federich Ebert Foundation.
Filtzer, D.A. (1991), 'The contradictions of the marketless market: self-financing in the soviet industrial enterprise, 1986–90'. *Soviet Studies*, 43(6).
Gradev, G. (1996), 'Privatization policies and the role of management in Britain and Bulgaria: a review of the literature'. Unpublished paper, Canterbury Business School, University of Kent.
Henderson, J., R. Whitley, G. Lengyel and L. Czaban (1995), 'Contention and confusion in industrial transformation: dilemmas of state economic management' in E.J. Dittrich, G. Schmidt and R. Whitley (eds), *Industrial Transformation in Europe*. London: Sage Publications.
Kabalina, V., P. Fairbrother, S. Clarke and V. Borisov (1994), 'Privatisation and the struggle for control of the enterprise in Russia'. Paper given to the ESRC East–West programme Workshop on Privatisation, London, June.

Kiss, Y. (1992), 'Privatization in Hungary – two years later'. *Soviet Studies*, 44(6).

Kornai, J. (1980), *Economics of Shortage*, Volume B. Amsterdam: North Holland Publishing Co.

Major, I. (1993), *Privatization in Eastern Europe*. Aldershot: Edward Elgar.

Markoczy, L. (1993), 'Managerial and organizational learning in Hungarian–Western mixed management organizations'. *International Journal of Human Resource Management*, 4(2).

Murrell, P. (1993), 'Evolution in economics and in the economic reform of the centrally planned economies' in C. Clague and G.C. Rausser (eds), *The Emergence of Market Economies in Eastern Europe*. Oxford: Blackwell.

Myant, M. (1993), *Transforming Socialist Economies: The Case of Poland and Czechoslovakia*. Aldershot: Edward Elgar.

Nolan, P. (1995), *China's Rise, Russia's Fall*. London: Macmillan.

Nuti, D.M. and R. Portes (1993), 'Central Europe – the way forward' in R. Portes (ed.), *Economic Transformation in Central Europe*. London: Centre for Economic Policy Research.

Petkov, K. and G. Gradev (1995), 'Bulgaria' in J. Thirkell, R. Scase and S. Vickerstaff (eds), *Labour Relations and Political Change in Eastern Europe*. London: UCL Press.

Petkov, K. and J. Thirkell (1991), *Labour Relations in Eastern Europe*. London: Routledge.

Przeworski, A. (1993), 'Economic reforms, public opinion, and political institutions: Poland in the Eastern European perspective' in L.C.B. Pereira, J.M. Maravall and A. Przeworski (eds), *Economic Reforms in New Democracies*. Cambridge: Cambridge University Press.

Thirkell J.,R. Scase and S. Vickerstaff (1994), 'Labour relations in Eastern Europe in transition'. *Industrial Relations Journal*, 25(2).

Thirkell, J., R. Scase and S. Vickerstaff (eds) (1995), *Labour Relations and Political Change in Eastern Europe*. London: UCL Press.

Thirkell, J., K. Petkov and S. Vickerstaff (1997), *The Transformation of Labour Relations: Restructuring and Privatization in Eastern Europe and Russia*. Oxford: Oxford University Press.

Thirkell, J. and E. Teseneva (1992), 'Bulgarian labour relations in transition: tripartism and collective bargaining'. *International Labour Review*, 31(3).

Thompson, P. and C. Smith (1992), 'Socialism and the labour process in theory and practice' in C. Smith and P. Thompson (eds), *Labour in Transition*. London: Routledge.

van Brabant. J.M. (1990), *Remaking Eastern Europe: On the Political Economy of Transition*. Dordrecht: Kluwer Academic Publishing.

Whitley, R. and J. Henderson (1995), 'Emergent capitalism: ownership, control and change in Hungarian enterprises' in H. Rudolph (ed), *WZB Jahrbuch 1995*. Berlin: Edition Sigma.

Whitley, R., J. Henderson, L. Czaban and G. Lengyel (1996), 'Continuity and change in an emergent market economy: the limited transformation of large enterprises in Hungary' in R. Whitley and P.H. Kristensen (eds) *The Changing European Firm*. London: Routledge.

10 Ideologies, Economic Policies and Social Change: the Cyclical Nature of Hungary's Transformation[1]

Laszlo Czaban

By the end of the 1980s, a general crisis had developed in Hungary. It was not only a crisis of the state socialist system, as the change of that system did not solve it. It was not only an economic crisis, since it affected other spheres of social life. In this chapter it will be argued that the central issue of this crisis was the incapability of the elites to put Hungary back into the mainstream of technological and economic development.

In the early 1990s the remedies advocated in academic and political circles for the problems of Eastern Europe started from the assumption that something revolutionary had happened in the region and this provided the precondition for a rapid transition to the free-market economy and to political democracy. These 'remedies' were based, implicitly, on the assumption that East European societies and their economies would become, and would have to become, similar to those of the advanced countries and any diversion from this would have to be strongly criticized. The recipe for the future seemed very straightforward: liberalization, deregulation, privatization and de-statization. Although most East European countries have made attempts to apply this recipe, the transition has proved to be relatively slow and, in many respects, has lacked a firm domestic social base. Experience in the first half of the 1990s shows that just as the introduction of state socialism did not have a script, the transition from state socialism has not had one either.

In this chapter it will be argued that the transition from state socialism in Hungary started much earlier than 1989–90; the changes of 1989–90 in many respects interrupted organic development; the domestic political and economic basis of the transition has been weak and has been further weakened by the manifestation of contradictory interests; these factors have resulted in periodical slow-downs and speed-ups of the transition; and that

224

the main forces of the transition in Hungary are the transnational companies and international organizations.

STATE SOCIALISM AND THE TRANSITION TO CAPITALISM

By the early 1960s in Hungary primary industrialization and the collectivization of agriculture (commodity producing agriculture) had been accomplished. With this the state socialist regime had achieved the basic modernization task that the bourgeoisie was unable previously to fulfil. Although this transformation provided for significant increases in productivity and reserves, the level of development (by international comparison) remained relatively low (Bekker 1973). The need for further resources demanded the modification of the existing social, economic and institutional system. However, international circumstances, the domestic situation, and the lack of experience, and supportive social movements and ideologies, made systemic reform impossible. Given this situation, the country's leadership chose to compromise with various factions within Hungarian society, and this eventually led to system stabilization in the mid-1960s.

The core mechanism of the system was central planning. Central planning was a bargaining process between branch Ministries and trade unions on the one hand and planning offices and central party bodies on the other. The role of the trade unions was crucial. Trade unions under state socialism were vertically integrated organizations: integrated and managed by enterprise managers and Ministry officials. Institutionally, management and employees were members of the same union. As a result, the behaviour of the trade unions was similar to that of other economic interest lobbies; namely, they acted to achieve advantageous conditions for the development of 'their' industrial branch *vis-à-vis* other branches.

The planning process was necessarily bureaucratic since it cut across production lines and along the boundaries of the industrial branches, as the interest groups associated with the branches (Ministries, trade unions and chambers of commerce) were organized on this basis. The planning mechanism, then, set the sectors against each other as the process of resource allocation proceeded.

The central planning process had three important consequences from the point of view of this chapter. On the one hand, its procedures help to explain the rather limited resistance of those who lost out in the transition of the early 1990s, and on the other it helps explain the necessity of marketization. Additionally, it also helps to explain the relatively limited change experienced since 1989–90.

Hungarian industrialization, for historical reasons, was largely based on heavy industry and this brought about two important consequences: investment funds were relatively low, even though the operation of the production system required additional resources; and the development of the higher levels of vertical integration (downstream processing) began to be pursued only in the second half of the 1960s. While existing industry did not provide for the necessary quantity of additional resources, reallocation of significant resources from other spheres (agriculture, consumption), mainly because of the experiences of the uprising of 1956, was unacceptable to the political leadership. There were two possible solutions to this situation within given conditions: either a slow and unstable development or the utilization of external resources. The structure of the existing institutional system privileged the second choice, as this would not endanger the political and social compromise or the allocation of power.

It was for these reasons that the tendency underlying the economic history of Hungary from the second half of the 1950s was a 'stop-go' cycle. Specifically, the need of the economic sectors for additional resources created foreign trade problems that exacerbated indebtedness. As a consequence, an austerity period was implemented but this threatened the priorities (extension of the production base, increasing living standards) of the political leadership. Thus as soon as the situation stabilized somewhat, restrictions were relaxed, and the cycle started again.[2]

Due to state ownership and the role of the Hungarian Socialist Workers Party (hereafter HSWP) in the regime, these economic problems always appeared as political problems. Decisions, then, had to be made at the political level, and thus trust in the bureaucracy was a precondition. However, economic competence within the bureaucracy was missing and this was one of the main reasons for the gradual and partial marketization of the economy in the 1960s.

Another major reason for the marketization of the 1960s was the need to weaken Hungary's unilateral political and economic dependence on the Soviet Union. Khrushchev's expulsion from power in 1964 was the signal the Hungarian leadership needed to initiate reforms (Kadar 1990).

Finally, the accomplishment of collectivization in agriculture was an important element in the reform. With collectivization, agriculture could appear as a unified interest represented by strong political figures. Since the reform was based on foreign trade expansion, in which agriculture was supposed to play a significant role, and because of the above-mentioned political priority of increasing living standards, the weight of demands from agriculture for industrial products and technologies (via licences) increased. Furthermore, Hungarian agriculture was collectivized on a different basis from the Soviet Union (the rich peasantry were prioritized and there was a larger role for household plots), and this required different regulatory methods.

As a result of these factors and as a solution to increasing macroeconomic problems, the New Economic Mechanism (hereafter NEM) was introduced in 1968. The name of the reform expressed the expectation of the political leadership that from then onwards, economic issues would be managed as technical, rather than political, problems.

Contrary to the general perception (as in Kornai 1993), the above-described institutional system was by no means monolithic. It reflected (and to some extent represented) not only the various particular interests, but also the different factions within the elite (politicians and technocrats, branch and functional Ministries, national authorities, and so forth) and their dependence on the prevailing form of political power.

The NEM was an attempt to overcome the irrationalities of direct and detailed regulation by introducing competition and (politically) neutral regulation; however, during the entire period of the NEM the main macroeconomic processes required constant adjustment. The NEM, instead of implementing feasible economic management and regulation, relied on a belief in the eternal rationality of market.

The NEM also exacerbated the structural problems of the Hungarian economy. Companies shifted their import purchases from the CMEA to Western sources, cooperative relationships between companies weakened, the debt-burdened balance-sheet structure of large industrial companies required capital injection by the state instead of the commercial financing assumed by the NEM, and the new regulations tended to support risk-avoidance behaviour and thus (unintentionally) worked to sustain the existing economic structure rather than modifying it.

These inherent contradictions of the NEM reinforced the struggles between the interest groups themselves as well as between the central governmental organizations and those groups. As the entire reform was based on projections of a fast-growing world economy, and this did not occur (as a result of the first oil shock and the 1973–5 recession), the country moved towards a general economic and social crisis. Clashes of interests obstructed the political will to reverse this tendency and consequently the latter was able only to moderate the speed at which the crisis developed.

To manage the situation, the reforms associated with the NEM were slowed down, and then reversed to some extent (in 1972–3). The power base for this development was the large industrial companies, and it resulted in a wide-ranging reshuffle in economic administration and a redesign of administrative authority. The new structure meant that the functional authorities (Ministry of Finance, Central Planning Office, National Bank of Hungary [hereafter NBH], National Price and Materials Office) gained an upper hand over branch Ministries and these bodies began to make political decisions. With these institutional and personnel changes, the fragmentation of the state and economic policy-making accelerated, and branch Ministries lost many of their functions of coordinating company interests (Carroll *et al.*1988, Henderson *et al.* 1995). Large companies began to bypass the Ministries and lobbied the central authorities directly (Szalai 1989).

DISINTEGRATION OF THE STATE SOCIALIST SYSTEM

As a result of the regulatory weaknesses of the NEM, policy decisions, the advice of the bureaucracy to base development and economic management on external resources (and the receptivity of the political leadership to such advice), and growing protectionism in export markets, Hungary slid into a debt trap and became virtually insolvent by 1979. The situation forced the political leadership to abandon its policy of stable economic growth with increasing living standards. At the same time, and based on its technical competence, the financial bureaucracy gained almost a free hand in the management of external economic relations, with the exception of those with the CMEA (Czaban 1990).

As early as the beginning of the 1970s, some advisers of the government and some groups in the bureaucracy proposed that Hungary should join the International Monetary Fund (hereafter IMF) and the World Bank. This, however, met resistance from the USSR. With the indebtedness of the country the situation changed. The financial and monetary faction of the bureaucracy claimed that the only way of avoiding insolvency – and its consequences – was membership in these two international organizations. Exclusion of Hungary (and other Eastern European countries) from international capital markets in 1981–2 reinforced their argument. Although political approval for joining the IMF and World Bank occurred only in 1981 it was clear that one of the reasons for reform of the NEM was to meet IMF membership requirements (internal government documents cited by Vigvari 1990). Therefore, from as early as 1979, Hungarian economic policy can be considered as IMF-conforming.

The differences between the economic policy priorities of the National Bank (NBH), the Ministry of Finance and the National Planning Office, led to a purge of high- and middle-ranking officials in the latter in the late

1970s. The position of the Ministry of Finance and NBH was further stabilized by changes in the structure of government. In 1980, branch Ministries were merged into a single Ministry of Industry. Preoccupied with shaping its new structure and finding its role, this Ministry could not participate effectively in government struggles. As a result, the motivation of companies to individually and directly lobby central authorities further increased and with this the fragmentation of the state caused instability for the companies themselves (Henderson *et al.* 1995).

From the perspective of economic transformation and its cyclical nature, these developments brought significant changes. Firstly, they speeded up the disintegration of the elite of the Kadar regime that had given the system its stability. The legitimacy of that elite derived from its ability to satisfy social needs. It had been recruited from the peasantry of particular regions, from skilled workers with second and third jobs, craftsmen, managers of small businesses, party bureaucrats, state administrators and from the managers of companies and cooperatives. However, engineers and academics became disillusioned as a result of income disparities and lack of political direction and weakening control damaged party and state administrations (Csaba 1992, Kardos and Vertes 1990). Additionally, those company managers who were to become private owners acquired new interests to pursue, while many others lost their legitimacy and position as economic difficulties increased and their companies began to collapse. Furthermore, with stagnating disposable income, many craftsmen, small businessmen and skilled workers slid down the social hierarchy.

At the same time, the structure of the pressure groups changed too. Although they remained a conglomerate of interests – of managers and employees, top bureaucrats, top managers of large state-owned enterprises and so forth – on the basis of their different functions in the organization of production and distribution, they developed particular (and conflicting) interests. With the disintegration of the state socialist system and its economy, factions of the elite began to recognize that transformation of the system was in their own interests. However, different factions of the elite arrived at this recognition at different times and by way of internal struggles.

Parallel with the disintegration of the Kadar regime's elite, a new elite (albeit with continuities of personnel) began to emerge. One of the first factions of this new elite to crystallize was in the financial bureaucracy. This group was interested in transforming the system into a capitalist one in which they maintained their existing leading positions. Szelenyi (1990) calls this group 'comprador intellectuals' because of the similarity in the functions of this group and the comprador bourgeoisie of developing countries.

In order to ensure transformation to a capitalist economy two important preconditions had to be met: political intervention had to be obstructed and the support of the large enterprises had to be gained. Developments along these lines were already underway by the early 1980s.

In 1984 a 'reform package' was introduced which contained proposals for a two-tier banking system, the introduction of value-added and personal income taxes, the abolition of Ministry control over enterprises (designed to eliminate the Ministry of Industry from economic policy formulation) and the extension of the legal scope of the private sector. In exchange for the acceptance of the reform package, reform economists promised economic growth (based on external borrowing again) to the political leadership (Vigvari 1991). However, the aims of the economic growth policies and the reform package contradicted one another, with disastrous results.

The leading position of the financial lobby within the emerging new elite was reinforced by the introduction of new institutions and the reform package in general. Between 1982 and 1984 the main objective of reform was the introduction of new ways of thinking and methods of marketization. Between 1984 and 1988 establishing new institutions beyond the control of the traditional party leadership and its supporting bureaucracy became the principal objective. These two phases established the ideological, personal and institutional preconditions for changing the system, while foreign indebtedness, membership of the IMF and World Bank and the Gorbachev reforms in the USSR were the external circumstances and mediations favourable to further reforms.

As the policy to accelerate economic growth degenerated into fatal disequilibrium (indebtedness doubled in three years) and consequently resulted in highly restrictive economic policies, managers of large enterprises, who were interested in growth, finally turned away from the state socialist system. As the Acts on Business Entities and on the Transformation of State Owned Enterprises offered them the possibility of becoming capitalists, they too became part of reforming elite.

The disintegration of economic policy-making was soon followed by the disintegration of the political elite. Tensions increased due to declining living standards, higher pressure from the West (the 'Brzezinski doctrine') and the withdrawal of the Soviet Union from the region.[3] As a result, by about 1986, the political centre of the HSWP – Kadar's principal power base – had fragmented and the right wing was in the ascendant.

The fragmentation of the centre and the rise of the right wing increased in 1988–9. By the beginning of 1989, sections of the Politbureau began to recognize that for a swift transition to take place, the Party had to be marginalized. This was necessary in order to advance negotiations with the emerging opposition (Kimmel 1990) and for them personally to achieve positions of power in the new system.

Although it began as an HSWP government, the Nemeth regime of 1989–90 became the government of the system change and prepared the ground for this change.[4] While opposition forces continued to call it a 'communist government' (to pave the way for establishing their own identity), it considered itself a Western European-style social democratic government, as the memoirs of the non-party member Minister of Justice show (Kulcsar 1993). The underlying ideology of the government was neo-liberalism and its economic policy was based on neoclassical principles. Since it was a government dedicated to the continuation of the reforms, its domestic powerbase was the technocratic bureaucracy and the managers of large state-owned companies. Its survival, however, depended on the goodwill of the IMF as, without foreign loans, insolvency was an imminent danger which threatened its collapse.

This description of Hungary's last 'communist' government highlights facets of an inherent contradiction in the transition. The basis for the bureaucracy's influence was the reform process and its neo-liberal underpinnings. Both of these sought the reduction of state involvement in the economy; however, this merely deepened the chaos of macroeconomic management at a time when the need for increased accumulation in the interests of servicing the external debt demanded pro-active state involvement.

Although two (technocrats, entrepreneurs from the informal economy) of the three (descendants of the pre-state socialist elite) potential sources of the new capitalist class supported the Nemeth government, it was much too weak to preserve the system or even to maintain its economic policy. The conception of utilizing foreign investment to finance debt service and to access modern technologies and skills, and the spontaneous privatization and implementation of loose regulations as bases of the transition, had failed almost as soon as the Nemeth government had been formed. With the changing political climate the road had been opened for new social groups to acquire assets and take over the role of macro- and microeconomic management to establish themselves as the new elite.

CONCEPTIONS OF MODERNIZATION IN HUNGARY

In the Hungarian economic literature two major conceptions of modernization were developed in the years 1989–90.[5] The first of these was, in effect, the programme of transnational capital. In principle, this programme was but the continuation and extension of the economic programme of the Nemeth government. Its theoretical basis was neo-conservative monetarism and supply-side economics and its ideal was Reagan's United States and Thatcher's United Kingdom. It sought to base the modernization of the country on the resources and interests of transnational capital. To encourage capital inflow, it proposed the widest possible liberalization and deregulation, and monetary restriction (strong control of the money supply, high interest rates, surplus state budgets). Additionally the object was to force less viable companies out of business. In exchange for freeing the economy for foreign investment, the representatives of this approach expected relatively easy access to international capital markets in order to help service the debt.

The Hungarian representatives of the programme of the transnational capital relied on their belief in free markets and did not address the problems that would arise from translating these beliefs into practice. They did not anticipate the social tensions created by the destruction of the existing production culture and by high unemployment and inflation. Nor did they question whether this economic policy would provide the necessary hard currency income to service the debt; specifically, they did not anticipate that pressure for export growth and the destruction of cooperative links between domestic companies would substantially increase demand for imports. Additionally it was not clear whether foreign capital would indeed invest in a socially and economically highly unstable country, and whether, in the event, the IMF would relax its constraints on external borrowing.

The second main conception was associated with the development of a national bourgeoisie. The model for the representatives of this conception was East Asia, though with modifications. In this conception the main role in the modernization process was to be a national bourgeoisie recruited from domestic entrepreneurs and managers. Consequently, preferential treatment for domestic investors in the privatization process – with administrative limitations on foreign access to specified sectors – was proposed. The central issue in this conception was the stabilization of the domestic market, since it was assumed that in the short to medium term, the new capitalist class would be capable of operating in this market only. The proposed methods were anti-inflationary and careful exchange rate policies, some market protection, and the avoidance of monetary restrictions.

Those who argued for this conception of transformation neglected the fact that some of the circumstances that were important in East Asia did not exist in Hungary; the significant international financial support for South

Korea, for instance, being a case in point (Henderson and Appelbaum 1992). Additionally, in Hungary the programme of the domestic bourgeoisie for economic growth, within the given circumstances, was in conflict with debt-service obligations, the principle of the free flow of capital and the programme of the IMF. This conception, therefore, pointed towards conflicts with the creditors and thus exclusion from world markets, which in turn would have meant stagnation, recession and ultimately economic collapse. Furthermore, this conception necessarily would have meant that the transformation would have been very slow.

ATTEMPTS AT SWIFT TRANSITION

The common problem of these two conceptions was that neither of them addressed the inherent contradiction of the transformation process indicated above: that the reasons for the changing the state socialist system were the main obstacles for the development of the new one. In particular, none of these approaches addressed the problem of indebtedness, technical backwardness and the socio-economic environment of ownership change.

Although the above-mentioned conceptions of modernization were associated with particular political parties, theoretical approaches can be attached to certain political parties, they were not consistently reflected in the programmes of those parties. Thus the Hungarian Democratic Forum (hereafter HDF), as the leading force in the new government (1990–4), did not follow the second conception as could have been expected, but opted for 'shock therapy'.

The main reason of the implementation of shock therapy was Hungary's financial situation and IMF and US government policy that prioritized systemic change in Eastern Europe in the interests of sustainable economic growth. Political uncertainty in Eastern Europe in 1989–90 and the suspension of the one-year IMF standby loan to Hungary led to a serious fall in international reserves which threatened the economy with insolvency. In these circumstances, the new HDF-led government had but one choice: the implementation of 'shock therapy', which was the only policy the IMF supported at the time.

Shock therapy is, by definition, an anti-democratic measure, since it aims at such large-scale transformation in such a short time that it inhibits popular participation in and social adjustment to the institutional changes that are involved in the process. In theory, it can only be implemented in exceptional circumstances, that is, when other scenarios have clearly become impossible and the public is ready to accept this fact, or where the government is able and willing to suppress public discontent. In 1989–90, neither of these conditions fully existed in Eastern Europe (Gowan 1995).

The first phase of shock therapy enjoyed the support of the main opposition party, the Alliance of Free Democrats (hereafter AFD) and its support was cemented on the basis of a pact between that party and the HDF. The basis of the pact was three-fold. First, there was strong pressure from the West to establish a coalition government. Second, the government's economic programme was close to the first conception of modernization, outlined above, and the main supporters of that conception belonged to the AFD. Third, the two parties agreed to replace the management of the large state-owned enterprises, thus opening the way for a new elite to emerge. Technically, the government ordered compulsory re-elections of the chief executives of state-owned companies by the company councils. However, the attempt failed as in most cases the company councils re-elected the former chief executives. The government's plan was frustrated even further when a few months later, under even stricter rules, the company councils re-elected the same persons.

At the same time, to reinforce the governing coalition, broaden its sources of popular support and compensate the heirs of some of the ownership classes of the pre-state socialist period for their 'lost' accumulation possibilities, the government submitted a limited restitution act to parliament. These steps symbolized the failure of the HDF to recognize two very important bases of stability in the late state socialist period, and thus of the transition: the politically strong and economically viable large-scale agricultural interests, and the significant number of small businesses operating in the informal economy. These two sectors supplied a large proportion of basic needs, absorbed significant proportions of household income and expanded the domestic market for industrial goods. When the government realized the importance of these interests, it was obliged to break with the Smallholders' Party (representing small-scale agricultural interests) and had to provide a quasi-legal basis for establishing and running small businesses. The implications of these developments on the behaviour and structure (fragmentation and underworld methods) of the developing bourgeoisie cannot be underestimated.

These developments, and a third attempt by the government to bring companies under its control, ended the pact between the HDF and AFD. The government began to understand that while its influence on the economy was less than its political power, its political power was sufficient to change this situation, and thus open the way for a transformation of the elite.

The government's solution was to modify the Act on Transformation of State Owned Companies. While the original act stipulated that transformation of the companies was optional, the modification made it compulsory. From then onwards ownership rights in all state-owned companies were to be exercised through an external board whose members were appointed by the main owner, that is, the government. With this the government began to build its influence over the boards and, since they exercised appointment rights, replacement of the chief executives became possible.

The compulsory transformation of state-owned enterprises was closely connected with the change in privatization policy. The government changed the legal status of the State Property Agency (SPA), which had operated as an agency under parliamentary control, and transformed it to a government agency. Subsequently the government announced the so-called 'active privatization' programme, in which the government offered a number of companies for sale to foreign investors within a centrally organized and controlled framework. By so doing, the government retained its control over decisions to sell, or not to sell, particular enterprises to particular foreign interests.

The success of the active privatization was crucial to shock therapy, since it was known that the deregulation and full liberalization would result in a large current account deficit and falling production. Capital receipts from the active privatization programme, then, were necessary to finance the burdens of the shock. Shock therapy, however, failed before it was implemented; this was partly because the programme contradicted the interests of the coalition partners and some of the major factions of the HDF, partly because of the government's diminishing popular support (as indicated by defeat in local elections and the taxi drivers' blockade of the Danube bridges), and partly because of deteriorating external economic conditions. These factors resulted in intra-government fights in which the Economic Policy Secretariat of the Prime Minister Office emerged as an opponent of shock therapy (Henderson *et al.* 1995). These intra-government fights limited the ability of the HDF to carry out the transformation of elites to which it was commited.

The second version of shock therapy was, in fact, not shock therapy at all, but was rather the implementation of the same deregulation and liberalization programme, but in a longer time-frame. During this period, almost all price, wage and foreign trade controls, and direct subsidies, were abolished. Parliament passed Acts on the Central Bank, Commercial Banks, Accounting, Bankruptcy and so on. Although all these steps were taken, the programme of liberalization and deregulation was defeated because of the problems of privatization. The failure of the active privatization programme showed that centrally directed privatization is too slow and could not be carried out without the support of enterprise managers.

Economic deterioration also pointed to the need to change general economic policy. By the end of 1991, the recession reached rock-bottom. The recession had caused not only social problems and further diminishing support for the HDF, but had created macroeconomic management problems. Although access to international capital markets was relatively easy, the current account, mainly because of the deep recession, showed a surplus and incoming foreign capital substantially eased debt-financing. Additionally, the contracting domestic market and the collapse of CMEA markets forced companies to try to increase their exports to Western markets. Inevitably this was done at the expense of their capital equipment, as the size of their excess capacities was beyond manageable limits. This factor, the lack of additional capital and the financial consequences of the restrictions (swift and large indebtedness of enterprises, and the effects of the financial loss on the operating profits) resulted in large devaluations of existing state assets, together with largely uncontrolled privatization through liquidation procedures.

These developments forced the economic leadership of the government to break with the policy of state withdrawal from macroeconomic management. This resulted in the setting up of the Economic Policy Working Group (hereafter EPWG) in November 1991, which was headed by the privatization Minister, and consisted mainly of the state secretaries of the Ministries. With the EPWG, a powerful opposition to the fiscal and monetary bureaucracy had emerged once again.

COMPROMISE OF ELITES

The EPWG submitted its report to the government in early 1992 (Economic Policy Working Group 1992). Besides widespread state intervention (export guarantees, credit consolidation, state involvement in R&D, setting up a state holding company for managing state owned companies and so on) and open criticism of the economic policy of 1990–1, the report stated that opposition to the current management of state-owned companies was destructive and had to be stopped, not only for economic reasons, but because these people would become one of the main sources of a new Hungarian bourgeoisie. The EPWG tried to mobilize support outside the government by, for instance, lobbying the Hungarian Association of Industrialists and powerful private-sector interests (Stumpf 1991). Such extra-governmental lobbying was, in effect, an admission that only a unified elite could manage and legitimate the transition.

Technically this compromise between various factions of the elite was realized through the so-called 'decentralized privatization' programme,[6] which meant that under a certain company size, management, with the assistance of consultants, were permitted to carry out privatization. The last element in this phase was the establishment of the State Holding Company. This development meant that substantial governmental power over state assets had been secured for a longer period of time. Privatization laws of mid-1992 legitimated the existing situation: exclusive government control over privatization and state asset management. With this, the government was able to offer a choice to a large part of the elite: if they cooperated with the government and the HDF, they could participate in the accumulation of private wealth and the management of the economy.

SWITCHES IN ECONOMIC AND PRIVATIZATION POLICY

The macroeconomic management problems, the slow-down in privatization, a relatively favourable external economic situation and the diminishing legitimacy of the government resulted in a change in the economic policy. The aim of the change was to help companies to stabilize their position. In the second half of 1992, the government established the institutions earlier proposed by the EPWG, and between 1992–3 spent HUF 300 billion (about 9 per cent of GDP) on the recapitalization of the banks and on release from indebtedness.

At the same time, and in connection with the changes in economic policy, a major change in privatization policy took place. The context for this was that the interest of foreign investors in Hungarian assets had fallen while domestic purchasing power remained negligible. As a result, proceeds from privatization were not sufficient to finance the budget deficit, not to mention repayment of state debt. On the supply side, the rapid deterioration of state assets and the free transfer of assets to social security funds and various quasi-political foundations reduced the quality (attractiveness) of the assets on offer.[7]

The government tried three ways to resolve the problem. First, the possibility of purchasing state assets on the basis of government loans was extended and interest rates subsidies associated with these deals were increased. Second, the government started preparations for privatization of large companies via capital increases (in order to achieve it, large restructuring programmes were initiated). Third, preparations for privatization of banks were suspended. There were three, partly contradictory, considerations behind the third move. Selling a large bank in Hungary would have meant more than merely selling an economic unit, because the banking sector, via the large amount of bad debts, was a *de facto* owner of a large number of enterprises. Because of the concentration of bad debts government support for economic growth was largely based on the banking sector (since it was expected that large capital injections would help the banks to reduce interest rates and make lending easier). Finally, as a result of the change in functions of the state budget and the National Bank, the banking sector became a major extractor of disposable income from the economy (through high positive real interest rates) in order to finance the servicing of foreign debts.

With these changes in privatization policy, the government expected a substantial extension of its political support as well as a slow-down in the devaluation of state assets. These changes also implicitly realized the aim of compromise within the elite as they transfered assets to those who were the potential source of the Hungarian bourgeoisie: the managers of state-owned companies, technocrats who had moved from the bureaucracy to business, the entrepreneurs of the 1980s and to some extent the descendants of the traditional middle class. These changes in privatization and general economic policy also reinforced the management role of the elite in state administration, while compensation schemes and employee buy-outs secured the neutral position of relatively broad social groups towards the transition.

With regard to political ideology, these changes required a shift to conservatism. Although this had always been a part of HDF's ideology, it had been restricted to issues of culture and social life. The new conservatism helped legitimate not only larger state involvement (state responsibility), but also the needs of the emergent capitalist class for ideological support to justify its acquired position *vis-à-vis* those who had lost out in the transition. The switch to conservatism, however, remained limited for two main reasons; first, because the nature of transition still required free-market methods and the introduction of free market-institutions, and second, because of the emergence of ultra-right-wing nationalism.

Ultra-right-wing nationalism emerged between 1990 and 1992 because foreign investors and domestic capitalist groups not close to the right wing of the HDF were the main beneficiaries of privatization. Additionally, the ultra-right understood that the compromise within the elite was designed, in part, to prevent further groups from becoming capitalists. The ultra-right, however, remained marginal, partly because the government turned against it (the ultra-right endangered Hungary's international obligations) and partly for ideological reasons. The ultra-right had added chauvinism and anti-Semitism to its ideological portfolio, but the issues they highlighted were not widely regarded as significant ones. Most importantly, the ultra-right was unable to establish a popular base, as the majority of the population considered state socialism to be the main alternative to transition, not the idealized future that they (the ultra-right) offered.

In 1993–4, the external economic situation and its reflection in the state budget became the main obstacle to stabilizing the elite compromise, and therefore to the stabilization of the transition. As the basis of economic growth was the import of capital goods and large state contributions, recession in the most important export markets meant that the current account had started to deterioriate rapidly by the end of 1992 with a record deficit being registered in both 1993 and 1994. At the same time, the growth of the budget deficit accelerated to such an extent that the growth of domestic savings could not keep pace, especially as growing household income began to filter through to consumer goods purchases, the bulk of which were imported.

As a result of these developments, Hungary slid into a fiscal trap. This trap, besides endangering the solvency of the country and making the current system of public finance unsustainable,[8] increased the cost of macroeconomic management, and froze the resources needed for creating and supporting sustainable growth and thus consolidating the transition. This situation, as in the 1980s, reinforced the leading position of the Ministry of Finance and the National Bank on economic policy issues and since 1995 fiscal and monetary policies have been designed to deal with structural problems, while alternative economic policies have been swept away.

Because of Hungary's indebtedness (and the political decision for handling the indebtedness, that is, 'repaying' the debt) one of the major tasks of monetary policy was to extract income from the economy equivalent to interest payments on external debt. Since between 1990 and 1992 the current account showed a surplus, the National Bank was ready to follow the easier path and left this income in the economy. This 'retained' income was one of the main factors for the increase in imports and the relatively small decrease in general living standards between 1990 and 1994 (in 1994, real wages even grew!). This meant that foreign investment and privatization income went mainly towards current expenditure between 1990 and 1994.

The prospect of insolvency in 1995 prompted the government to withdraw not only income equivalent to the interest on foreign loans from the economy, but privatization income too. Monetary policy became very restrictive and aimed at reducing the spending of every economic agent and using their savings to finance the national indebtedness. This was a new stage of monetary restriction, since it aimed directly at reducing investment resources (while inflation reduced mainly household purchasing power). In practice it helped create a mutual interest between employers and employees in opposition to the government. This produced a stronger-than-ever ideological and public relations campaign by the Ministry of Finance and the National Bank against any alternative policy. Clearly proposals for using privatization income for investment, infrastructure or job creation implicitly questioned monetary restriction and, therefore, the dominant positions of the two institutions.

The Ministry of Finance and the National Bank recognized the danger of alienating large sections of the elite and inserted new priorities into the austerity package of March 1995. As a consequence this was the first economic programme in Hungary since World War II that openly declared that the burdens would have to be carried by the lower classes and, at the same time, burdens on entrepreneurs and high income earners would have to be reduced. Although many elements of the package failed due to the resistance of the trade unions, some factions of the principal government party – the Socialist Party (which had been elected in mid-1994) – and because some components were unconstitutional. Thus economic policy explicitly, and dismantling the welfare state implicitly, became the routes to the reduction of real wages.

With these steps, and in spite of modifications implemented in 1996, the financial bureaucracy of the state and the upper echelons of the financial sector in general have secured their leading position within the Hungarian elite. They have also averted conflict with other elite factions (who have been concerned that monetary restrictions have delivered competitive advantage to foreign companies, and threaten social harmony) with measures that provide investment resources and improve living standards. Additionally, while continuing to circumvent the problem of foreign indebtedness and without entirely subordinating sustainable growth to IMF-required policy measures, the National Bank and the Ministry of Finance have managed to maintain the support of the international financial community. Whatever the short-term success of these policies, however, they effectively divert attention from the need to deal with the causes of the general crisis of Hungarian society and its economy.

At the political level, the Socialist Party-AFD coalition is in effect an expression of the balance of interests within the elite that I have described above. The Socialist Party continues to have strong support from managers, much of the state bureaucracy and the banking sector (as well as workers), while the AFD can deliver the support of sections of the former groups as well as that of a large proportion of intellectuals.

CONCLUSION

In Hungary, the composition of the new capitalist class has already been determined. The elites that have managed the transformation thus far have learned that factional in-fighting could endanger the entire transformation process. On the other hand, the internal struggles of the elite show that the dominant positions have not yet been stabilized and that the leading role is under constant challenge. The periodic return to dominance of the financial faction of the elite is dependent on macroeconomic factors and the open support of the international financial institutions. Maintenance of their dominant position also requires state support for other elite groups.[9] As a result of these developments, other sections of the emergent capitalist class (entrepreneurs and others) remain heavily dependent on the state and the political process. In this situation the state-bureaucratic faction of the elite, while pursuing their own interests, have had to maintain this delicate balance within the elite. Accomplishing these tasks has not yet required the search for solutions to the structural crisis of Hungarian society and economy and nothing makes it inevitable that it will. As the legitimacy of the transition derives from the need to solve the crisis, however, the dominant position of the elite remains problematic, and with it the stability of the transition.

Transformation, then, has not solved the most crucial problem of Hungary's economic development: the reallocation and development of investment resources. As a consequence the economic cycle has continued to be locked into a 'stop-go' sequence, and to be coupled with dysfunctional state interventions. The main difference between the economic cycles in the state socialist period and the current ones is that behind the latter now lie fragmented capitalist groups in addition to bureaucratic factions.

The nature of the economic cycle addressed in this chapter has been the predominant influence on the speed of the transition and is the underlying cause of the periodic economic reversals that stretch back to the 1960s. Since 1979, the most important element has been foreign indebtedness, and thus the influence of the IMF. While the HSWP was unable to control its own bureaucracy, the IMF was able to control the most important bureaucratic factions of the state socialist system. Today, while the new capitalist class is unable to control the state bureaucracy in order to achieve a more favourable basis for competition, the IMF is able to exercise pressure and control the most important bureaucratic factions of the state. Though insolvency and its consequences will not inevitably result from resisting the IMF, the risk is simply too great to be taken by any social strata.

Since 1989 foreign ownership has become significant in Hungary and owing to foreign indebtedness, loss of markets and lack of capital, further foreign investment is a primary interest of the Hungarian elite. The question is not whether Hungary needs foreign capital but rather the conditions foreign capital will require in order to invest further. The shift in export markets, the recession and the operation of foreign-owned companies has already changed Hungary's economic structure and domestic market. When all these processes are taken into account, it becomes clear that the dominant position in developing Hungary's systemic change lies – and is likely to continue to lie – with international companies and international financial organisations.[10] It is these forces that will shape the nature of Hungary's version of industrial capitalism for the foreseeable future.

NOTES

1. I am grateful to the Economic and Social Research Council for funding the project *The Development of Firms and Markets in Hungary* (grant R234422) on which this chapter draws.
2. For example, in 1977 after two years' slow growth of output and stagnating real wages due to restrictive economic policies, the Politbureau, in spite of opposition from the Central Planning Office, decided to stimulate economic growth. The result was the disastrous current account deficit of 1978.
3. In one year – 1985 – the half-billion dollar Hungarian surplus on foreign trade with the Soviet Union in convertible currencies disappeared and never returned.
4. For example, with regard to privatization it enacted the legislation on 'Business Entities', 'Transformation of State Owned Enterprises', 'Protection of Foreign Investment', and it established the State Property Agency, etc.
5. There was a third conception represented by intellectuals associated with the social democratic-Marxist wing of the HSWP, but this one received little publicity and had almost no impact. Their argument was that the state enterprises should be converted into worker-owned ones and that an economic system based on self-management, democratic planning, interest reconciliation, support for the domestic market, cooperation with foreign capital, etc., should evolve. In effect it was a proposal to adapt the Scandinavian model – minus a dominant capitalist presence – to Hungarian circumstances.
6. Between 1990 and 1991 there were 30 'expert' submissions to the government regarding privatization strategy, but none of them were accepted (Vigvari 1992). Between 1992 and 1993, however, most submissions were accepted. This suggests that by the latter period, various elite factions had reached a compromise.
7. While in 1991, 78 per cent of privatization revenues came in the form of foreign exchange and the proportion of cash income was 97 per cent, the figures for 1992 were 56 and 85 per cent respectively. By 1993 foreign exchange income from privatization had dropped to 33 per cent, and cash income to 56 per cent (in spite of the sale of the Hungarian Telecommunications Company, the largest single privatization in Eastern Europe).

8. In 1995 the net interest payment was HUF 263.5 billion, or 93 per cent of the total budget deficit.
9. Such as for domestic banking interests whose position is threatened by loans from foreign banks.
10. Foreign-owned companies now produce over 50 per cent of industrial production (*Figyelo* 1995) and annual servicing of the foreign debt amounts to about 10–12 per cent of GDP (calculated from National Bank of Hungary 1994).

REFERENCES

Bekker, Z. (1978): *Novekedesi utak, dinamikus agak* (Growth paths, dynamic branches). Budapest: KJK.

Carroll, G.R., J. Goodstein and A. Gynenes (1988), 'Organisations and the state: effects of the institutional environment on agricultural cooperatives in Hungary', *Adminstrative Science Quarterly*, 33: 233–56.

Commission of the European Union (1991–5), *Eurobarometer.*

Csaba, L. (1992), 'Kolteszet es valosag a magyar gazdasagpolitikaban' (Poetry and reality in Hungarian economic policy), *Valosag*, 11.

Czaban, L. (1990), 'Magyarorszag nemzetkozi penzugyi helyzete 1982–1989 kozott' (Hungary's international financial situation between 1982 and 1989). *Gazdasag es Tarsadalom*, 3.

Economic Policy Working Group (1992), *A Gazdasagpolitikai Munkacsoport Jelentese a Kormanynak* (Report of the Economic Policy Working Group to the Government). Budapest: Hungarian Government.

Figyelo (1995), 'Top 200 companies in Hungary in 1994'.

Financial Research (1990), *Reports from the Tunnel 3.*

Gowan, P. (1995), 'Neo-liberal theory and practice for Eastern Europe'. *New Left Review*, 213: 3–60.

Henderson, J. and R.P. Appelbaum (1992), 'Situating the state in the East Asian development process' in R.P. Appelbaum and J. Henderson (eds), *States and Development in the Asian Pacific Rim*. Newbury Park: Sage Publications: 1–26.

Henderson, J., R. Whitley, G. Lengyel and L. Czaban (1995), 'Contention and confusion in industrial transformation: dilemmas of state economic management' in E. Dittrich, G. Schmidt and R. Whitley (eds), *Industrial Transformation in Europe*. London: Sage Publications: 79–108.

Kadar J. (1990), 'Feljegyzese a Politikai Bizottsag reszere 1964' (Janos Kadar's note to the attention of the Politbureau 1964) in Koltai and Brody (eds), *El nem egetett iratok* (Documents that were not burnt). Budapest: Szabad Ter Kiado.

Kardos, P. and A. Vertes (1990), 'Korforgas. az 1987–1989 es idoszak gazdasagpolitikajanak elemzese' (Turning around: an analysis of the economic policy of 1987–1989). *Kulgazdasag*, 5.

Kimmel, E. (1990), *Vegjatek a Feher Hazban* (End-Game in the White House). Budapest: E. Kimmel.

Kornai, J. (1993), *A Szocialista Rendszer* (The Socialist System). Budapest: KJK.

Kulcsar, K. (1993), *Ket vilag kozott* (Between Two Worlds). Budapest: Akademia.

Mandel, M. (1996), 'Bankokracia' (Bankocracy). *Tarsadalmi Szemle*, 1.

National Bank of Hungary (1994), *Annual Report.* Budapest: National Bank of Hungary.

Stumpf, I. (1991), 'Partosodas es valasztasok Magyarorszagon' (Development of parties and elections in Hungary) *Tarsadalomtudomanyi Kozlemenyek*, 1–2.

Szalai, E. (1989), *A Nagyvallalati Erdekrol* (On the Interests of Large Companies). Budapest: KJK.

Szalai, E. (1995), 'A kastely' (The Castle). *Kritika*, 9.

Szelenyi, I. (1990), *Uj Osztaly, Allam, Politika* (New Class, State, Politics). Budapest: Europa.

Vigvari, A. (ed.) (1990), *Adossag* (Indebtedness). Budapest: SZGTI.

Vigvari, A. (1991), 'Reform es rendszervaltas' (Reform and change of the system). *Eszmelet*, 9–10.

Vigvari, A. (1992), 'A tulajdonvaltas es erdekek' (Change of ownership and interests). *Tarsadalmi Szemle*, 3.

Index

.